Dedication 4
Introduction 4

Chapter 1: Restoration Supplies 5
  Manufacturers and Suppliers 5
  Al Knoch Interiors 8
  Top Flight Automotive (Corvette America) 8
  Corvette Central 9
  Eckler's 9
  Corvette Pacifica 10

Chapter 2: Tools 11
  Basic Tools 11
  Specialty Tools 14
  Panel Removal Tools 16

Chapter 3: Seats and Interior Components 17
  Seats 18
  What to Order 18
  Seat Disassembly 19
  Seat Back Hardware 22
  Prepping the Foam 29
  Installing the Cover on the Seat Bottom 32
  Adding the Hardware 37
  Anchor Access 38
  Backrest Cover 38
  Perimeter Listings 40
  Trim Installation 45
  Final Assembly 46
  Ready to Drive 49
  Late C3 Seat Covers 49

Chapter 4: Door Panels 60
  Removal 60
  Door Trim 62
  Teardown 63
  Panel Assembly 65
  Molding Installation 67
  Finishing Touches 69
  Panel Flush Washers 71
  Armrest Preparation 72
  Cover Installation 73
  Armrest Assembly 78
  Panel Installation 78
  Door Hardware 80

  C3 Door Panels 82
  Panel Conversion 88
  Armrest Repair 93

Chapter 5: Carpet 94
  Teardown 94
  Clean Up 101
  Carpet Pad 102
  New Carpet 104
  Dimmer Switch Grommet 119
  Installing Seat Belts 119
  Armrest Pad 120
  Trim Panels 121
  Finishing 121
  C3 Carpet 121

Chapter 6: Trim Panels 123
  Hand Brake Cover 123
  Rear Compartment 129
  Hardware 136
  A-Pillar 141
  Dash Pads 143

Chapter 7: Convertible Tops 144
  What Makes a One-Piece Top? 144
  Variations 145
  Inspecting the Frame 153
  Top Frame Adjustment 155
  Clean and Paint 157
  Top Latches 158
  Fitting a New Top 158
  Top Pads 159
  Prepare the Top 162
  Attach the Top 163
  Rear Bow Detail 167
  Top Decking 167
  Wire-on Welt 168
  Front Weather Seal 171
  Rear Weatherstrip 172
  The Finished Top 173
  Header Bow Repair 174
  Broken Screws 174

Source Guide 176

DEDICATION

A special thank you goes out to my best friend, Larry; my cousin Dana; and a great mentor, Ron. You all have inspired me, and for that I am forever grateful.

INTRODUCTION

It's undeniable that when the Corvette was introduced in 1953, it was truly a unique sports car. The interiors of the Corvette are also very unusual and broke all the rules of design and assembly.

Throughout the many generations of Corvettes, style changes to the interior have made restoration a challenge. Many small changes and year-specific details not only make it challenging to obtain the correct parts but it also gets expensive.

I have been working on these cars for almost 50 years and have truly come to love their beauty and distinctive styling. Restoring Corvette interiors is my specialty, and each one has given me hours of joy and pain, but in the end, they are well worth the effort to bring them back to life.

These cars are special and need the care and unwavering attention to detail they deserve to bring them back to their full glory. Time and patience allow you to achieve the goal of a fully restored Corvette interior. Do not get discouraged when things get tough; persevere and you will be rewarded with a job well done.

RESTORATION SUPPLIES

Restoration of a classic Corvette interior can be a very expensive and challenging experience. Knowing what is needed and where to get it will aid in making better choices and reduce the risk of obtaining the wrong supplies. Overspending can easily happen when a part needs to be repurchased because it was not the quality you expected or was not the correct piece needed for the project.

Almost every part needed to restore a car can be obtained from a box house, and getting the correct materials is not difficult. If help is needed when placing an order for parts, it is best to ask a salesperson for assistance. He or she can suggest additional items that may be needed to make your project come together and turn into the brightly polished gem that you dream it should be.

Cutting corners to save money by omitting parts and materials that should be replaced will most likely cost more in the long run. Many interior pieces can be reconditioned and reused to complete the interior, but beware of retaining the old soft goods, such as seat foam, convertible top pads, and carpeting. These items are often overlooked, and you will later wish that you had replaced them.

Manufacturers and Suppliers

With an internet connection, it is possible to find many manufacturers and sellers of quality Corvette

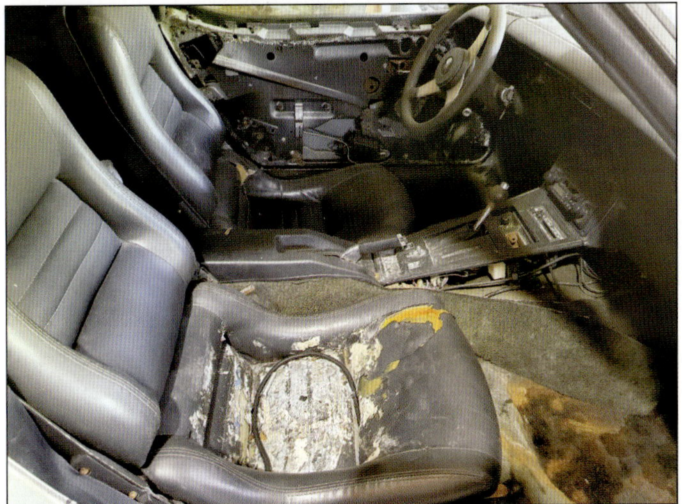

Years of neglect and weather ruined this late-model C3 interior. It will take a lot of time and effort to return the upholstery of this Corvette back to its original condition. Thousands of dollars in labor cost can be saved, and the satisfaction of a job well done can be earned by doing the work yourself.

After just seven months of use, this is the result of installing a new seat cover over the old, worn-out foam. The bolster on the lower seat cushion is already wrinkling and starting to develop a hole in the leather. Please don't let this happen to your Corvette.

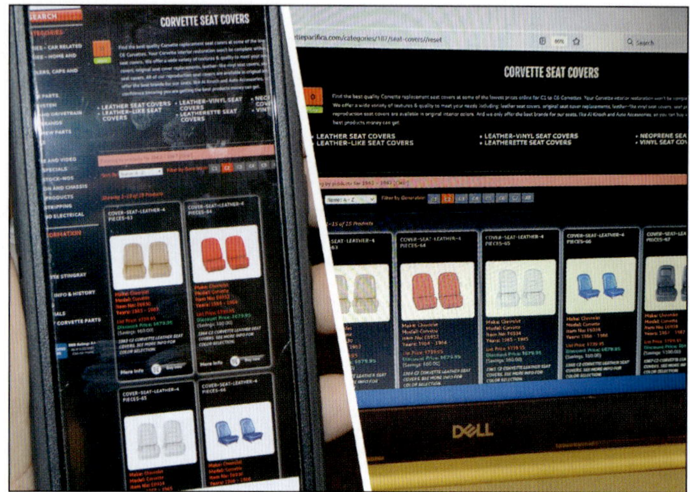

Ordering online is an easy process, but if you are unsure about an item listed on a website, a simple call to the vendor is recommended. Suppliers should be willing to help guide you through the process of obtaining the correct pieces for your model of Corvette.

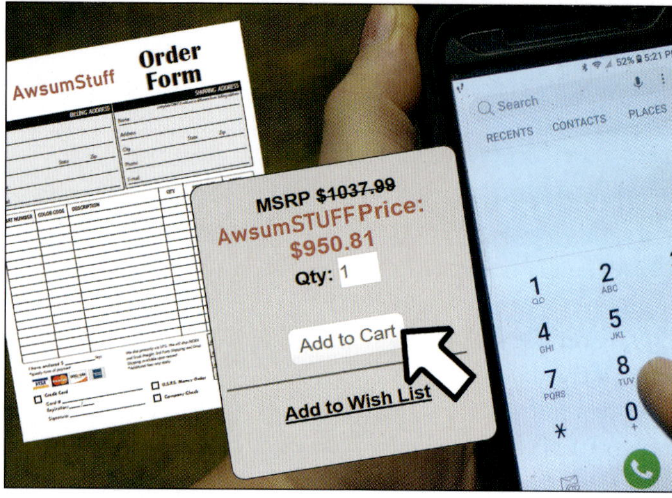

Old-fashioned paper order forms are seldom used in this day of modern technology. Websites are set up with "click" to order and then place the items in a virtual shopping cart. An order can also be placed over the phone if you feel more comfortable talking to a real person.

restoration parts. Not all of these suppliers are specialists in Corvettes, so ask questions about the fitment of parts before ordering them. This saves time and money, minimizing the need to return an incorrect part.

To ensure that you get the correct parts for your project, have the VIN number and paint code at hand. This will help identify if the car was from an early or late-year production run.

Set up an Account

Ordering parts from a vendor is easier if an account is established with them. It takes a few minutes to fill out the online registration with your name, physical address, email address, and the year and model of your car. With the car info, the vendor can catch items that might not fit your particular project.

One benefit of having an account is that checking out is faster. An account also allows for tracking order status. Some vendors offer registered buyers special discounts and email offers.

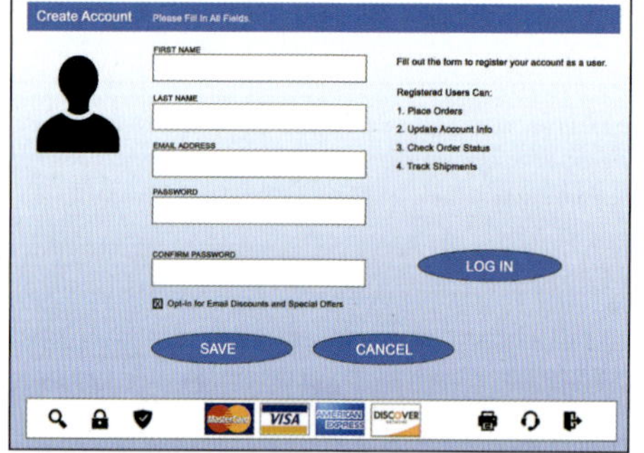

It's quick and simple to register with an online merchant. They ask for name, address, and email to ensure that the order is shipped to the correct destination. Faster checkouts and online discounts are some of the advantages of setting up an account with a vendor.

Place an Order

Before placing an order, make a list of the parts needed and include the vendor part number from its catalog or website. If you are confident with the parts selected, simply select the items, place them in your cart, and submit the order. If you are not sure about a particular part, calling the merchant is the best way to order parts.

Be sure to ask questions about fitment and if the parts are in stock and ready to ship. These questions can be answered by the sales staff. Also, ask if the supplier has any additional parts the project might require that may not be listed.

Shipping Charges

Do not be surprised when it comes to the shipping charges. Each vendor has its own way of calculating the handling and packaging of items for shipment. Packages may be measured for size and not necessarily weight. Oversized boxes of seat foam can be very light and still cost as much as the product to ship. Actual shipping costs are determined at the time the items are packaged for delivery.

Some retailers calculate shipping costs based on the sale price of the items ordered, which leads to overpaying to get the parts to your door. Watch for free shipping specials, which can help you save a lot of money on an order. Ask the vendor if they can combine items into one box, which can save you cash and change the shipper options, such as USPS over UPS and FedEx.

Other Charges

Do not be surprised by additional charges for handling, insurance, drop shipments, and cash-on-delivery (COD) orders. These nonstandard charges can be added to an order at the merchant's discretion for preparing a package. Always ask the vendor what the actual shipping costs will be before finalizing an order.

How to Pay

When placing an online order, a shopping cart is created listing the parts chosen. Before finalizing the purchase, verify that the parts selected are correct for your project. Changes can be made by increasing quantities or adding or deleting items. Special discount codes can also be entered at this time, along with your shipping information.

When the selections are complete and you are ready to check out, enter a major credit card or other accepted form of payment. Make sure that the browser page is secure before entering any personal information or credit card numbers. Some people do not like to enter this information online, so it is possible to call the merchant to place the order and pay.

Returns or Exchanges

Sometimes a part is ordered and turns out to be defective or doesn't fit your car. When this happens, look up the vendor's return policies. This will guide you through the process of how to return an item. It is your responsibility to read and understand the merchant's terms before an order is placed. You may not be able to get a full refund, and there also may be more shipping charges for the returned part.

The next step is to contact the vendor's customer service department. It will issue a return merchandise authorization (RMA) number and instructions on where to ship the item so that it can issue a credit. Do not just send an item back. Most merchants require an RMA, otherwise items get lost, and there is no way to issue a refund or exchange.

When shipping or returning anything, remember to get a tracking number for the parcel. A tracking number allows you keep an eye on your package so that you know it has arrived safely at its destination.

Be Polite

When calling to get an RMA number, it is in your best interest to be patient and kind to the operator. Going in with a poor attitude and a hostile disposition will only slow the process, and it most likely will not end the way you would like it to. Take a deep breath and calm yourself before reacting to the customer service representative. Thank them for taking the time to help, and avoid using bad language; you will receive better results if you are kind.

Restocking Fees

Some vendors may offer a full refund, a credit, or an exchange if the product is returned within a specific period of time. After the grace period, be prepared to pay a restocking fee. These fees are typically 25 percent of the purchase price. The fee is assessed to cover some of the costs incurred by the vendor for handling and repackaging parts.

Shipping Damage

Sometimes packages are delivered damaged. It happens, but do not panic, as this is just a small part of doing business by mail order. Take photos of the box and any broken items and then contact the vendor immediately either online or by

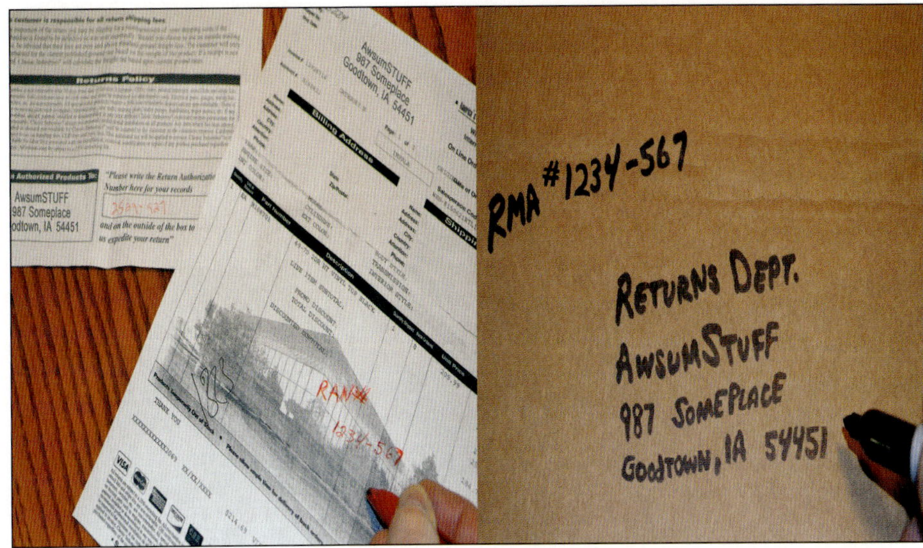

If a part arrives damaged or doesn't fit the project car, call the vendor; it will help resolve the problem. Returns are just another part of doing business. Before a part can be returned, request a return merchandise authorization (RMA) number from the vendor to ensure your account is credited properly.

phone. Provide them with as much information as possible along with the pictures of the damage. A reputable merchant will most likely replace the item without any additional costs to you.

To file a damage claim, the seller will provide a return merchandise authorization (RMA) number. Instructions will be provided for if and how the item should be returned, and there will most likely be a return tag issued for shipping.

After the package is received, a replacement will be sent out. Be patient during this process, as it can take a few extra days to get the new item packaged and shipped. Remember that the merchant is trying to help the best that it can.

Al Knoch Interiors

For more than 50 years, Al Knoch Interiors has produced the most accurate and authentic Corvette interiors that money can buy. Many restorers have achieved Bloomington Gold and NCRS awards by completing the interiors of their prize Corvettes with an Al Knoch convertible top and upholstery.

Attention to detail and customer service are just parts of what makes Al Knoch successful. The true reason for the success is that Al Knoch is not distracted from his goal of creating the most accurate interior pieces, and that is why he does not produce wheels, body panels, or T-shirts and hats. The retailer concentrates only on producing high-quality restoration interiors and convertible tops.

Top Flight Automotive (Corvette America)

Located in Reedsville, Pennsylvania, are the good people at Corvette America. Dan LeKander founded the company as part of Auto Accessories of America, and it has been making replacement Corvette interiors since 1977.

Along with interiors, Corvette America houses a complete line of Corvette parts, wheels, and accessories for all generations of Corvettes to help complete a restoration. For those looking to make their Corvette go faster, Corvette America also provides access to a full line of performance parts by other top manufacturers. You can find all these parts online or in free catalogs.

No one wants to see a package that looks like this showing up on their doorstep, but it happens. Having an order arrive with a damaged box is all too common today, but don't panic. Take photos, check the package for broken or missing pieces, and then contact the merchant to get a replacement if necessary.

When an authentic reproduction Corvette interior and convertible top is needed, Al Knoch will have it. All the pieces made by Al Knoch Interiors are manufactured from scratch at its 100,000-square foot facility in Canutillo, Texas. (Photos Courtesy Al Knoch Interiors)

For more than 42 years, Top Flight Automotive has helped the Corvette community grow by supplying American-made Corvette interiors and accessories. The retailer makes seat covers, door panels, dash pads, headliners, rear quarter panels, armrests, sun visors, kick panels, and more in its Pennsylvania facility. (Photo Courtesy Corvette America)

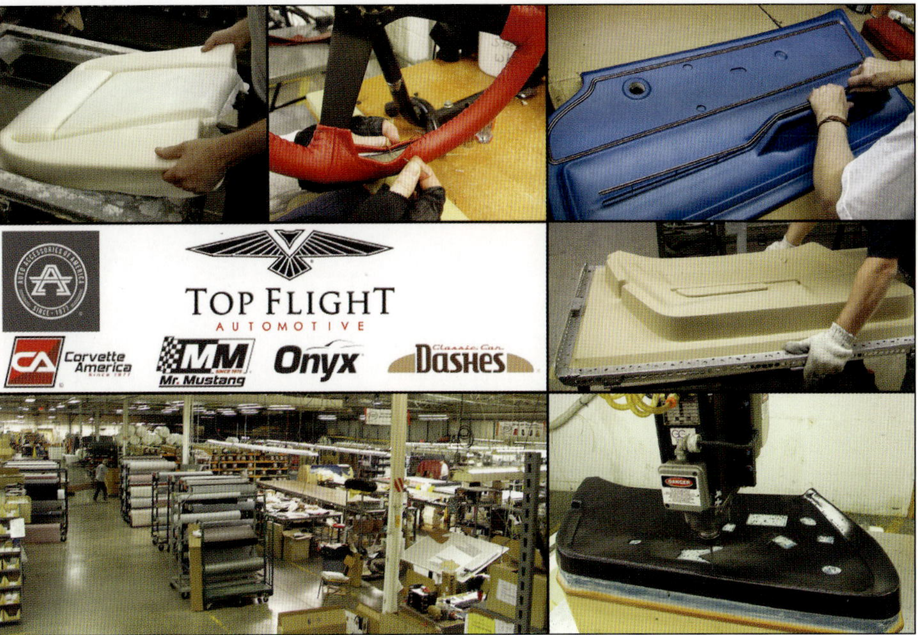

Corvette Central

Before catalogs and the internet, people purchased restoration parts at car shows and swap meets. New parts were hard to find, and when someone did come out with a re-pop, the quality was not as good. In the mid 1970s, Corvette enthusiast and tool-and-die maker Jerry Kohn began to make hard-to-find parts for his 1958 Corvette. Soon, he began producing parts for other Corvette owners, and that grew into the empire that exists today.

Corvette Central produces more than 3,000 parts at its facility in Sawyer, Michigan. It also lists more than 60,000 parts and accessories in seven full-color catalogs. High quality and service has made Corvette Central a giant in the Midwest, and it continues to grow, meeting the requests of customers looking for better parts.

Eckler's

Eckler's Restoration and Performance Parts started in 1961 as a one-man body shop in Rock Island, Illinois, when Ralph Eckler fabricated a new hood for a damaged Corvette. This led to making more fiberglass pieces for other car owners who had no other place to get parts for their wrecked Corvettes. The customizing trend of

After 40 years, Corvette Central has grown to produce more than 3,000 different parts in-house to restore six generations of Corvettes. This family-owned business stocks all the Corvette restoration products needed to get your project across the finish line. (Photo Courtesy Corvette Central)

the mid-1970s was a blessing for the company, and business flourished.

In the late 1990s, Eckler retired and sold the company. In the years following, acquisition of other companies led to the expansive empire that Eckler's is known for today. One of the acquired companies was Mac's in 2012.

Mac's brought a new dimension to the Eckler's family of parts companies by adding Ford parts. Mac's had already developed the Cartouche brand of upholstery for 1909 to 1950s Ford cars and trucks, adding more choices for the restoration market.

The main headquarters for Eckler's is still located in Titusville, Florida, with the Mac's branch in Lock Port, New York. You are welcome to visit their showrooms during business hours.

Corvette Pacifica

When looking for everything Corvette, this is the place. Corvette Pacifica was established more than 35 years ago with a passion to provide quality, reliability, dependability, and service to the Corvette enthusiast. The company sells only products that meet or exceed the standards required to get a car into top shape.

Having an extremely knowledgeable staff that can give the technical support needed and can answer questions, Corvette Pacifica helps guide you to getting the correct parts needed for C1 to C7 projects. Trim shop owners can take advantage of wholesale pricing by visiting the retailer's website, where thousands of available high-quality parts are easy to locate by category and generation.

Many people may think of Eckler's as just a source for interior and bolt-on parts for Corvettes, but times have changed. The retailer has now grown to include a full line of components for other popular classic cars, such as Chevy, Camaro, and now Ford with their Cartouche brand of auto upholstery. (Photo Courtesy Eckler's Restoration and Performance Parts)

Your Corvette deserves the best parts and accessories along with the most knowledgeable salespeople in the industry to help guide you to a successful restoration. With thousands of parts to choose from, Corvette Pacifica has everything that your Corvette could ever need and a staff that really cares about your project. (Photo Courtesy Corvette Pacifica)

TOOLS

Before beginning to work on the interior of a Corvette, assemble the proper tools to be able to properly remove and restore the worn and failing interior components. Most of the tools required can be found in a standard tool kit, but there are a few that may need to be obtained or made to achieve the desired results that a Corvette deserves.

Basic Tools

Many of the following items can be found in a basic toolbox or are obtainable at a local hardware store.

Screwdrivers

A variety of screw types and sizes are used to secure the interior trim panels to the car. Using the correct screwdriver prevents damage to the fastener and interior trim panel. Having a good variety of flat-blade and Phillips-tipped screwdrivers ensures that the screws can be safely removed.

Specialty bits are also an option to have in the toolbox. Larger screws and fasteners may require more torque to remove. Some 3/8- and 1/2-inch-drive bits are the perfect choice for these hard-to-remove

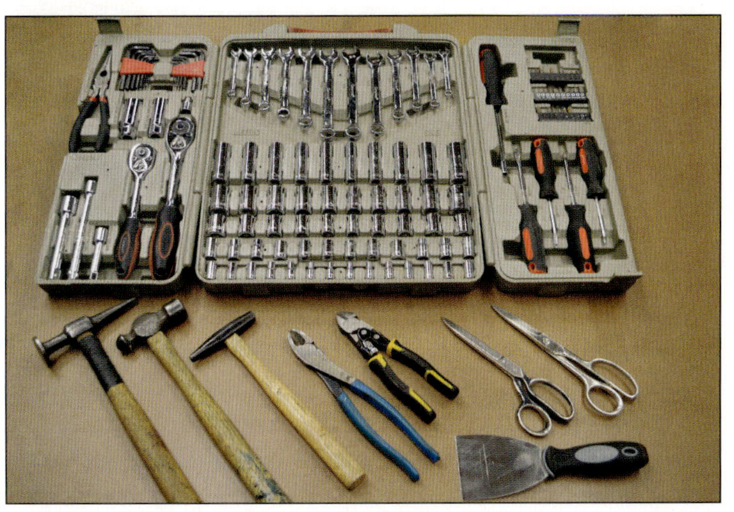

Fasteners can be removed with standard screwdrivers. However, there are many different sizes and types of screwdriver bits and sockets that can get into those hard-to-get-at places. Larger screws are easily removed with #3 or #4 Phillips-head socket bits as well as interchangeable bits for manual handles.

pieces. Torx bits are another type of fastener remover that come in handy when a standard screwdriver is not an option.

Power screwdrivers can speed up the work, but they can slip and break the head of the screw during extraction. Caution is also needed if using a power tool to reassemble the interior. Many screws are driven into fiberglass, and overtightening a fastener can cause tear-out, preventing the screw from holding properly.

Most car enthusiasts already have a collection of tools for working on their car projects. A basic set of wrenches, sockets, and screwdrivers along with an assortment of hammers, pliers, and wire cutters is a good start. However, you may need to add a few special tools to remove the upholstery.

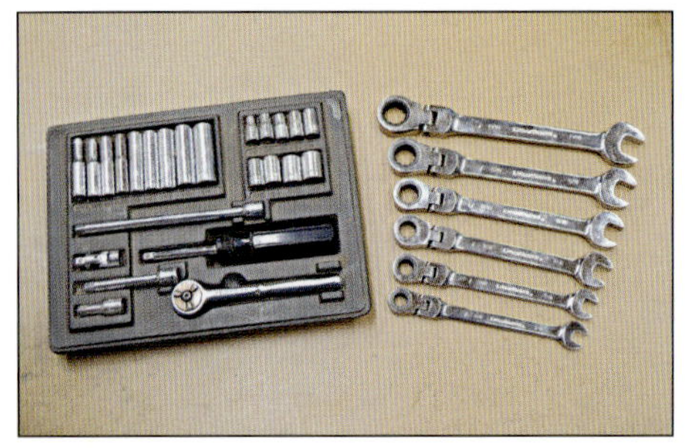

Most interior trim panels and upholstery can be disassembled with a standard 1/4-inch-drive socket set. Larger seat track nuts and bolts are best removed with a combination wrench. To speed up the process of removing a bolt, a ratcheting wrench can get into tight places that a socket cannot access.

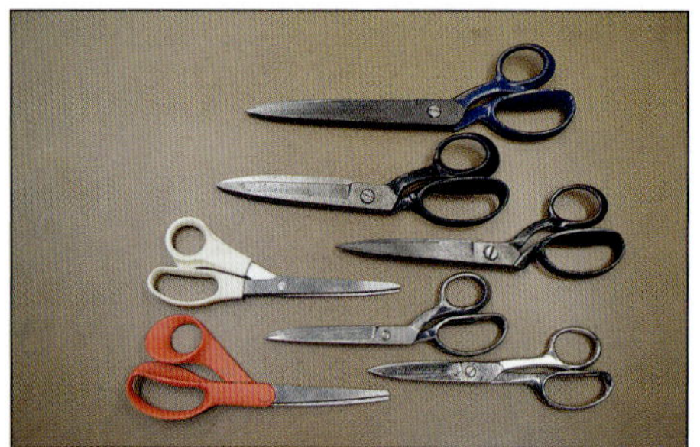

The blades of common plastic-handle household scissors are just not strong or durable enough to cut through auto carpet and leather without damaging the material. A good pair of heavy-duty scissors are sharper, and they will make the task of trimming a lot easier and safer.

Nothing beats a good pair of diagonal cutters to remove hog rings from seat covers. When shopping for a good cutter, look for a pair with long handles. These take less effort to operate by producing more leverage and make cutting easier like a double-action cutter.

Wrenches and Sockets

Open-end and box-end wrenches are great for removing nuts and bolts. They are able to get into tight places to loosen fasteners, but they are not very efficient while they are removed and reset to advance the fastener from the car.

Sockets attached to an extension and ratchet handle can get at hard-to-reach fasteners and speed up the process of removal. It is advised to use a 6-point socket on hex-head nuts and bolts. The socket grips the fastener much more securely than a 12-point socket and prevents rounding of the fastener due to slippage.

Scissors

Trimming the heavy materials used to upholster a Corvette interior requires the use of scissors that are very sharp and much stronger than what is around the house. A basic pair of scissors can actually create more problems by breaking or harming the interior and the user.

Plastic-handle scissors with stamped metal blades work well for cutting paper or lightweight fabric. They are usually assembled with a rivet and are difficult to sharpen when they become dull.

Professional scissors are heavy duty and are assembled with a screw, not a rivet. The blades and integrated handles are made of solid steel and can be sharpened if they become dull. Expect to pay $35 to $70 for a pair. It may seem like a lot compared to the few dollars you would shell out on a lesser pair, but it is worth it in the long run.

Wire Cutters

The handle length of a diagonal cutter directly affects how much force is needed to cut through a hog ring. Having an angled cutting head also makes getting into hard-to-reach places much easier. Specialty lever-action cutters are designed to greatly reduce the effort needed to cut through wire fasteners.

End nippers are another type of cutter used for getting under the heads of rivets, clipping them flush with the panel surface.

Hammers

Persuading stubborn parts to move can require the assistance of a few love taps. A hammer is a very useful tool to make adjustments and set fasteners. There is a large variety of choices when selecting the right hammer for your purpose.

Traditionally, a magnetic-tipped tack hammer is a great addition to any tool kit. They are useful for picking up small washers and can get into tight places. Machinist (ball-peen) hammers are handy for many jobs, and the very useful dead-blow hammer provides that little extra push without the effort.

Having a good assortment of hammers helps get a project through any situation. When it comes to reshaping metal or setting a panel fastener to secure a trim panel, using the correct mallet will make getting the job done safer and a lot easier.

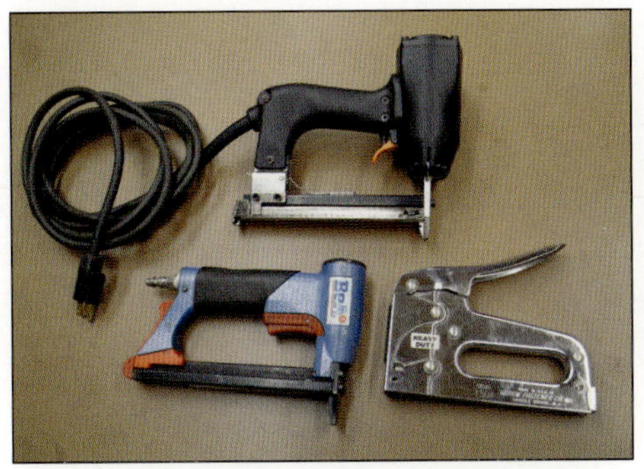

Most upholstery projects will require the use of a staple gun to finish the assembly of an interior component. A simple hand-operated mechanical stapler will usually finish a project just fine, but a pneumatic or electric stapler can help speed up the job with a lot less effort.

Wide-blade scrapers make the task of interior component removal and cleanup much faster. Smaller stiff-bladed scrapers are much better at getting into tight places and getting under tough, glued-on carpet pads.

Aerosol spray glue may be convenient, but it is messy and can get very expensive. Professionals purchase contact cement in 5-gallon drums and use siphon feed cup guns to apply the glue. Check out the local hardware store for 1-inch chip brushes and quarts cans of contact cement.

It is not advised to use your fist as a hammer, so make the appropriate choice for the task at hand. Using the correct hammer will prevent accidental damage to your project.

Staplers

It is not necessary to spend a lot of money on a stapler to finish your project. Each type of stapler has advantages and disadvantages. Hand-operated staple guns require you to squeeze a lever to activate the device. This repetitive action can be fatiguing. This type uses a spring action to drive the staple, which can limit the depth the fastener can be embedded into a tacking strip.

Electric staplers are able to drive a staple with greater force and are effortless to use. Light-duty staplers are underpowered and are not recommended for upholstery work due to their smaller magnetic coil, which can overheat with continuous use. A professional-quality electric stapler can be expensive, but it will perform for many years of heavy use. They are also heavy and can be large and awkward to handle.

Pneumatic staplers are inexpensive and work well. The light weight and slim profile of the tool make it easy to use, but they require an air compressor to make them function, which can be an expensive acquisition.

Scrapers

To make the task of cleaning old materials from interior trim panels quicker, use a scraping tool. It is possible to obtain a variety of narrow- to wide-blade broad knives from any hardware store.

Heavy or stiff blades work well for removing glue and scale from the floor and interior trim panels of the car. A beveled edge on the blade cuts through and separates materials with greater ease than a flat blade. I have found that scrapers with wooden handles that are riveted to the blade are more durable and comfortable to use.

Glue Gun

Many interior components require some glue to bond them to the car. Applying glue to interior trim panels can be done many ways. Prepackaged adhesives sold in an aerosol spray can are convenient, but there are other considerations when compared to bulk adhesive. The first is cost, as each can does not provide much glue for the money spent. Next, the spray tips tend to clog easily, which makes getting the glue onto the surface you wish to bond impossible. Another issue is that most aerosol sprays are most likely to fail and end up with the cover material peeling away.

It is best to use bulk contact cement that is sold in quarts or gallon cans. The adhesive can be sprayed from a simple siphon-feed paint gun. This provides better control of the spray pattern and coverage on large areas with less waste.

The downside to spraying glue is that an air compressor is needed, which can be expensive but very useful for many other tools around the workshop. Bulk contact cement can also be spread with a small 1-inch chip brush. This is a great way to apply glue to smaller areas neatly and with better control.

There are many different styles of rivet tools. To get the best results when joining pieces together, select the tool and fastener that will handle the job with the most efficiency. A loose rivet will cause problems by failing and damaging the interior.

Avoid using the cheap and agricultural hog ring pliers to fasten seat covers. They will work, but they are not designed to get into the deep recesses of the foam to securely fasten the seat cover upholstery to the foam and seat frame. Professional-grade hog ring pliers can do this with ease.

Rivet Tool

Choosing the right tool depends upon the project and your budget. Pop rivets are a simple way to join materials together when making a repair. Manual rivet tools are inexpensive and come in many styles that can perform the function they were designed for. Power rivet setters cost more and are great for large projects without causing fatigue from repetitive squeezing.

Rivets are available in a variety of sizes and lengths to accommodate the thickness of the project you are working on. They are also made of aluminum or steel, depending on the strength requirements you need for a repair. Most tools and fasteners can be found at a local hardware store.

Specialty Tools

Installation of Corvette seat covers and interior panels often requires the use of very specific tools to complete the task at hand. Many of these tools can be obtained for just a few dollars, and some can be fabricated from common materials.

Improvising to get a project finished can result in a poor result. Using the right tools will not only get the project together faster but will also look better.

Hog Ring Pliers

It pays to have a good pair of hog ring pliers when installing seat covers. There are many styles and types of hog ring pliers from which to choose. Some work better than others, and some should just be avoided altogether.

Originally, hog ring pliers were designed for agricultural use. A farmer would cinch several hog rings into the nose of a hog to help prevent it from rooting up the soil. These are not well suited for the upholstery trade.

Most suppliers of kit interiors offer the option to buy a simple set of hog ring pliers. These are made from round stock and are joined together with a single rivet. One large flaw with this type of pliers is that the handles are too short to get

a proper cinch. The riveted design is very weak, and they tend to wear out very fast.

Professional hog ring pliers are typically made of cast iron and come in straight- or bent-handle designs. The longer handles make the tool much easier to use, and they last a lifetime. Pliers with a bend or angle are used to get into the deepest part of a seat cushion. The professional-grade hog rings are also stronger and sharper than those supplied with the simple pliers kit.

Seat Cover Installation Hook Tool

A special hook tool is used to reach through the foam cushion and grab the listing retainer on a Corvette seat cover. This tool simplifies the installation of the seat cover. After the listing retainer has been pulled through the cushion, it can then be attached to the retaining wire on the bottom side of the foam, securing the cover in the correct place.

Using zip ties and needle-nose pliers to attach a Corvette seat cover is just not the proper way to get the

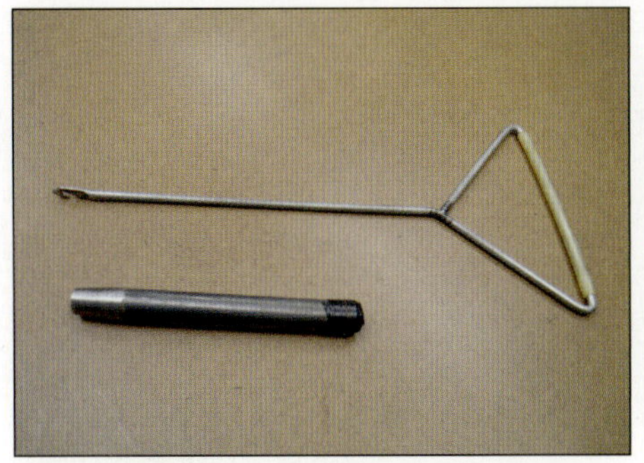

There are special tools needed to install Corvette seat covers. A hole must be made in the seat foam for the seat cover retainer clip to pass through. This hook tool is designed to reach through the foam to grab the retainer and secure it to the anchor wire on the back side of the foam.

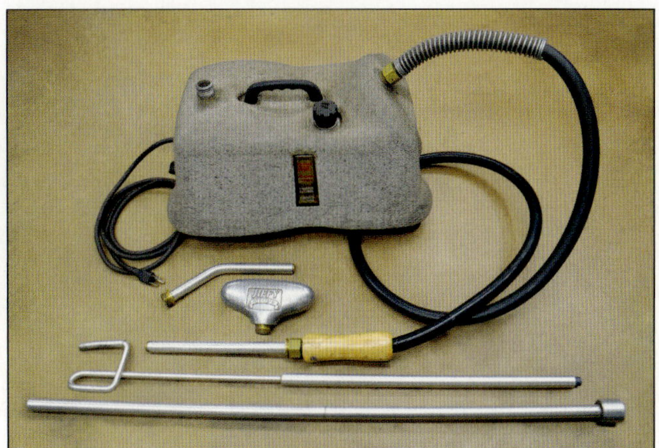

Stubborn wrinkles can easily be removed from a seat cover with a steamer. When working on carpet or a convertible top, a professional-grade steamer with the proper appliance head can reach those difficult places that a garment steamer cannot.

A heat gun is a great way to help relax a vinyl or leather seat cover to help smooth out any wrinkles that may have formed during the installation process. Always use the greatest of care to not scorch the surface of the material.

job done. It is worth the few dollars to invest in this tool.

Foam Hole Cutter

A hole cutter does just what the name implies: it makes a hole in the foam seat cushion to allow the passage of the seat cover retainer. This is one of those tools that can be made in a home shop for little to no cost from a small length of tubing.

Holes in the foam should be 1/4 to 3/8 inch. Sharpening the end of the tubing creates a tool that will get the job done. Some people use a power drill with a 3/8-inch bit. Drilling through foam is not safe, and it can travel and tear up the foam. It will also leave a ragged hole.

Steamer

A steamer is a finishing tool used to remove wrinkles in upholstery. Small garment steamers work well for clothing, but when it comes to seat covers or a convertible top, a better grade of steamer is needed.

Some steamers are equipped with a standard flat head for removing wrinkles on larger flat surfaces such as seat covers or carpeting. Steamers that have interchangeable heads are more useful to the upholstery trade. When working on a convertible top, a wand-type head works well for getting into the small, tight areas that need a little help.

Steamers with a remote water tank and long hose are also better suited for working on upholstery. They are less likely to spill water on the surface material when the head is moving around.

Heat Gun

Dry heat is applied to the surface of materials with a heat gun to help the material contour to a desired shape. Heat guns come in a variety of heat ranges and are designed for specific tasks.

Consumer-grade heat guns gen-erally have a preset heat range and no cooling fan. These devices work great for small projects, such as stripping paint or softening caulk for removal.

Professional heat guns have replaceable heating elements and can be adjusted to a range of temperatures to meet the needs of a particular task. They also have a fan mode to cool down the tool, which will prolong the life of the heating element.

Great care must be taken when using a heat gun. The surface area of the tip can be extremely hot and melt whatever it touches. The tool must always be kept in motion to prevent burning or melting the surface of your project. Always check the electrical requirements of a heat gun to see how many amps it will draw. If it is plugged into an extension cord

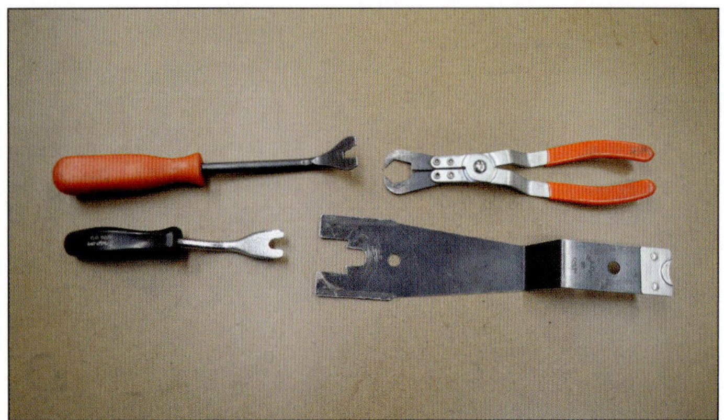

Blind fasteners used on window cranks and trim panels have always been a challenge. Always use the correct tool to remove door handles and trim panels. These tools make life simpler by reaching into those impossible places to remove a fastener without causing damage to the upholstery.

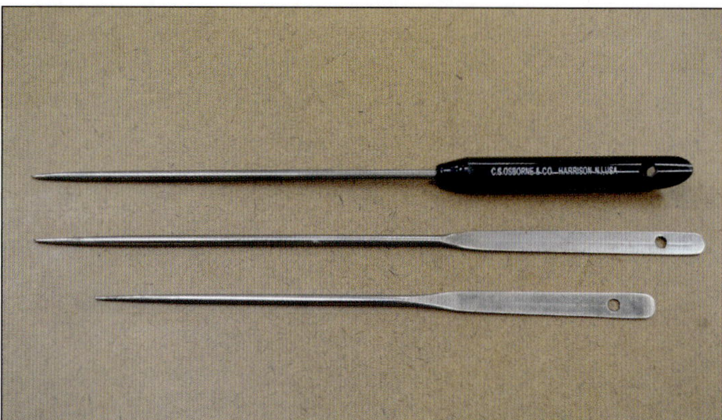

Upholstery regulators are very versatile tools. They are useful for locating and aligning the screw holes in panels to make assembly easier. They can also tuck material into tight places that a finger can't reach and are available in 8- and 10-inch lengths.

that is not able to carry enough current, it could blow a fuse or melt the extension cord.

Panel Removal Tools

A panel or lift tool is used for getting behind a trim or door panel to free it from the car. There are several different types of lifter tools, and each has a purpose. Plastic lift tools are great for getting into places without scratching the surfaces. Although they are flexible, they do not have a lot of pulling power. Metal lift tools have the strength to get behind a door panel and lift it away from the surface of the car.

Some of these tools have longer handles to reach deeper into the panel to get to the fasteners. The forked head shape of the tool varies depending on the type of fastener being removed.

Window cranks and lock knobs have a retainer clip that prevents them from popping off their posts. Reaching the spring clip located on the back side of the device requires a special tool that can be purchased at most auto parts stores.

Regulators

One of the most useful and must-have tools in any trimmer toolbox is a regulator. This needle-like tool was originally designed to help adjust the padding underneath the cover material of furniture. It can get into very tight places to tuck, glue, or locate screw holes in trim panels.

Regulators come in different sizes, and some have handles attached. This has always been my favorite tool to use.

SEATS AND INTERIOR COMPONENTS

Without a doubt, the Corvette has one of the most difficult-to-install interiors of any American car. These seats and interior components are not designed like any other vehicle, and it takes a lot of experience to be able to correctly install the upholstery.

The early C1 models (1953–1962) have inner spring support along with a molded foam pad. The individual coil springs are sewn into muslin and burlap bags, and that is what gives the individual springs the correct tension for support and comfort while driving the car. A molded foam rubber cushion is then placed over the spring unit, giving the seat its distinctive shape.

Attachment of the seat cover is similar to that of a traditional car seat. Listings are hog ringed to the springs to hold the insert in position,

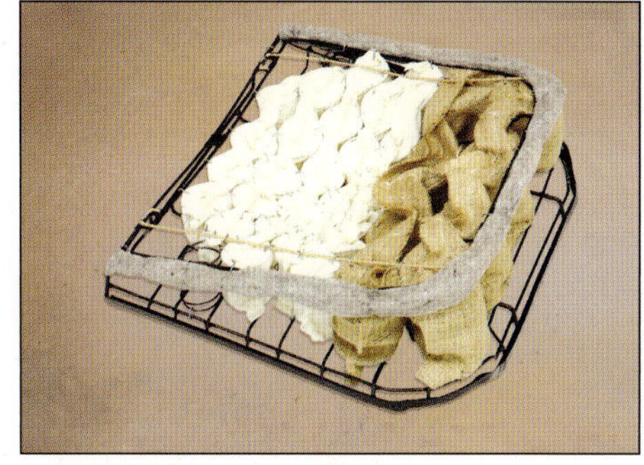

Many different sizes of springs are used to provide comfort and proper support for the seat cushion. This lower C1 seat frame has been cleaned and refitted with new original-type replacement springs. It is now ready to be covered with new burlap, foam, and upholstery.

This 1954 Corvette sports an all-new interior that has been reconditioned with brand-new materials. The seats are not adjustable, as they are designed to fit the body of the car, giving the driver the most comfort and legroom for such a small cab.

Do not let this happen to your Corvette. Someone did not use the correct seat cover installation kit and opted to used zip ties to attach the seat back cover to the old foam. Several hog rings were linked together to fasten the bottom seat cover to the seat frame.

and the cover is then pulled over the foam and hog ringed to the bottom edge of the seat frame.

The C2 and later models rely more on the molded foam to give support to the seat cover. The nontraditional attachment hardware is what makes the process of installing a Corvette seat cover difficult. The actual hardware is often misunderstood, and it also requires a special tool to pull the listing clips through the foam so that they can be anchored.

I have seen many different and creative ways that Corvette seat covers have been installed. Among the top methods some have tried to secure a seat cover is the use of zip ties and chain-linking hog rings together. These fastening techniques are innovative, but they are just not acceptable ways of installing a Corvette seat cover.

Seats

For this project, I have chosen a C3 seat from a 1974 Corvette to demonstrate the proper way to attach the new seat cover and foam.

It is never a good idea to put a new seat cover over the old foam. As you can see, when the foam ages, it shrinks. The seat cover becomes misshapen, and replacing just the worn upholstery will only result in a poor-fitting seat cover.

Although this is a high-back seat, the principles used are basically the same for all seat cover installations from 1963 to 1978.

Another thing to know about this era of Corvette seats is that they are not left or right specific. Instead, they are a universal design that can be fit on either side of the car. Seat-back locking mechanisms did not appear on the seat backs until late 1967 and continued until 1978.

What to Order

There are a few things to know when it comes time to place an order for new seat cover materials. The first is determining what type of material the seat cover is made from. The original seat covers could have been leather, vinyl, or a combination of

There is just no way to make this original leather seat cover look good again. The seat must be completely stripped down to repair the bent frame, preparing it for the new upholstery. All-new original-type materials will be used to bring the seat back to life.

To make the seat look factory fresh again, a new set of seat foam and original-style leather seat covers have been ordered to replace the worn and damaged upholstery. Additional support hardware will also be needed for this project.

both. If you are trying to restore the car to original condition, the material does not matter as much as the correct seat pattern. The sewn or embossed pattern changed every year, but the seat frame did not.

Another thing to order is new seat foam. Yes, new foam is needed. As the seat ages, the foam breaks down, shrinks, and becomes compressed. If the new seat cover is installed over the old seat foam, it will be baggy and wrinkles will form right away, resulting in deep creases that will turn into holes. The seat will also be very uncomfortable to sit in.

It is possible to spend a lot of time trying to recondition the old, rusty, and damaged hardware that was removed from the seat, but it just doesn't make sense when new replacement pieces are readily available at a reasonable cost.

Yes, an installation kit is needed to get the proper fit for the new upholstery. Without one, too much stress will be put on the tensioning wires. Do not risk damaging the new seat cover by reusing the old hardware. This seat has the new kit preinstalled.

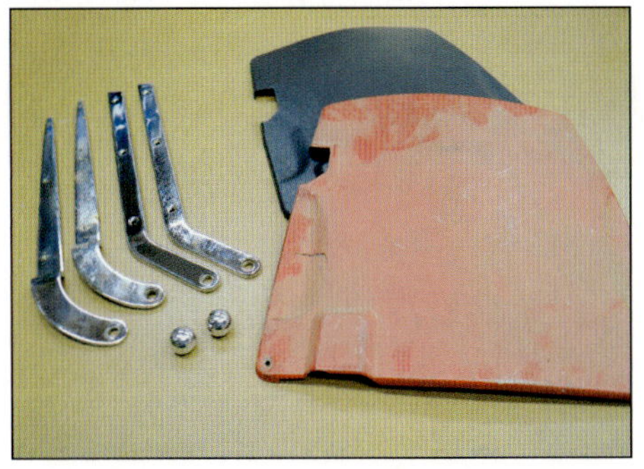

The exterior components of the seat can take a pretty good beating over the course of 45-plus years of service. Pitted chrome side irons, worn adjuster knobs, and cracked fiberglass seat backs can be replaced with exact fit, ready-to-install reproduction parts.

Finally, all the support items are needed to attach the seat cover, such as rubber and plastic bumpers, pivot bolts, and a seat installation kit. The installation kit includes all the tensioning wires, listing anchors, and attaching clips. Some manufacturers include this kit with the seat cover set, and others sell it to you separately. Do not reuse the old installation kit, as it has most likely fatigued with use and will surely fail shortly after being put back into service.

Optional items that may be needed or replaced include the adjuster knob, seat backs, and side irons. These parts show signs of wear, rust, and pitting. Because they are mostly cosmetic, updating them with new pieces gives your seat that factory-new appearance.

Seat Disassembly

Remove the seat from the car and place it on a workbench where it can be worked on at a comfortable level. Before the seat back can be removed from the bottom cushion, the locking seat back release strap needs to be unbolted. If the strap is not removed prior to the pivot bolts, the metal strap can become damaged from excessive twisting.

Depress the release button to allow the backrest to tilt forward. Then, use a 3/8-inch socket to loosen the two bolts located on the lower bracket of the release strap.

You could bag and tag all the pieces that are taken off the seat, but that would be a lot of extra work. I use a large parts tub to retain all the removed screws and hardware. This way, I can easily retrieve the pieces during the reassembly of the seat.

Pivot Bolt

Locate the pivot bolts on the outer sides of the bottom seat cushion. Depending on the year and model of seat, there are three different styles of pivot bolts that hold the seat back in place.

From 1963 to early 1970, the pivot bolts had a smaller Phillips head on a short shoulder bolt.

Late 1970 to 1973 models used pivot bolts with the same heads and a longer shoulder bolt that also used a locking nut on the inside of the frame.

In 1974, the shoulder bolt was changed again. This time it had a larger head on a long bolt with a locking nut. It was used until 1978 when Chevrolet introduced the pace car, which had the clamshell style of seat.

Seat Tracks

To gain access to the lock nut, the seat tracks need to be removed. Begin by unscrewing and then removing the adjuster knob on the end of the lever.

Depress the adjustment lever to allow the track to slide backward, exposing the track bolt. Use a ratchet wrench and 3/8-inch socket to extract the bolt. Slide the track forward and remove the rear bolt.

Remove the seat track from the frame and place it in the parts bin. Repeat the process with the other seat track.

Lay the seat on its side and remove the lock nut from the inside of the frame with a 1/2-inch wrench. The shoulder bolt can then be removed with a #4 Phillips screwdriver bit. Under the shoulder bolt is a plastic bushing. The bushing takes up the slack in the pivot hole, allowing the seat to fold without binding. It also prevents the shoulder bolt from wearing into the pivot hole of the inner side iron.

When removing the pivot bolt, be aware that between the pivot arm of the seat and the cushion there is a thick spacer washer that prevents the side iron of the seat back from tearing up the upholstery of the cushion. This spacer will need to be reused or replaced if it is missing or damaged. After the pivot bolts have been removed, separate the two halves of the seat.

Removing the Seat

1 The bolts holding the baseplate of the locking backrest release strap are removed with a socket wrench. The thin spring metal band can be easily damaged from twisting if it isn't freed from the seat bottom before the pivot bolts of the backrest are removed.

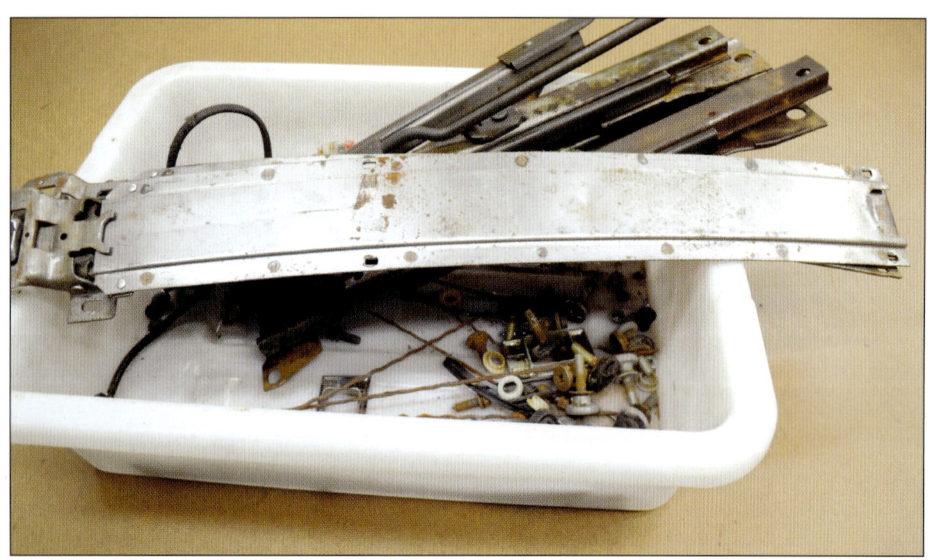

2 A large wash bin is used to store and keep the seat components together after they are removed during the teardown process. Having open access to the pieces will help speed up the sorting, cleaning, and assembly of the seat.

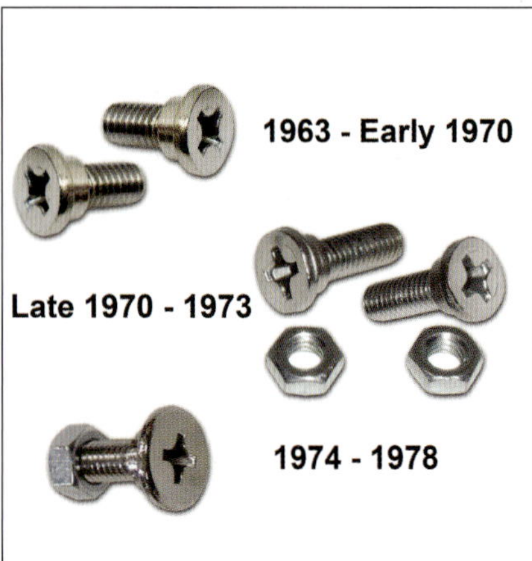

3 There have been many changes to the pivot bolt hardware over the course of 16 years. Choosing the correct part can be tricky if you do not know what the differences are. It is always best to compare the old parts with the new.

4 Before the seat track is removed, the adjuster knob must come off to allow the locking rod to pass through the adjuster handle guide bezel. The seat adjustment knob comes off by rotating it counterclockwise until it is free of the adjustment lock lever.

5 *The lower section of the seat track is moved backward and then forward to get access to the seat track retainer bolts. A socket wrench can then be used to remove the retainer bolts from deep inside the channel of the seat tracks.*

6 *After the seat tracks have been removed from the bottom of the seat frame, the lock nut for the pivot bolt can be easily accessed for removal. An open-end wrench is used to reach and loosen the nut from the stud on the pivot bolt.*

7 *To prevent damaging the shoulder bolt, a #4 Phillips screwdriver bit has been fitted to a 1/2-inch-drive ratchet to aid in the removal of the pivot bolt. It takes a lot of pressure to remove the rusted-in bolt from the seat frame.*

Seat Back Hardware

Earlier models (1968–1969) have a release lever that goes through a chrome trim bezel with a knob fastened to the end. Place the backrest facedown on the workbench and remove the back-release knob. It takes an Allen or hex wrench to loosen the small set screw that locks it in place.

The bezel piece is held in place with two oval-head trim screws. Remove the screws with a #2 Phillips screwdriver and lift the bezel away from the seat back. Place the trim pieces in the parts bin.

Adjustable Headrest

An adjustable headrest is mounted to the top of the early C3 seat back. Under the headrest is a chrome trim bezel that needs to come off before the seat cover can be removed. Remove the headrest by pulling straight up, and then angle it to the right to release the post from the seat back. Unscrew the trim screws and remove the bezel.

Seat Belt Retainer

With the headrest removed, the seat belt retainer located on the top outer shoulder of the seat back can be accessed. Remove the two trim screws that hold the retainer in place.

Release Button

Later high-back models (1970–1978) have a release button on the back side of the seat. It is located in the center of the headrest. Two oval-head trim screws must be removed to free the bezel from the seat.

The release button is attached from the back side with a single machine screw. The screw can be accessed after the release strap assembly is removed from the seat.

Shoulder Harness Loop

Another variation that may be encountered is on the convertible seats. They may have a shoulder harness loop on the back of the seat. Remove the two screws that hold the trim piece to the seat.

Cover Panel

Attached to the back of the upper seat frame is a large, solid cover panel that conceals the locking mechanism for the backrest. Removing the screws in the lower corners of the fiberglass panel allows it to slide upward and off. There are metal brackets mounted on the inside of the back panel near the top that hook over tabs attached to the seat frame.

To remove the panel, push upward from the bottom edge toward the top of the seat back to clear the brackets from the tabs. Do not try to lift the panel off, as this can damage the panel by ripping the small screws holding the brackets out of the fiberglass panel.

There are two threaded bumpers on the bottom of the backrest that are removed by unscrewing them from the seat frame. The rubber on the bumper may be damaged from the stress of pressing against the bumper stop on the seat bottom. Worn or damaged bumpers should be replaced with new parts.

Trim Molding

One last trim piece needs to be removed before the seat cover and foam can be replaced. Accessing the fasteners requires removing the backrest locking release mechanism. With the backrest facedown on the workbench, remove the hog rings from the short listings at the top of the seat cover opening, just below the back panel tabs. This allows you to open the overlap fastener enough to expose the retainer nuts on the release mechanism.

Release Mechanism

Use a 7/16-inch socket wrench to remove the two nuts located at the top of the mechanism. There are four more hex-head sheet-metal screws that hold the main body of the release mechanism to the seat frame. Use a 1/4-inch socket to remove the sheet-metal screws. Now, lift the entire mechanism from the backrest.

The trim molding on the front of the headrest area is secured to the seat frame by three speed nuts deep inside of the seat frame. To remove the trim molding, lift the foam padding on the back side of headrest to expose the speed nuts attached to the posts that extend through the seat frame. Use a 3/8-inch socket to remove the fasteners from the posts. Pull the trim molding straight outward from the front of the backrest and place the hardware in the parts bin.

Stripping the Cover

Hog rings are used to attach the perimeter listings to the backrest frame. Place the backrest facedown on the workbench and use a diagonal cutter to remove the hog rings along the bottom and then the sides of the seat cover.

Anchor Listings

On the back side of the foam pad are the corrugated anchor listings that hold the seat cover to the foam. The curvy listing wires are secured to the seat springs with hog rings. To free the foam and seat cover from the frame, carefully remove the hog rings without damaging the seat springs.

At this point of disassembly, the backrest frame should be free and can be lifted out of the old seat cover and foam. The frame should be thoroughly inspected for stress cracks and the springs for signs of wear and fatigue.

Disassembling the Seat

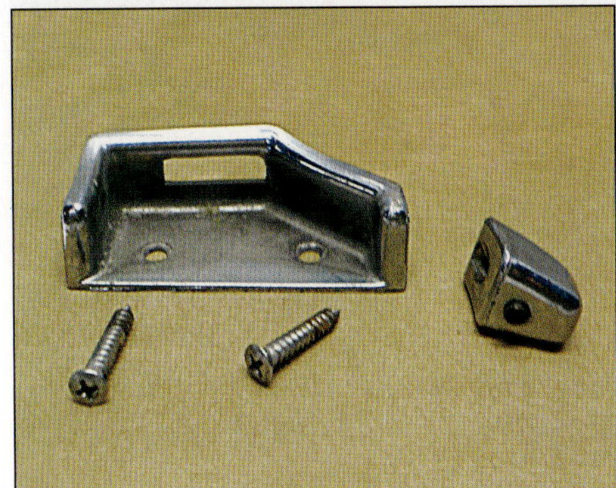

1 *This latch lever knob and cover plate was used on 1968–1969 seat backs. A hex wrench is used to loosen the set screw on the release knob and trim screws securing the trim bezel are extracted with a Phillips-head screwdriver.*

2 *The adjustable headrest has been removed from the seat by pulling it up and out of the post slot, exposing the headrest trim bezel. A Phillips screwdriver will be needed to remove the trim screws that secure the trim piece to the top of the seat.*

3 *Trim parts usually hide the raw edges or fasteners of the seat cover. The trim bezel for the release button does that and more. It also helps hold down the overlapped fastener section of the rear seat cover. It only takes two screws to hold it in place.*

4 *Applied solid seat backs were only used on C2 and C3 Corvettes. Early models were secured in place by the chrome side irons attached along the outer edges of the backrest. C3 seat backs were attached by cleats on the upper back side and two trim screws.*

5 *The top of the seat back panel is held in place by small cleats that slide behind metal tabs that point upward from the backrest frame. The small screws that hold the cleats are prone to pulling out of the aged fiberglass panel from lifting the panel outward.*

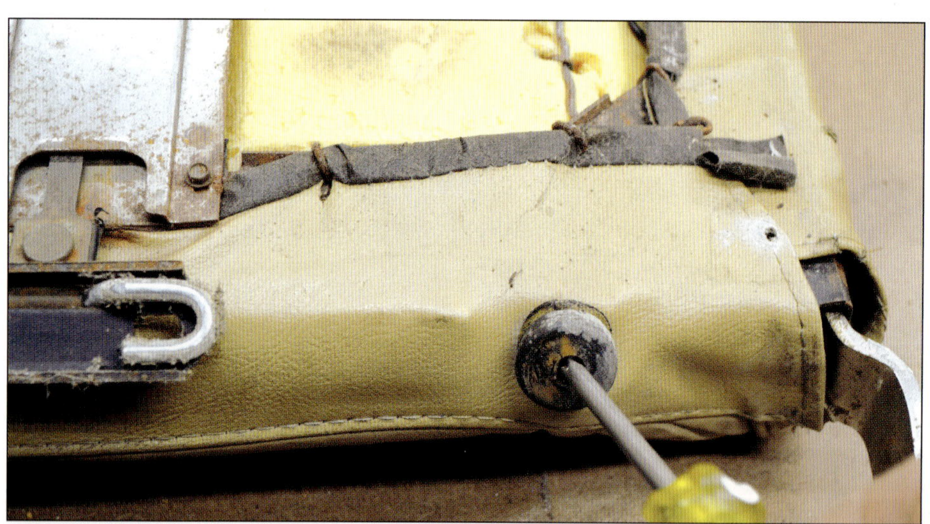

6 *Rubber-covered backrest bumpers are used to help limit the amount of recline applied to the backrest. These simple threaded devices are fully adjustable. By turning them in or out, they can accommodate the personal comfort of the driver.*

7 *To help with the fitting of the backrest cover, a hidden tuck-under fastening system is used to join the two halves of the rear panels of the backrest. When the seam is opened, the internal hardware can then be removed or serviced.*

8 *A socket wrench is used to remove the upper retainer nuts that hold the seat-latching mechanism to the seat frame. Access to this mechanism is made easy by peeling back the seat cover to reveal the underlying hardware.*

9 *Additional sheet-metal screws are removed from the seat latching mechanism with a socket wrench. Replace the pitted-chrome release button and thoroughly clean and lubricate the mechanism to ensure its proper operation.*

10 *Under the headrest foam are retainers for the seat trim. It takes a few turns of a socket on a nut-driver handle to release the speed nuts that hold the trim molding in place. The fragile posts are made of pot metal and can snap off, so be careful.*

11 *Getting the old seat cover off the backrest frame is no different from other seats. The seat cover and foam are attached to the back side of the seat frame as a unit. A diagonal cutter is used to remove the hog rings along the inside perimeter of the seat frame.*

12 *Hog rings have been used to secure the anchor listings to the seat springs. Use a diagonal cutter to carefully cut away the fasteners from the backrest springs to allow the removal of the seat cover and foam assembly.*

13 *With more than 45 years of rough service, the seat frame is bound to have some structural condition issues. After it is separated from the old upholstery, all the necessary repairs can easily be made to bring the backrest back to a serviceable condition.*

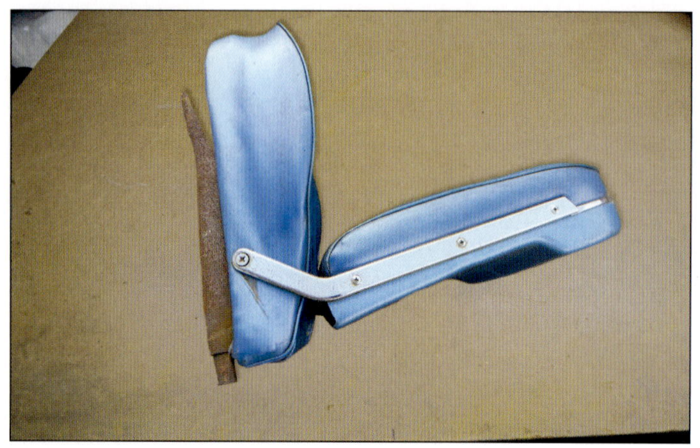

The side trim on this C2 Corvette seat is not only decorative but also very functional. The side irons allow the seat backrest to tilt forward. They also cover the seam between the seat upholstery and the solid backrest cover.

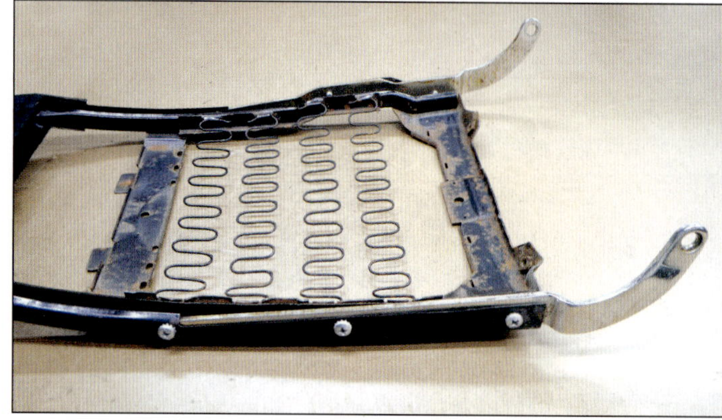

A built-in headrest was just one of the major changes made to the backrest on the C3 Corvette seat. The high-back design still had external pivot arms but brought the side irons inside the seat upholstery for a sleek and softer appearance.

Side Irons

On 1963–1967 seats, the backrest is attached to the bottom seat cushion with external side irons. These are the chrome-plated hockey stick–shaped pieces that conceal the edge of the seat back cover and provide a pivot point for the backrest. Each side iron is held in place with three large Phillips oval-head trim screws.

Chevrolet changed the seat design in 1968 to a high-back bucket seat. Then, the side irons were attached to the backrest frame and concealed by the seat cover, with only the chromed pivot arm portion of the bracket exposed.

Inspect the chrome for pitting and damage, and then decide if the side irons need to be replaced. The attaching hardware should also be inspected and replaced if it shows signs of damage.

Bottom Cushion

There are only a few items that need to be removed from the rear rail surface of the bottom seat frame before the cover and foam are ready for removal. Early C3 seats had a lower latch and backrest stop bumper. Two

The latching hardware is much easier to see with the seat back removed on this early C3 (1968–1969) seat. A rubber bumper and metal catch are fastened to the rear rail on the bottom seat cushion while a plastic backrest stop is secured to the bottom of the backrest.

small hex-head machine bolts secure the catch to the seat frame, and a Phillips-head machine screw holds the rubber stop bumper in place. Use the appropriately sized tool to remove the fasteners and place them in the parts bin.

From 1970 to 1978, Corvette seats had two metal bumper bolts that act as a nonadjustable stop that mate with the rubber bumpers on the backrest. The lower stop is removed with a #4 Phillips screwdriver bit.

Use some penetrating oil on the threads of the bolt to help during the extraction of the bolt.

Turn the seat frame facedown on the workbench and remove the bottom frame adjuster guide bezel bracket. This provides more room to attach the seat cover and the opportunity to clean and repaint the bracket. Remove the two small sheet-metal screws holding the bracket in place with a 1/4-inch socket and then place the parts in the bin.

Accessing the Seat Foam

1 *A large Phillips screwdriver bit is used to remove the large seat stops from the rear rail of the lower seat cushion. Often the stops can be hard to remove due to years of corrosion and the possibility of being bent from stress.*

2 *Pulling the old seat cover off is difficult enough without having extra parts in the way. It will help to remove the seat adjuster guide from the bottom frame. A socket is used to remove the two small sheet-metal screws holding the bracket in place.*

3 *Unlike other car seats, the Corvettes use blind fasteners to attach the bottom seat cover to the frame instead of ordinary hog rings. The clips slide upward and off the seat flange with the help of a flat-blade screwdriver.*

4 *The seat belt warning switch and upholstery are attached to the bottom seat frame springs. Cautiously, use a diagonal cutter and make sure that only the hog rings are cut and not the springs or wires of the warning switch.*

5 *This lower seat frame has just been cut away from the old seat foam, and it looks like it is in need of some major cleaning. The edges of the metal seat frame are sharp and rusted, so be careful when handling the old frame.*

Cover Removal

Special S-clips are used to hold the seat cover to the perimeter of the seat frame. The clips can be easily lifted by prying up on them with a screwdriver. Use the seat frame as a fulcrum to apply leverage on the clip. Push down on the screwdriver, and the clip will slide off the frame.

Just like the backrest, the corrugated anchor wires are attached to the seat springs with hog rings. Carefully remove the hog rings without damaging the springs. When all the fasteners have been removed, the seat frame can be lifted off the foam.

It is not necessary to disassemble the old foam from the seat cover, but it is possible to salvage some of the fasteners and corrugated wires. The seat cover can also serve as a reference guide for locating the new hardware during reassembly. After the new seat covers are installed, the old foam and covers can be discarded.

Frame Repair

All Corvette seat frames are designed and built from stamped sheet metal that has been spot welded together. The design of the seat frame is very weak, and in most cases, the metal is fatigued and needs some repair.

Our seat frame shows the typical stress cracking at the rear rail. This is caused by the force put on the backrest, which creates a great downforce on the thin metal frame. There are reinforcement plates available from parts suppliers to help beef up the seat frame. These panels can either be welded or bolted in place to strengthen the seat frame.

In most cases, the metal can be reshaped to its original position and welded back together. This repair can be done at home or by a local body

I have seen this type of stress crack on every Corvette seat frame I have worked on. The frame takes a lot of abuse from the rider being thrown back against the backrest, and this is the result. After a cleaning, it can be repaired better than new.

The damaged seat frame is set on an anvil. With just a few blows from a body hammer, the metal is straightened out and ready to be cleaned and welded. The repair will make the frame stronger and give better support to the backrest.

Welds were made to both sides of the seat frame to give the metal more strength and integrity. The top weld was ground smooth to create an even surface for the bumper stop to mount to. A nice coat of gloss enamel is applied to prevent corrosion.

shop. After the repair has been made, the frame can be cleaned and prepped for a new coat of gloss enamel. Painting the frame protects it from further corrosion.

Reconditioning Parts

Although a worn or damaged part can detract from the restoration of a seat, some parts can be cleaned up and put back into service. This saves you money and provides an extra sense of satisfaction with your project.

Cleaning a part is half of the battle. Parts can be washed, scraped, and sanded to remove scale and rust. Deep cleaning comes from bead blasting, wire brushing, and chemical baths. After cleaning, the damage can be accurately assessed to see if the part can withstand being reused.

Seat Tracks

Some parts require special attention to make them perform as they should. The restoration of seat tracks can be done in many ways. The first course of cleaning should be a good degreasing. There are many solvents that can be used to remove years of caked-on goo that can free the internal roller bearings. It is not a good idea to bead blast the tracks, as the grit is very difficult to remove afterward.

Paint

Proper surface preparation for priming and painting the surface can bring a part back to life. This prevents further corrosion and makes it look new and fresh again.

Prepping the Foam

A little cleanup on the molded seat foam is needed before the new

A wire brush can quickly remove rust and dirt from a part. After a thorough cleaning, the part is washed, masked off, and given a nice coat of paint. Moving parts are coated with an appropriate anti-corrosion covering and lubricated.

These tracks were corroded to the point that they would no longer slide. After the tracks were soaked in a parts washer, they loosened up and became functional again. The brackets were taped off and painted to look better.

Years of wear left the finish on the original seat backs dull and scratched. The backs were checked for damage and found to be in great condition. After a good cleaning, several light coats of matching spray dye were applied to make them look new.

seat cover can be installed. There are many sharp, hard edges that remain from the molding process. These hard lumps and bumps will show through the cover material, so they must be removed.

Dry Fit

It helps to first dry fit the foam to the seat frame. It may be a little long in places, and that excess amount of foam can simply be trimmed off. Scissors can be used to trim the crusty foam along the edge.

Run your hand over the surface of the foam to check for other hard spots. When the foam is clear of imperfections that can blemish the seat cover, it is time to clear the openings for the seat anchor fasteners.

Fasteners

To get the correct locations for the fasteners, line up the seat cover on the foam and fold back the bolster. The seam of the seat cover should lay in the channel. This is where the holes for the fasteners are to be made. Use a permanent marker to mark the fastener location on the foam.

Making Holes

There are many ways to make a hole through the foam. Making a clean hole safely is easily done with a 3/8-inch hole cutter. It only takes a few minutes to make a hole cutter from almost any scrap tubing. I made one out of a gas pipe nipple by tapering one end of the pipe on a belt sander. The other end was wrapped in electrical tape to make it safer to use.

To make a hole in the foam, the cutter is twisted back and forth with a slight downward pressure. The sharpened end of the pipe cuts cleanly through the stiff foam with very little effort. After the hole has been made, clear the core out to make room for the wire fastener to go through.

Preparing the Seat Foam for Installation

1 *After the new foam cushion was dry fit to the frame, it was found to be too long. A little trimming is needed to make it fit the frame properly. If it was left as is, the seat cover would be very hard to install, and it would look overstuffed.*

2 *Getting the new seat cover to fit correctly is a matter of preplanning. Positioning of the seat cover on the foam and getting the seat fasteners to land in the correct places takes just a few minutes and some minor adjustments.*

3 For a good fit, make sure that the listings line up with the recesses in the foam. It helps to use a permanent marker to mark the location of the seat fasteners. This will make the installation go a lot smoother and give the seat cover a better appearance.

4 The new seat foam does not always have the fastener holes cut through in the correct places. Making a hole in the foam is actually quite easy. This small piece of ⅜-inch gas pipe makes a perfect homemade hole cutter.

5 Many tools can be purchased, but sometimes it is just as easy to make them. The end of the pipe was tapered to a sharp edge with the aid of a benchtop belt sander. Take it easy and do not force the process by overheating the metal.

6 The end of the pipe may have threads or a bur that can harm you. Treat the end with a few wraps of electrical tape to soften the edge. This will prevent the palm of your hand from getting cut when using the tool.

7 *Cut a hole through the foam by rotating the cutting tool back and forth over the indicated location for the seat fastener. The tool cuts a clean hole in the cushion as it is twisted and advanced through the foam.*

8 *It is important to remove the unwanted core section after the hole is made. Leaving the core in the foam will make it difficult to insert the seat cover fastener. If the cutting tool is blocked with foam, it will become more difficult to cut the next hole.*

Installing the Cover on the Seat Bottom

Traditionally, the foam and cotton padding are attached to the seat frame and springs before a seat cover is installed. Our Corvette seat cover is attached to the foam cushion, and then the assembled unit is fit to the seat frame.

Another difference is how the seat cover is attached. Corvette seat covers are attached to the seat foam with wire fasteners resembling a paper clip. The smaller loop in the fastener is attached to the seat listing wire, and the larger loop is then pulled through the foam and connected to a corrugated anchor wire

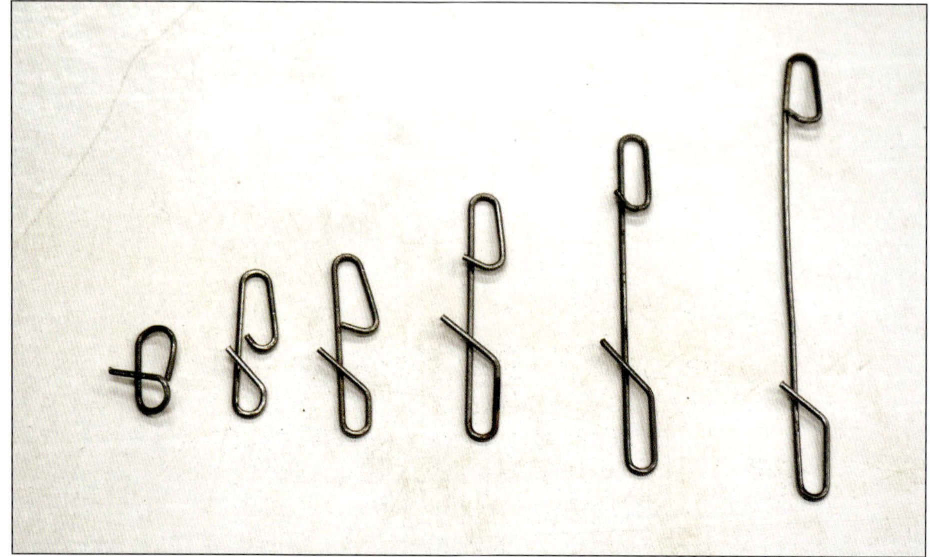

These special fasteners are used to attach the Corvette seat cover to the seat foam. A graduation in fastener size will give just the right amount of tension on the seat cover without creating a distortion in the upholstery.

that rests against the back side of the foam. It really doesn't matter the direction of the large loop end. I suggest facing them all in the same direction, as this makes it more convenient when they are connected to the anchor listing.

It takes a special hook tool to grab the end of the fastener and thread it through the foam and onto the anchor listing. As mentioned earlier in the chapter, some people can get really creative with this process and end up with a seat cover that just does not fit or perform well.

Listing Fasteners

Start with the insert listing fasteners, as they are accessible before the bolster listings are secured. Insert the hook tool from the back side of the foam and latch onto the loop of the listing fastener. Pull the fastener through the foam and allow it to capture the anchor listing.

The split end of the fastener loop is designed to open enough to allow the listing to seat inside and then close again. Make sure that the loop end of the fastener is closed and that it is inside the foam and not pinching the foam. It may be hard to pull the fastener through the thick foam, so push down on the anchor listing, compressing the foam. Repeat the process with the bolster fasteners and anchor listings.

Anchoring the Assembly

Double-check that all the fasteners are properly seated on the anchor listings before fitting the unit to the seat frame. It helps to turn the outer edges of the seat cover inside out to properly align the foam with the frame.

Hog Ring the Anchor Listings

Turn the assembly facedown on the workbench and hog ring the anchor listings to the seat springs where they intersect. The anchor listings should be in a straight line, so do not distort them as they are fastened to the springs. When all are attached, turn the unit faceup.

Clear the Foam

Before the edges of the seat cover are attached to the frame, clear the foam from the hardware anchor holes. Lift the rear section of the seat cover and locate the anchor holes for the baseplate of the backrest release strap.

Use the hole-cutting tool to remove the foam blocking the anchor points. Rotate the unit and cut away a small portion of foam covering the pivot-bolt anchor point. Taking time to do this now makes fitting the hardware much easier later.

Attaching the Cover

The bottom edge of the Corvette seat cover does not attach to the seat frame with a traditional perimeter listing and hog rings. Special spring clips are used along the bottom edge of the seat cover. These clips grab a fiber strip that is sewn to the edge of the seat material and are turned over the edge of the seat frame. The inside portion of the spring clip secures the seat cover to the frame.

Anchor the Cover

As with most seat covers, the rear portion of the cover is attached to the seat frame first. This anchors the upholstery so that it can be pulled and stretched onto the frame. If the front section is attached first, it will be very difficult to turn the rear edge to secure it correctly, and then the seat cover will have wrinkles in the sides that are almost impossible to remove.

Applying the Cover

Work the corner of the seat cover over itself to prevent it from bunching up. After the corners have been set, turn the bottom edge of the seat cover over the edge of the frame and slide the fastener down onto the frame. The edge of the cover should be neatly tucked behind the seat track support posts with the material smoothed outward to the corners.

The process is similar along the front of the seat cover. Work the corners over and down. Compressing the seat foam with your thumbs while inching the material over the corner helps the material lay out nicely. Turn the bottom edge over the front of the seat frame and slide the fasteners down onto the frame.

Now, work the sides one at a time from front to back. Make sure that the seat foam does not roll over the edge of the seat frame. It should remain flat and smooth around the perimeter of the seat frame.

Attach the fasteners to the sides of the frame from front to rear. If a fastener is in a position that it cannot be clipped to the frame, move the fastener over to prevent it from distorting the cover material. The seat cover should lay smoothly around the seat frame. Make any adjustments necessary to make the cover look nice.

Installing the Cover on the Seat Bottom

1 A special hook tool is used to work the seat fastener through the foam cushion and attach it to the anchor listing. The tool has a long shaft that can easily reach through the foam cushion and grab the fastener.

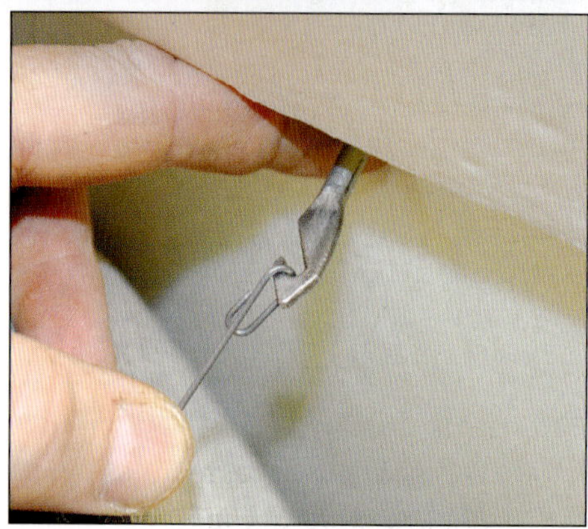

2 This is how the hook end of the tool should grab the fastener. Sometimes it must be worked by feel because the end of the fastener cannot always be seen when attaching the seat cover. After hooking the fastener, it can be pulled through the foam.

3 After the fastener emerges on the back side of the foam, it is looped over the anchor listing. The split loop should close again and rest inside of the fastener channel. Pushing down on the anchor listing will also help with the attachment.

4 C2 Corvette seats from 1963–1967 require a special burlap base pad that has thin spring steel wires woven through it. The corrugated anchor listings lay on the surface of the burlap, creating a firmer seating foundation than just the seat springs.

5 *The seat cover fasteners are not attached to the seat springs, just the anchor listings. Hog rings are used to secure the anchor listings to the springs. This prevents the foam from shifting position when it is being sat upon.*

6 *A little preplanning will save a lot of work on the simple task of bolting on hardware. Cutting away the foam from an anchor point prevents the bolt from binding and the possibly of cross threading. A nicer fit results from this action.*

7 *Excessive padding can lead to many unforeseen problems. Making room for the pivot bolt to be installed properly will save time in the long run. The seat will also function better if bulk is removed before final assembly of the seat.*

8 *The seat clips are designed to slide onto the edge of the upholstery and the metal flange of the seat frame. The wider partition of the fastener grips the upholstery, and the thinner section matches the perimeter edge of the frame.*

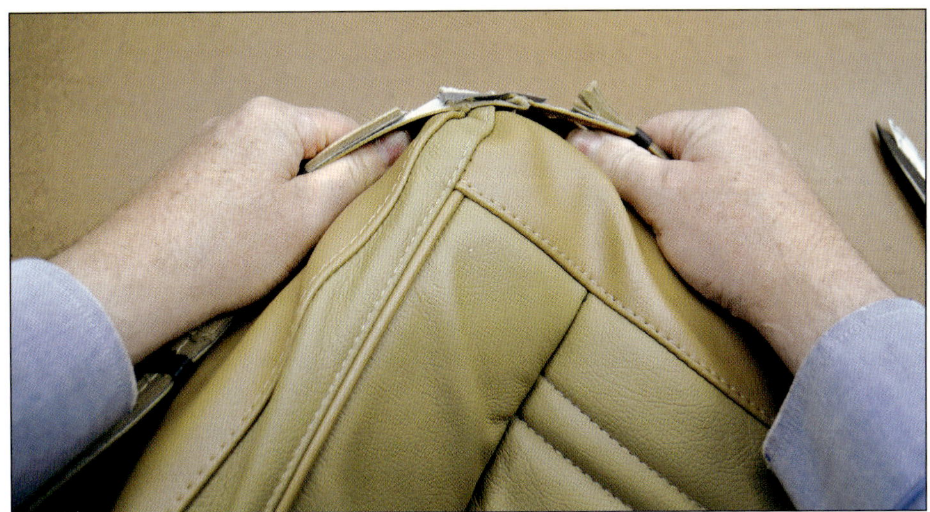

9 *Getting the corners of the seat cover to come out right is not always an easy task. It helps if the seat cover is turned inside out and the cover material is slid over itself as it gets worked down the corner of the seat frame.*

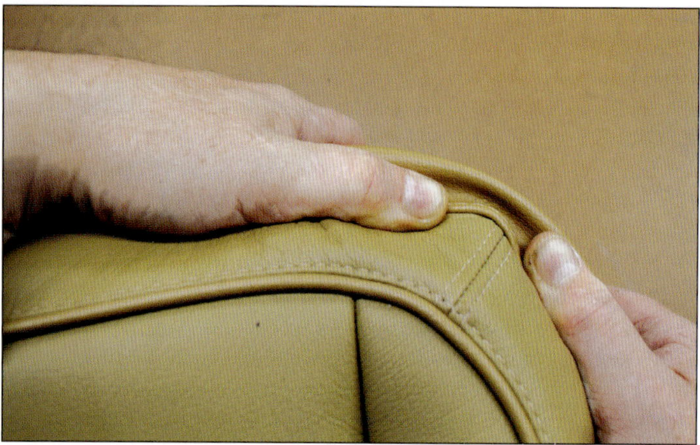

10 *Having the back edge of the seat cover anchored first gives a better foundation to work from. The special fasteners hold the seat cover tight to the frame and keep the material from bunching up. This looks a lot neater with no wrinkles.*

11 *A great trick to help a tight seat cover go on easier is to compress the foam cushion as the material is worked over the edges. Having less bulk to fight actually gives you more material to work with, preventing the cover from damage.*

12 *Getting the seat cover to conform and fit the front of the frame is a lot more challenging because the foam along the front of the seat is much thicker. When the cushion is crushed and compressed, the material is much easier to handle.*

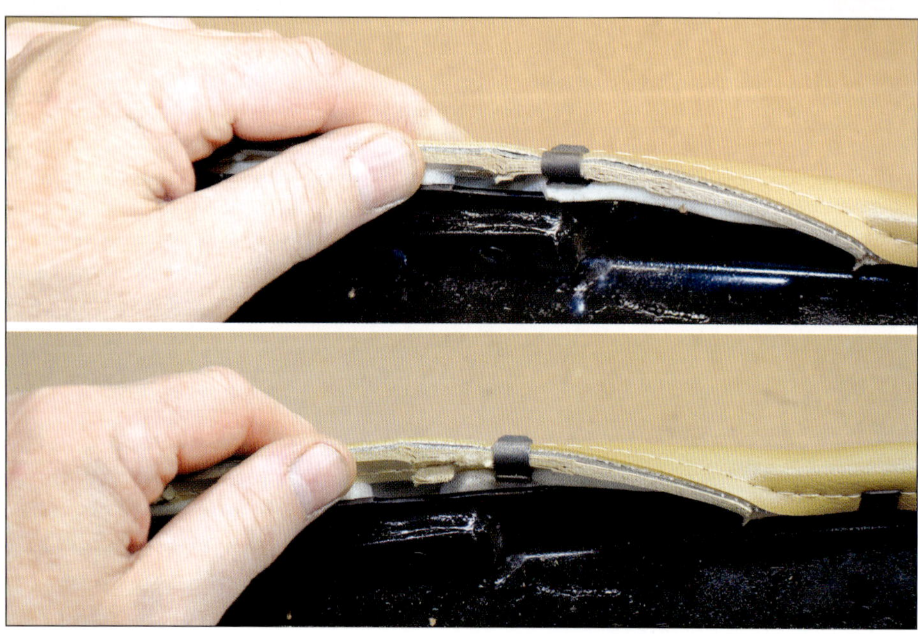

13 *This really isn't a problem. The factory installed these clips on the seat cover, and they interfere with the pivot anchor that is welded to the seat frame. It will only take a moment to remove the clip and reposition it to a more suitable position.*

Adding the Hardware

With the seat frame facedown on the workbench, reinstall the seat adjuster guide bezel in the corner of the seat frame. Locate the mounting holes of the bracket with the anchor holes by using a regulator. Set the small sheet-metal screws in the openings and tighten them down with a 1/4-inch socket. Be careful not to overtighten the screws.

Refit the nylon guide bushing in the lever opening of the bezel. A channel in the bushing should allow the part to just snap into place and fit securely without any adhesives.

At the rear of the seat frame, use a regulator to make a guide hole through the seat cover to allow the stop bumper bolt to pass through. There is already a void in the foam, so it is necessary to squeeze the seat cover against the rear rail of the seat frame when making the hole in the cover material.

Turn the unit faceup and use a round-shafted screwdriver to enlarge the bolt hole. Clear the hole by cutting away a very small portion of the cover material with scissors. Place the plastic gasket on the bottom of the stop bolt before inserting the bolt

Little details like this nylon guide bushing are important. The bushing protects the metal adjustment lever of the seat track from rubbing directly on the bracket. This prevents the lever from being damaged when it is used.

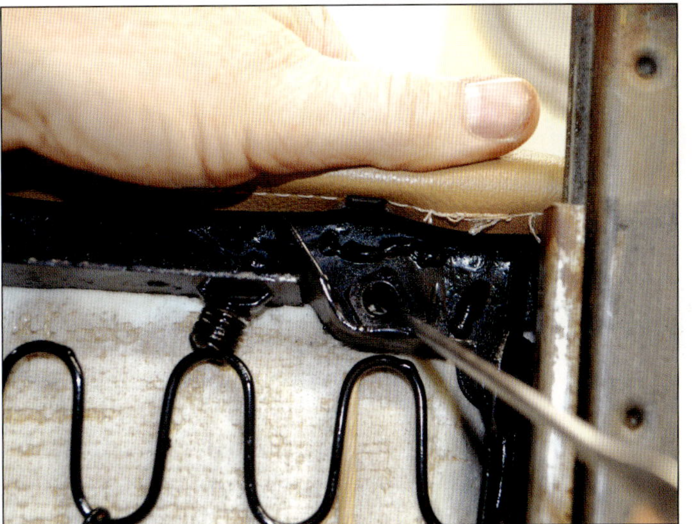

To avoid making a hole in the wrong place or making too large of a hole in the seat cover material, a small reference guide hole is made from the underside of the seat frame with a regulator. When the seat is turned over, a larger hole can be made.

To make the guide bezel fit properly, the metal seat fastener is repositioned to allow the bracket to fit properly. It is a tight fit and a hard place to get a tool into. A deep-well socket is used to tighten the retainer screws.

A larger reference hole is made from the top of the seat cushion with a screwdriver. Before the bumper bolts can be installed on the seat, the bolt hole will be cut open with scissors to make an unobstructed path for the bumper bolt.

To protect the seat cover material from becoming damaged or cut by the bumper bolt, place a protective plastic gasket on the bottom of the metal stop bumper. Little details like this are important to the longevity of the seat cover.

Using improper or the wrong-size tools can flair or scuff the surface of a part. To avoid damaging the metal stop bumper, it is hand tightened first and then the proper-sized tool is used to secure it in position.

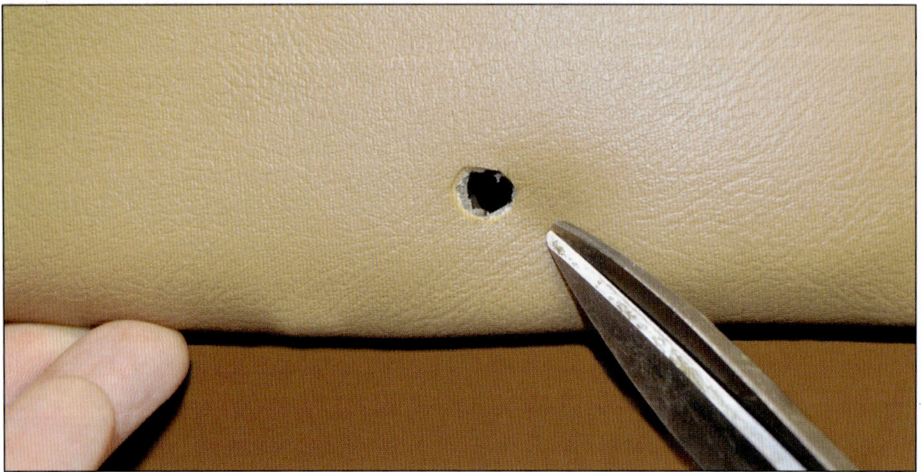

After a threaded anchor hole is located, the cover material is carefully trimmed away to allow the hardware to pass through without harming the seat cover material. Excess material can cause the threads of a bolt to bind or break off.

into the seat frame. Hand tighten the bolt to prevent it from cross threading in the anchor.

Use a #4 Phillips screwdriver bit to tighten the stop bolt to the seat frame. It is normal for the seat cover material to distort as the bolt is tightened. Just be careful that the material does not twist or bind during the installation of the stop bolt.

Anchor Access

The bottom seat cover has been secured and can be set aside until final assembly. Before the backrest can be attached, the anchor holes for the pivot bolts and the locking backrest baseplate should be cut into the cover material.

Use the same process as the bumper stop bolts to create the access holes: Use a regulator from the back side of the seat frame to create a reference hole in the seat cover. Expand the hole and then cut a very tight circular opening in the cover for the threaded bolts to pass through.

Backrest Cover

When assembling the backrest, there are a few differences from the lower seat cushion. The backrest on the high-back seat from 1968 to 1975 has a trim molding in the headrest area. The outer edges of all the high-back seat covers are attached to the frame with hog rings as well.

Prep the Foam

To prepare the foam, fit it to the frame and clear the headrest molding mounting holes. There are three posts on the molding that are used to align and secure it to the seat frame. Use the molding as a guide to locate the position of the holes and mark the post locations on the foam with a permanent marker. Use a hole cutter to clear the foam.

Dry fit the seat cover and mark the positions for the seat cover fasteners. Remove the foam from the seat frame and create the fastener holes in the channels. Then, finish by trimming and cleaning up the edges.

Anchor the Foam

The upper seat cover is installed to the seat foam just like the lower cover. Carefully position the cover on the foam and then turn the unit facedown on the workbench. Attach the fasteners first with the use of the hook tool. Pull the fasteners through the foam and attach them to the anchor wire on the back side of the foam. Then, continue with the bolster fasteners.

Position the assembled unit on the seat frame and use hog rings to secure the anchor listings to the seat springs. Recheck the position of the foam and cover to ensure that the alignment of the headrest trim molding is correct.

Trim Molding

From the front of the seat cover, set the headrest trim molding in place. Insert the guide pins through the seat cover, foam, and seat frame. To secure the trim molding, turn the backrest facedown and place a 10-inch-long 2x4 block under the molding to support it while it is fastened to the seat frame.

The molding is attached to the frame with speed nuts. A 3/8-inch socket wrench is needed to tighten the speed nuts. Because the trim molding is made of pot metal, it is important to be cautious when tightening the speed nuts, so avoid accidentally breaking off the post.

To fasten the trim molding, push down on the seat frame to get the posts of the trim molding to extend past the seat frame. Getting the speed nuts started can be difficult, considering all the downward pressure and working a nut driver. Gradually tighten the nuts a little at a time until they are seated evenly.

Internal Hardware

Inspect the condition of the release button on the latch mechanism. If it shows signs of pitting or wear, replace it. There is a small machine screw on the back side of the button that holds it in place. Use a Phillips-head screwdriver to remove the screw and lock washer. Swap out the worn button with a new one and reinstall the fastening hardware.

Set the seat-latching mechanism over the two studs located in the upper section of the seat frame. Square up the latch vertically and locate the anchor holes for the small sheet-metal screws. Install the upper set of screws and tighten them with a 1/4-inch socket. The lower screws will be added later. Next, secure the upper part of the latch in place with the washer nuts and tighten them with a 7/16-inch socket.

Fitting the Cover

To help the shape of the seat and soften the mechanical elements, an additional piece of foam is added to the back side of the headrest area. It would be much more difficult to assemble the seat if the foam was made in one piece, so this section of foam is glued in place after all the hardware has been installed.

Contact cement is brushed onto the edges of both pieces of foam, and then they are assembled. If they are not glued together, the foam sections

would shift, and the seat cover would not look full and smooth. Make sure that the edges are even and smooth before proceeding with finishing the fit of the cover.

After the glue has set on the foam, the upper section of the seat cover can be worked over the corners of the headrest area. The seat cover is split in the back to allow the cover to be installed without tearing the cover material. Be careful not to damage the cover while getting it over the top of the seat. It helps if the foam is compressed as you work the cover. This gives you extra material to work with. The foam will resume its shape to fill the cover when done. Do not fasten the top section of the seat cover to the frame at this time.

Now, focus on turning the bottom corners of the backrest cover. Begin by working the wrinkles from the seat cover from the top of one bolster down to the bottom corner. Pulling and stretching the material downward will turn over the corner without any trouble.

After both sides have been smoothed and turned, secure the bottom listing to the inner portion of the lower frame rail. It helps if you run the palm of your hand down the insert of the seat to flatten and smooth the material as it wraps around the bottom of the seat frame. The bottom listing must be tucked under the locking mechanism before it is hog ringed to the seat frame. Only fasten the listing at the inner points of the frame for now.

Upper Section

There should be a good stretch on the seat cover at this point. Most of the wrinkles in the face of the seat should be gone. Now, we can concentrate on the upper section of the seat cover.

Look at the seat cover and locate the blind overlap fastener in the center of the headrest area. To close this section, the sides need to be pulled inward and down to bring the blind fastener into the very center of the seat back. Begin with the right side or bottom part of the blind fastener and pull inward as you hog ring the short listing on the seat frame. Don't worry if there is not enough pull on the cover at this time; adjustments can be made later.

Repeat the procedure with the other side of the upper blind fastener section. The blind fastener should be close enough to slide together but do not fasten it yet.

Perimeter Listings

Work the sides of the seat cover from the top downward. Pull and stretch the material down and inward, hog ringing to the seat frame as you go. The bottom of the side cover should then tuck under the bottom listing. Finish fastening the bottom listing in place and then use a hog ring to cinch the two listing wires together in the corner.

Add the two remaining sheet-metal screws to the bottom of the locking mechanism to secure it to the seat frame. Use a 1/4-inch socket to tighten the screws. Insert the locking release strap back into the channel of the mechanism.

Blind Fastener

To seal the two halves of the seat cover, a tuck-under system has been sewn into the rear of the headrest section of the seat cover. Installation of the seat cover would be much more difficult if the seat cover was not split, so the tuck-under, or blind, fastener was added to simplify the cover installation.

To close the opening, simply pull the top or left section over the bottom or right section and hook the upper tab under the lower tab. You will encounter a battle here, as the seat cover is too tight, and the seam will not stay together on its own. This is because the new foam and cover material have not yet been allowed to relax and conform to the new contours of the seat.

Do not use glue on the blind fastener. This will not hold and will only create a mess. The only physical fastener to help keep the seam together is the lock button release bezel. After the bezel is fit, two trim screws hold the bezel in place and pinch the seam closed.

To fit the bezel, use scissors to cut away the cover material from around the release button. Do not make the opening any larger than necessary, and by all means, do not cut into the stitching on the seat cover.

Place the chrome-button bezel in the opening and locate the retainer screw anchor holes with a regulator. Secure the bezel in place with the correct oval-head trim screws. When the bezel is tightened up, it will pinch off the top of the blind fastener, preventing it from coming open.

Reassembling the Seat Back

1 Accurate reference marks will help achieve a better result on the seat cover installation. Taking the time to dry fit and prepare a part for assembly will save time and money by avoiding costly errors and damaged parts.

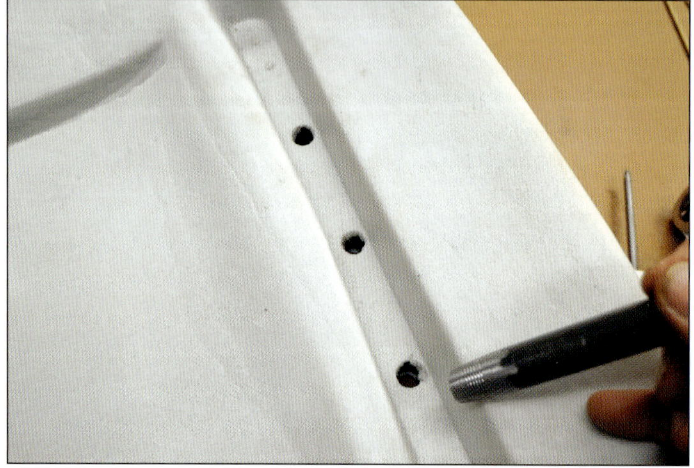

2 Clearing the through holes for a trim piece is a good practice. Many parts are made of fragile pot metal, and they can break if they are jammed into a tight place. Having a trim part fit properly and securely results in a better-looking seat cover.

3 *Each seat cover fastener hole has been cleared to allow for a better installation of the seat cover. The unobstructed fastener path makes this task of installing the seat cover much faster and allows the material to fit better.*

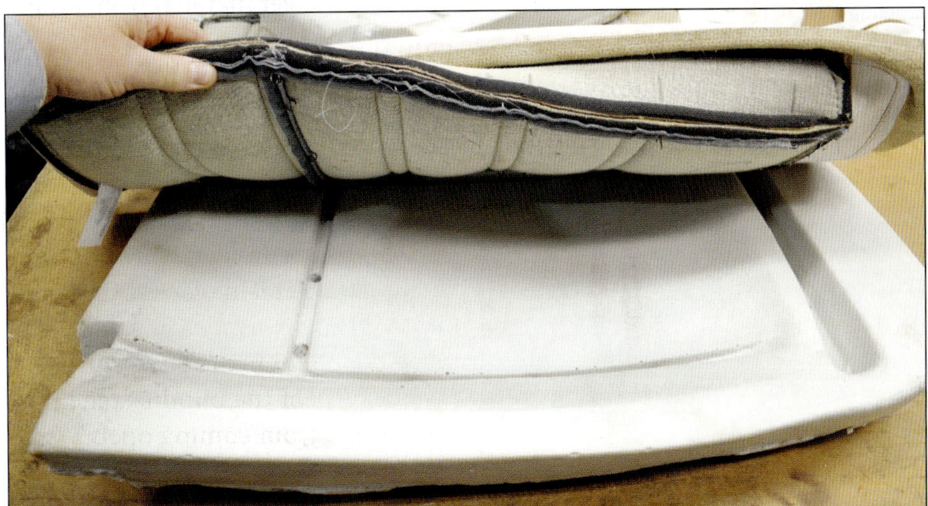

4 *Getting the fasteners and seams to line up with the foam is part of the job. Careful alignment of the seat cover to the foam cushion is vital for the appearance of the uphol- stery. No one wants to look at a crooked seat cover.*

5 *A hook tool is used to guide the seat fastener through the foam and onto the anchor listings. Having the right tools makes the job go much faster. Imagine trying to fasten the seat to the anchor listings without the hook tool.*

6 *The correct alignment of the seat cover assembly to the frame is a vital step if the headrest trim molding is to fit properly. The anchor listings are fastened with hog rings along the seat springs to keep the unit from shifting position.*

7 *A decorative trim molding is applied to the high-back seat. This molding fills the recessed area in the headrest portion of the seat. After the molding is set in place, it is attached internally with three small speed nuts.*

8 *To aid in fastening the trim molding, a block of wood is used during the installation process. The block helps fill the space between the workbench and the recess in the seat frame, giving much needed support to the molding.*

9 *The seat frame is pushed down against a block of wood that supports the molding while it is being fastened to the seat frame. Speed nut fasteners are carefully tightened with a nut driver to keep the trim molding attached to the seat frame.*

10 *After the seat back locking mechanism is set in place, it is secured to the seat frame with nuts and small sheet-metal screws. The only part of the locking mechanism that shows is the chrome release button located at the top of the device.*

11 To protect the seat cover from the underlying mechanical parts, an extra piece of foam padding is used to fill in the back of the headrest. The foam is glued onto the frame to keep it in the correct place during installation of the seat cover.

12 Even though the seat cover is designed to be installed with ease, a little finesse is applied to the seat cover as it is pushed over the top of the seat frame. The underlying foam fills the seat cover and gives the headrest a full, wrinkle-free finish.

13 A good downward stretch is applied to the seat cover to help it wrap around the bottom rail of the seat frame. This action helps remove wrinkles and makes it easier to add the hog rings that retain the cover to the seat frame.

14 A lot of inward pulling is done to get the upper cover to settle into place. Wrestling the seat cover over the foam seems like a tough job, but it is necessary to get a good fit. If the cover was loose, it would become baggy and not look very good.

15 *Attaching the sides of the seat cover is nothing more than a little pulling to work out the wrinkles as the cover is attached to the seat frame. Just a few hog rings along the frame rail and the seat cover is wrapped and wrinkle free.*

16 *With the seat cover all secured, more hardware is added to the seat-back latching mechanism to keep it in place. The small sheet-metal screws are tightened with a socket wrench before the locking release strap is installed.*

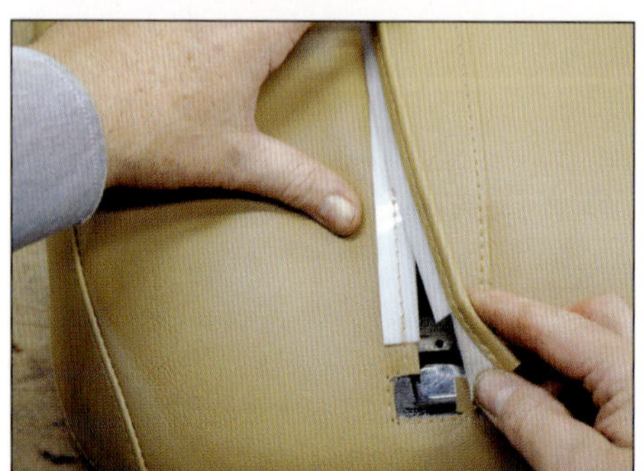

17 *To keep the outside of the seat cover looking sleek and stylish, a non-hardware fastener is used to close the gap in the back of the seat cover headrest area. The fastener just tucks under itself to make a flawless seal.*

18 *A little trimming is required to the back of the headrest before the latch release button trim bezel can be fit. Use extreme care along with scissors to remove just the right amount of seat cover material from the bezel opening.*

19 *After the trim bezel is set in place, small oval-head trim screws are used to secure the trim bezel to the seat back. The bezel is not only decorative but also serves as a retainer that keeps the blind fastener from opening.*

Trim Installation

The rear of the backrest is covered with a solid panel that hides the mechanicals and fastened edges of the seat cover. The lower portion of the blind fastener will also be held in place by the solid panel backrest cover. The panel cover has a pair of cleats on the top that slide over a retainer tab in the seat. The cleats are secured with pan-head trim screws along the inside top edge of the cover panel.

The retainer tabs can be located under the seat cover. To expose the tabs, press down on the cover material around the tab to reveal the profile of the tab. Use scissors to make a small cut across the base of the tab.

Continue pushing down on the cover material, and the tab will eventually pop through the cut in the material. When released, the cover material resumes its previous shape, leaving the tab exposed.

Installing the panel cover over the tabs can be a bit difficult unless you give them a little help. I like to bend them upward a little to help compensate for the new foam. This also prevents the seat cover material from becoming scraped by the panel cover when it is installed.

Place the top edge of the panel cover about 1½ inches above the retainer tabs with the blind fastener material centered in the notch at the top center of the panel cover. While pressing down lightly, slide the cover panel down over the tabs.

Use a regulator to index the cover by locating the anchor screw holes in the seat frame through the holes in the cover panel. Insert the oval-head trim screws and tighten them with a Phillips-head screwdriver. Do not overtighten the screws or they will crack the fiberglass cover panel.

Tabs on the back of the seat frame are designed to retain the rear cover panel. The tabs are revealed from under the seat cover when a small cut is made at the base of the tab and the cover material is stretched around the tab to expose the fastener.

When the seat cover material is fastened tight enough, it responds and gives results you can't imagine. Just a little downward pressure applied to the seat cover helps expose the retainer tab, and the material closes back up.

A small upward adjustment is made on the retainer tabs to make fitting the rear cover panel a much easier task. The tab is gripped with a hog ring plier to tweak it into a better position to receive the cleat on the rear panel.

Locate the anchor holes for the adjustable rubber bumpers and cut out a small access hole in the cover material. Insert the threaded bolt of the bumper and screw it into the bottom of the backrest until it bottoms out, but do not tighten the bumper bolt completely.

Final Assembly

Please be careful when reassembling the two seat halves. The assemblies are bulky, and the seat cover can be easily damaged. Cover the surface of the workbench with a clean towel to protect the surfaces from becoming scuffed.

Pivot Bolt

Begin by laying the seat bottom and backrest on their sides and carefully straddle the bottom with the pivot arms of the backrest. Place one of the heavy spacer washers over the pivot bolt anchor hole and then position the pivot arm over the washer.

Insert a new nylon bushing in the pivot arm. The bushing allows the seat to tilt without binding, and it also prevents the pivot arm from wearing against the pivot bolt. Install a new pivot bolt through the bushing, pivot arm, and spacer washer.

Because of the stress that is put on the pivot bolt, I like to replace them. Inspect the shoulder bolt for damage and reuse them if you like, but the replacement cost is low, new bolts look nice, and they are less likely to fail. The bolt is then tightened with a #4 Phillips screwdriver bit.

Next, add the locking nut to the bolt on the underside of the seat frame. Tighten the locking nut with a 1/2-inch wrench. Then, carefully turn the seat assembly over and repeat this process to the other side of the seat.

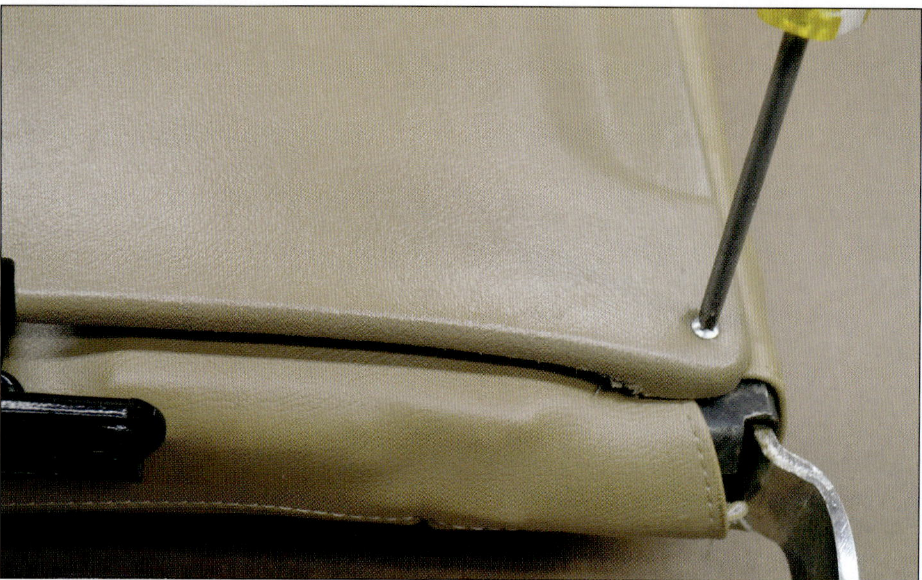

Oval-head trim screws are used to secure the rear cover panel to the rear of the backrest. The trim screws are tightened just enough with a screwdriver to keep the cover in place without causing the cover material to crack.

The top portion of the rear cover panel seals against the back of the headrest. A cutout has been formed into the panel to accommodate the shape of the blind fastener to eliminate a gap when the cover is set in place on the backrest.

Adjustable rubber-covered bumpers are screwed into the bottom of the backrest with a #3 Phillips screwdriver. The bumpers prevent the seat from tilting too far backward, which can cause premature wear on other parts of the seat and frame.

Plastic Backer

Set the seat upright and press the release button on the locking strap to allow it to extend out of the backrest. Place the plastic backer under the base of the release strap and align the base with the mounting holes in the bottom frame rail.

Insert the mounting bolts and tighten them down with a 3/8-inch socket. Please note that the correct positioning for the release strap is with the pivot loop toward the rear.

Bumper Adjustment

Latch the seat and then look at the bumper positions. Note that they do not touch each other. This condition will put unnecessary strain on the pivot points and cause the seat to tilt back too far. Ideally, the bumpers should meet and still allow the seat to latch and unlatch without any strain.

To make the adjustment, pull the backrest forward while it is still latched. Make a mental note of the distance that needs to be filled. Unlatch the seat and unscrew the rubber bumper to the desired length required and then latch the seat. Continue to make small adjustments until the bumpers touch, and the backrest will easily latch and release without excessive force on the button.

Seat Tracks

Turn the seat upside down to allow the installation of the seat tracks. Insert the adjustment lever through the opening in the bezel guide and position the track on the bottom of the seat frame. Depress the lever to allow the sliding portion of the track to move backward, exposing the mounting hole.

Insert the track bolt in the channel and tighten it with a 3/8-inch socket. Adjust the track forward and insert the rear bolt and tighten it. Repeat the process with the other seat track.

Finish the installation by screwing the adjuster knob onto the threaded end of the adjustment lever. The knob makes it more comfortable for the passenger to adjust the position of the seat.

Finalizing the Seats

1 *Don't forget the heavy washer. This small item has a lot of responsibility, and the seat needs it. The spacer prevents the pivot arm from tearing up the seat upholstery while also providing a solid base for the pivot bolt to bottom out on.*

2 *If the backrest begins to feel loose or sloppy when it tilts forward, it is time to replace the nylon bushing. The pivot bolt goes through the bushing and centers the pivot arm, preventing the two metal pieces from grinding together.*

3 *Because there is a lot of stress that is forced on the pivot bolt, a new pivot bolt is used. The new bolt will provide years of service without the worry of failing. A large socket bit is used to tighten the bolt to the seat frame.*

4 A wrench is used to tighten the locking nut that prevents the pivot bolt from coming loose. This safety measure was added to ensure that the backrest would not accidently work itself free and harm the passengers.

5 Because we took the time to clear the foam from the rear rail of the seat base, it is easy to mount the base of the locking release strap. The base sits on a plastic pad and two bolts are used to secure the base of the strap to the seat bottom.

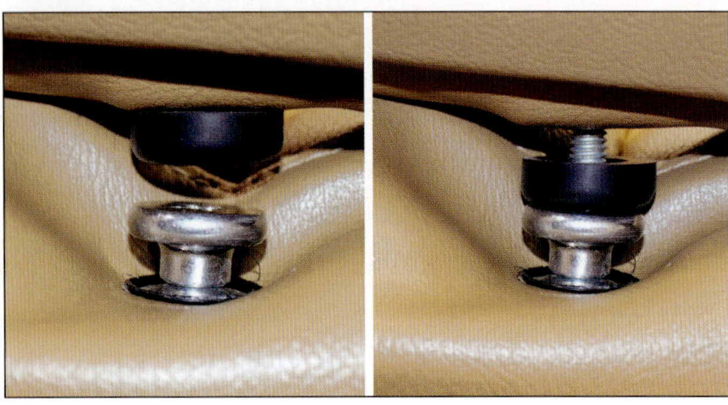

6 Keeping the backrest properly adjusted will prevent damage to the frame and make the seat safer to use. Prior to being adjusted, left, the bumpers do nothing, and this is not good. After the adjustment is made, the seat will function just like new.

7 Each seat has a pair of tracks but only one with an adjustment lever. The track with the adjustment lever mounts on the right side of the frame and the lever threads through the slot in the guide bezel before it can be secured to the bottom of the frame.

8 *The seat tracks are secured to the set frame with small bolts on each end of the track. When the track is fully adjusted front or back, the mounting hole is exposed in the channel. After the bolt is inserted, it can be tightened with a socket wrench.*

9 *A new adjuster knob is installed on the seat track adjustment lever. The chrome ball simply threads onto the end of the lever shaft without any tools. After the new shiny hardware is installed, it makes the seat look brand new again.*

10 *These fully reconditioned seats are now ready to be reinstalled. Every detail has been addressed to make them look and perform as if they just came from the factory. The owner will enjoy the new leather and comfort for a great driving experience.*

Ready to Drive

The Corvette seat has presented us with many different challenges not found on other types of car seats. New tools, procedures, and hardware only make getting to the end of the project much more rewarding. Tackling a project like this can be a little overwhelming if you are figuring it out on your own, but with some guidance, the experience isn't too bad.

Late C3 Seat Covers

A dramatic change in seat style happened with the 1978 Corvette pace car. The unique folding design earned the seat a nickname as "the clam." This seat was used up to the last production model of 1982. Servicing the seat is simple but has perplexed owners on how it operates and is disassembled. This section will help you better understand the seat and how to repair and update the upholstery on this type of seat.

It is only fitting that one of the most recognized Corvettes produced was equipped with a very special set of bucket seats. The seat design proved to be comfortable and stylish, and the change became permanent and lasted throughout the end of the regular manufacturing in 1982.

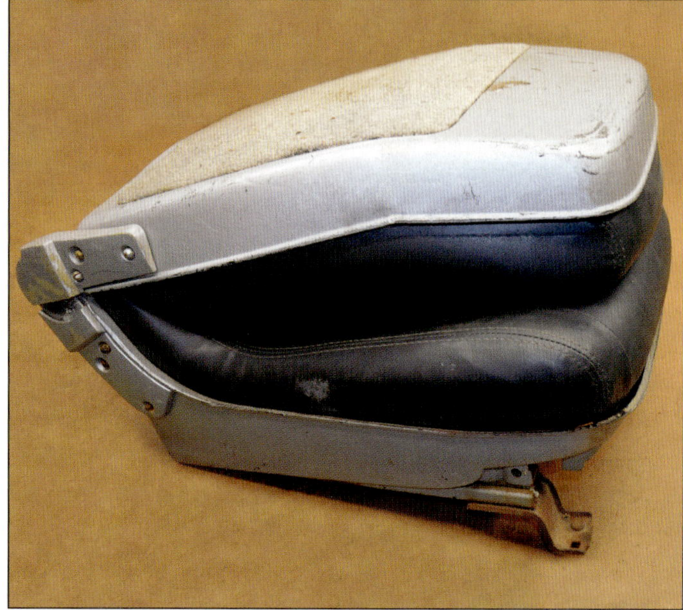

Late-model C3 Corvette seats could be folded in half, earning them the iconic nickname of "the clamshell seat." This was quite fitting due to the physical appearance of the seat when it was folded forward to allow passage into the rear compartment of the car.

Removal

Getting the seat out of the car for new seat covers can be done two different ways. The first is to unbolt the seat from the car. This is done from under the car. The seat track bolts go through the floor and are secured with a flared nut and washer. Use a 1/2-inch socket to remove the nut and then carefully lift the seat out of the car.

Traditionally, the whole seat is removed and then disassembled on the workbench, but these seat cushions can also be removed without unbolting anything. Each cushion has a built-in wire loom that is retained by a spring clip attached to the seat shell. There are four clips on the backrest and two on the bottom cushion. Simply push inward on the side of the backrest to release the retaining wire from the clip. Repeat this on the other side, and the cushion will come right out.

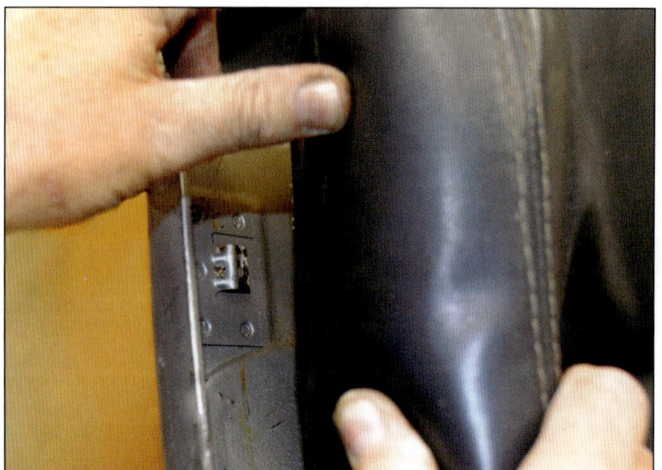

Retaining wires built into the foam cushion slid into metal spring clips mounted to the inside of the seat frame. This unique feature of the seat cushion made it easy to remove for servicing without any tools. One simply pushed in on the foam bolster.

An upper and lower spring clip is attached along the outer edges of the inner seat back. The opposing retaining wires in the foam are slid in these clips and hold the upper seat cushion securely in the seat frame.

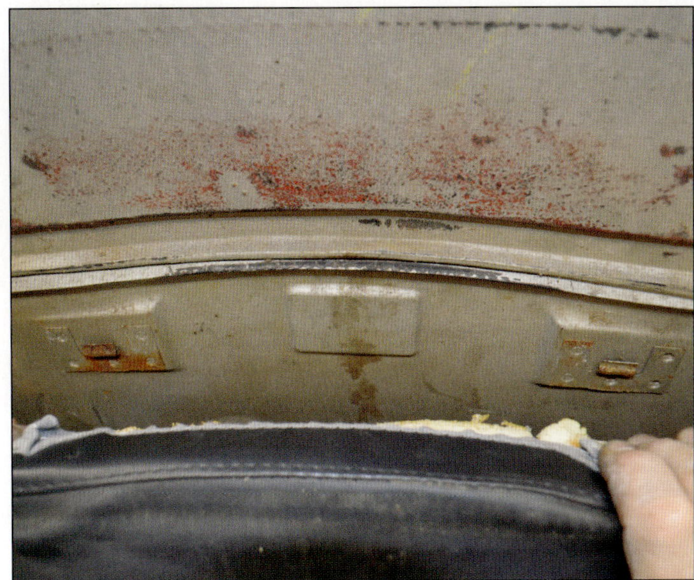

Along the upper edge of the lower seat frame is a pair of spring clip retainers. These clips are used to keep the lower seat cushion in place. Freeing the lower cushion is accomplished by lifting along the top edge of the cushion with a quick snap.

A listing wire with forward-facing extended tabs is attached to the underside of the lower cushion foam. These tabs hold the front of the lower cushion in place by tucking under raised retainers that have been formed into the bottom panel of the seat frame.

Lower Seat Cushion

Removing the lower cushion is just as easy. Push down along the upper back edge of the cushion to unclip it from the shell and then lift the back edge upward to slide the front hooks from under their retainers. The seat shell can remain in the car unless the plan is to replace a damaged panel or the carpeting on the back side of the shell.

A tailor's tape is used to make a quick measurement on the inside bolster of the backrest cushion. This is done to determine the correct foam and seat cover size before an order is placed. You should get a measurement of either 2 or 4 inches.

To service the shell, remove the four nuts that attach it to the seat tracks with a 7/16-inch socket wrench. If you are cleaning and lubricating the seat tracks, they can be unbolted from under the car.

Seat Cover Options

There are some options for restoring the C3 seat cushions. Seat covers are available in the original colors and materials that came with your car. Leather, vinyl, and a combination of the two along with other custom offerings are available

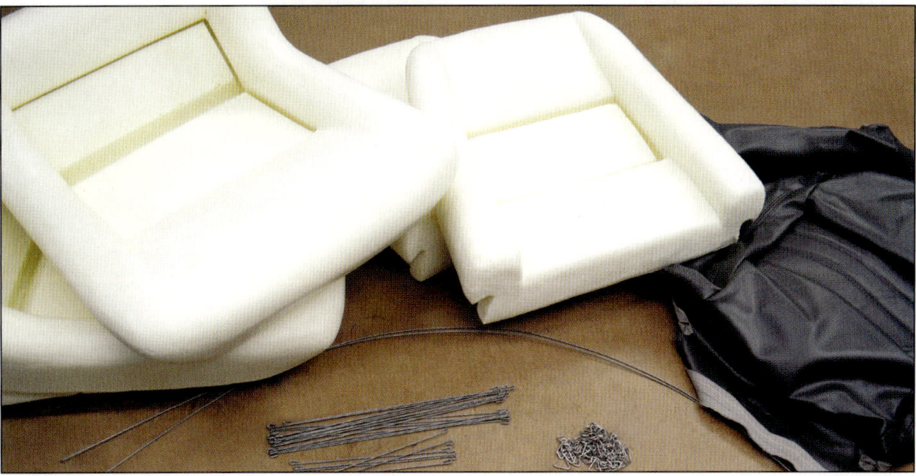

All new materials are used to create the seat cushions for the 1981 Corvette. Fresh foam ensures that a wrinkle-free fit is achieved by filling out the new seat covers, and the new installation kit secures the cover to the foam without the fasteners failing.

through parts dealers. You do not have to go with the factory options if you choose to make upgrades to suit your own taste.

The first option is to just replace the seat covers. If the seat foam is not torn or deteriorated, this might be the least costly way to proceed, but it also takes the most effort. Before a new seat cover set can be ordered, the bolster size needs to be determined for the upper seat cushion so that the covers will fit your existing foam.

Begin the process by measuring from the inside edge of the horizontal pleated insert to the center point of the French seam on top of the bolster. This measurement can only be 2 inches or 4 inches.

Taking these measurements can get confusing, and since these numbers cannot be intermixed, it is in your best interest to order new foam to go with the new seat covers. This ensures a proper fit and the best result in the long run.

When ordering new seat covers, make sure to get a seat installation kit as well. You cannot trust reusing the old listing wire fasteners, and the listing wires themselves are often corroded or broken.

Some manufacturers sell their seat covers with the installation kit already installed at no additional cost. Ask the dealer if the installation kit is included to avoid making a double purchase. Along with the installation kit, order the special hook tool needed to grab the wire fasteners to secure the seat cover to the foam and a good pair of hog ring pliers.

The best option is to order the seat covers already installed on the foam. This costs just a little more money, but it saves time, and you will not have to purchase any additional items to complete the project.

Seat Cover Disassembly

If you are replacing just the seat cover, the old cover material needs to be removed. Begin by turning the seat cover upside down on the workbench to access to the perimeter hog rings. The hog rings can be removed by grabbing them with a heavy-duty wire cutter and then twisting them off. This can get a little tiring on the wrist after a few dozen have been removed.

Cutting the hog ring is also an option, but be careful of flying debris. Wear eye protection and use a long-handle pair of cutters to make the task less fatiguing. Compound cutting pliers will also work with a lot less effort. Make sure that all the little hog ring pieces are removed

A good pair of diagonal cutters is necessary to remove the hog rings from the perimeter listings that secure the seat cover to the back side of the foam cushion. The hog rings can either be cut or twisted free of the anchor listing that is molded inside of the foam.

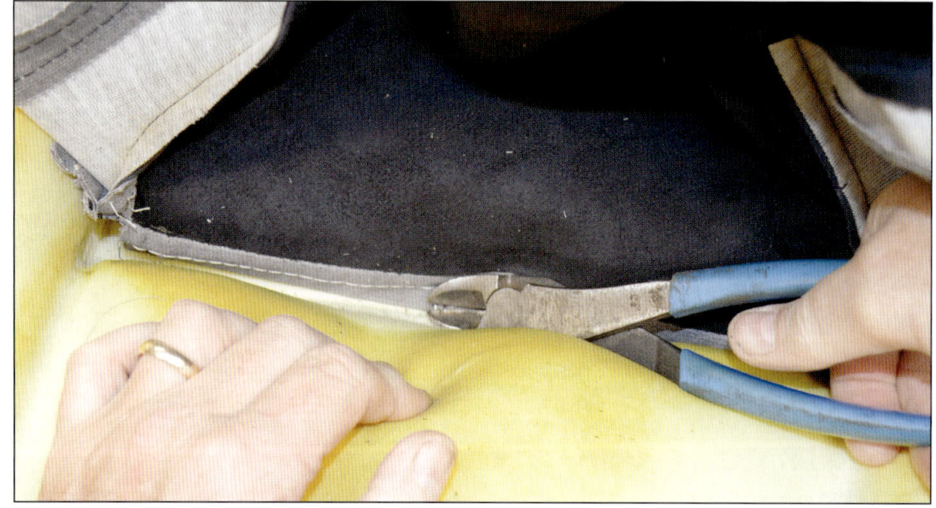

A wire cutter is the quickest way to remove the small anchor fasteners that are attached to the inner seat cover listings. New fasteners are used for the installation because the old retainers have become weak and corroded from years of service.

and then sweep up to prevent tracking them all over.

Next, turn the outer cover upward to expose the inner listings. These are held in place to the foam by small wire fasteners. The fasteners can be very sharp and are most likely covered in rust after many years of service. It is best to just cut them off rather than try to unhook them from the foam. On the lower cushion, there is an external anchor listing at each end of the insert. This listing sits on the outer surface of the foam. After cutting away the fasteners, remove the anchor listing and throw it away. It will be replaced with a new one from the installation kit.

Remove the old cover and be cautious of any sharp fasteners that may still be stuck to the old listings. At this point, the foam should be completely exposed. It can be inspected to see if it should still be used. Do not reuse the old foam if it shows any signs of mold or mildew or it has been chewed up by mice. It would be best to use new foam under the new seat cover, as it will not only be cleaner but it will also fill out the new cover. This will help avoid the new cover becoming prematurely baggy and wrinkling, which will lead to creases and holes in a very short amount of time.

Seat Cover Installation

There are a few things that need to be done before the new seat cover can be attached. If not already installed, the listing wires will need to be inserted into their corresponding listing sleeves. Then, three new wire fasteners can be evenly placed along the long listings and two on the shorter side listings. The fasteners should be at least 3/4 inch from the end of the listing and one centered on the insert.

Additional anchor listing wires are used on the back side of the lower cushion foam to secure the seat cover. The old, weak listing wires should be discarded, and new listings should be used along with the replacement foam to ensure that the seat cover is properly attached.

After the old seat cover was removed, it was clear to see that the old foam has shrunk quite a lot. It only makes sense to install the new seat cover on new foam. This will give the passenger much more comfort and prevent the seat cover from bagging and wrinkling.

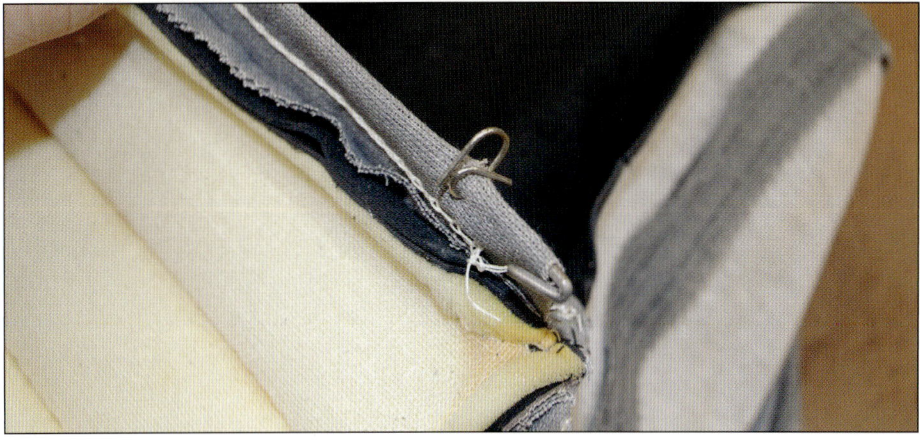

After the listing wire has been inserted in the sleeve, new wire fasteners are carefully installed on the listing. These small retainers are easier to use than hog rings and hold the seat cover securely to the new foam cushion.

A little time is taken prior to the cover installation to align and mark the pre-installed fastener positions. This step makes installation of the seat cover much faster by knowing exactly where the location of the underlying fastener is on the listing.

A hole cutter makes a clean passage for the wire listing retainers. With just a few twists of the simple homemade cutting tool, a perfect circle of foam is cut and ready to be removed. This simplifies the preparation needed to install the new seat cover.

I like to insert the wire fasteners so that the open end of the anchor loop is facing outward. It really doesn't matter the direction as long as the base is around the listing wire. The outer perimeter listing wires can be installed after the insert has been anchored to the foam. The perimeter will be hog ringed to the foam, as there are not any wire fasteners used to attach the perimeter of the cover.

After all the wire fasteners are in place, the seat cover can be dry fit to the seat foam. The listing should be set deep into the foam listing channel. Mark the position of each wire anchor fastener with a permanent marker.

When all the anchor positions have been marked, the seat cover can then be removed and set aside. A through hole will need to be made

in the listing channel at each marked point. Use a hole cutter to carve out a small hole no larger than 1/2 inch in diameter into the channel.

A heavy wire should be embedded in the foam. This is where the anchor wire will be attached to the seat foam. Press a finger into the hole and feel for the location on the back side of the foam. Complete the hole on the back side of the foam. When all the

Using the correct tool to get a project completed makes all the difference. The special hook tool easily grabs the wire loop fastener and draws it through the foam so that it can be slipped over the retainer wire embedded in the foam cushion.

Due to design and manufacturing costs, the factory does not always incorporate all the anchor points needed into its products. An external anchor listing wire is used across the back side of the foam for the listing fasteners to hook on to.

Hog rings are used to secure the seat cover around the perimeter of the cushion. For a better fit and finish, the top listing of the bottom cushion should be hog ringed first at the top center and then worked outward to the corners.

To prevent accidentally damaging the new seat cover during installation, the seat cover is gradually worked over the corner of the foam by turning it inside out and then inching it into place. More material can be gained by compressing the foam as you fit the cover.

through holes have been created, start installing the new seat covers.

Bottom Cushion

Begin with the lower seat cushion. Dry fit the seat cover to the foam, paying attention to the insert listings. Before pulling on the wire attachment fasteners, the listing should be pressed deep into the listing channel of the foam, as this will make the attachment process much easier. To simplify the installation, follow this sequence, otherwise you will end up fighting the seat cover.

Center Horizontal Insert Listing

The first listing to be attached is the centermost horizontal insert listing. Insert the hook tool through the center through hole from the back side of the foam and hook the loop of the fastener. Carefully pull the fastener through the hole until the open end of the fastener clears the anchor wire in the foam. Hook the clip on the anchor wire and remove the hook tool. Do the same with the outer wire fasteners.

Upper and Lower Horizontal Listings

Next, get one of the longer listing wires included in the installation kit. This will be used as the anchor wire for the upper horizontal listing. It will rest on the back side of the foam, and the listing fasteners will get attached to it.

Begin by pressing the upper horizontal listing into the top listing channel and hooking the center wire fastener, as was done with the last listing, pulling it through the foam and attaching it to the external listing wire. Continue outward with the other fasteners and then repeat this process with the lower horizontal listing. Check the positioning of

the seat cover to make sure that it is properly centered in the foam and make any adjustments as necessary.

Vertical Insert Listings

Now, begin with the vertical insert listings. Attach the longer bottom listings one side at a time before moving up to the shorter upper listings. These listings attach to the internal anchor wires embedded in the foam. After the listings have been attached, check the fitment, making sure that all the insert material has been neatly tucked into the listing channels before moving on.

Working the Seat Cover

As with all lower seat cushions, fit the rear of the cover over the foam before the forward section is fit. This provides the proper stretch needed get the seat cover to look nice. Start by inserting a medium-sized listing wire into the perimeter listing and

work it around to the top of the seat cover.

Gradually work the seat cover over the top of the foam until the listing is in close proximity to the anchor wire set in the foam. Hog ring the center point of the listing to the anchor wire and then check the fit of the cover. There should be equal amounts of material on both sides of the hog ring.

Now, turn the corner of the seat cover inside out and then work the cover over the corner of the foam with your thumbs. There is a heavy piece of chipboard glued to the upper back side of the foam cushion that helps define the shape of the cushion. The seat cover must go over the top of the chipboard. Once the seat cover has been positioned, add another hog ring to the top outer perimeter listing and repeat for the other side of the seat cover. There should only be three hog rings in this listing.

After the front of the lower seat cover has been attached to the underside of the foam and the material has been fit over the corners, side-panel wrinkles can be eliminated by adding evenly spaced hog rings from the front to the rear along each side.

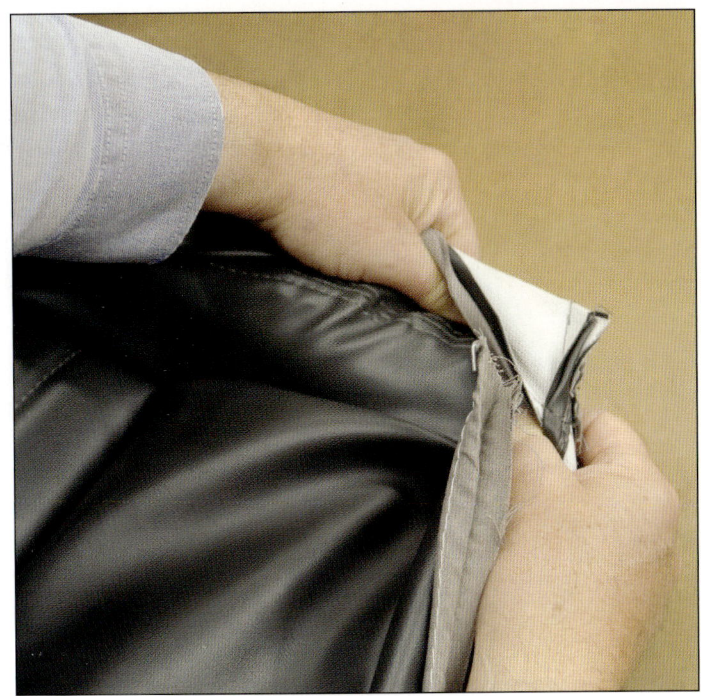

Getting the seat cover to fit properly over the soft foam corners of the upper cushion is always a bit of a challenge. The lower corners are turned first and then the cover can be hog ringed to the foam. This ensures that the cover will not be torn by pulling on the material.

Hog rings are installed along the back side of the foam from the center point outward. This prevents wrinkles from forming in the cover. After the lower stretcher has been secured, the foam in the upper cushion can be adjusted to fit perfectly.

Some additional foam will need to be removed from around and beneath the anchor listing in the foam cushion. Taking the time to do this makes the newly covered seat cushion a little easier to install into the seat frame.

Hog rings are only used between the anchor openings in the foam. There is only enough room in the seat cushion anchor clip for the anchor wire, so the anchor wires must be clear of all obstructions to ensure a trouble-free installation into the seat frame.

Applying a little heat to the new seat cover will help relax some of the wrinkles and make the new seat cover look a lot smoother. Care must be taken when applying heat so that the seat cover does not get damaged.

Seat Cover Attachment

To attach the bottom section of the seat cover, the very long listing wire is first inserted into the perimeter listing and then centered into position. Fit the bottom section of the seat cover just like the upper: hog ringing the center point of the perimeter listing first and then working the corners over and securing the cover with another hog ring. Again, only a total of three hog rings are needed for this section.

To create the corner, the listing wire should be shaped to curve around the underside of the foam cushion. The listing will not want to lay down along the side of the cushion right away. To help it, add a hog ring at the front, just behind the raised seat anchor, and continue working toward the rear by adding a hog ring about every 3 inches. Work one side at a time, making sure there are no wrinkles in the cover material as it is attached to the seat cover.

At this stage, the vertical riser will have to be attached to the foam cushion. Insert a medium-sized listing wire in the perimeter listing and work from the top down, adding a hog ring at the top and one at the bottom of the listing wire.

Backrest

The backrest is attached much the same as the bottom cover, but it has fewer listings to work with. Fit the seat cover into the foam and attach the upper and then lower horizontal listings followed by the vertical side listings.

Fitment

The bottom of the upper cushion is attached first. There is a large flap or stretcher on the bottom of the upper seat cover that attaches along the back side of the foam. The seat cover is fit by turning the lower corners of the cover inside out and then working them over the foam.

Now, insert a medium-sized listing wire into the perimeter listing. Hog ring the center point of the listing to the anchor wire in the foam cushion. Check for centering and then add a hog ring to each end of the listing to secure the flap in place. There should only be three hog rings in this listing.

Excess Foam

Before the upper section of the seat cover is fit, it is a good time to clean the excess foam from the mounting points. There are two of these on each side of the backrest. With the cover out of the way, there is less chance of damaging the listing. Place the upper cushion facedown on the workbench and use scissors to trim away the foam that surrounds the opening of the mounting point.

More Fitment

Add the long listing wire into the perimeter listing. Carefully work the seat cover over the foam and secure the cover with a hog ring at the top center point. Again, check the alignment of the cover, and when you are satisfied with the fit, add one more hog ring on each side of the center along the top.

To attach the sides of the seat cover, ease the listing wire around the curve of the foam and place a hog ring about 1½ inches below the bottom of the mounting point. Place a second hog ring the same distance up from the lower mounting point and then an additional hog ring in the center of the listing. The mounting points must remain clear or else the seat cover will be impossible to fit back into the seat frame.

To help tighten up the lower section of the seat cover, place a hog ring in the seat cover material below

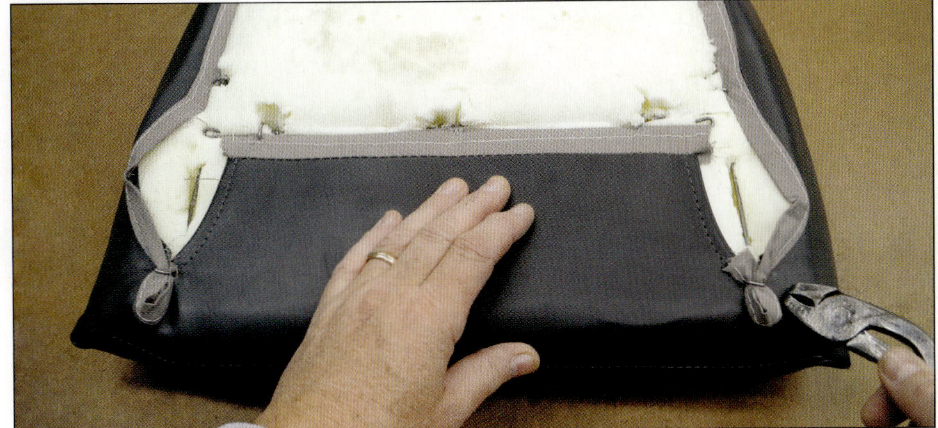

An extra hog ring is placed in the lower portion of the seat cover to help form the lower corner properly. Placing the hog ring well below the anchor opening prevents any difficulty during the cushion installation.

After all the effort of installing the new seat covers on fresh foam, our seat cushions are now finished, and they are ready to be installed in the car.

the mounting point. For the best hold and to avoid the cover material from tearing out, try to crimp the hog ring just on the outsides of the listing stitching. The listing gives the hog ring something to hold, and if the threads are not cut with the hog ring, it will hold forever.

Finishing

These particular seat covers are notorious for having wrinkles in the bolster seam. To help make them look nicer, apply a little heat to the wrinkled area to help relax the material. Be very careful when doing so, as too much heat can damage the seat cover.

If using a heat gun, put it on its lowest setting and just warm up the material by moving the nozzle back and forth. Once the material is warm to the touch, place a hand on one end of the bolster and move the other hand in the opposite direction to stretch out the seam. It is not necessary to pull hard; just a small amount of pressure will help. Hold the seam until it cools and you should have reduced the distortion considerably.

Once the seat covers have completely cooled, wipe them down with a damp cloth to remove any fingerprints or smudges that may be left over from the installation process. The finished seat cushions are now ready for installation.

Cushion Installation

Fitting the new cushions in the seat frame is just as easy as it was to remove them. Start with the lower cushion and tilt the front into the seat pan, making sure that the retainer tabs are under the raised anchors. Lower the cushion into the pan and set the mounting wires by making sure that they are lined up just below the anchor clips. While pushing backward on the cushion, lift it up to snap it into the retainers.

The backrest cushion is installed by aligning the inside retainer clips with the anchor wires and pressing back and to the inside all in one motion. The outer retainers are set the same way: pushing back while pulling toward you. Verify that the cushions are secured by lifting along the edges.

DOOR PANELS

Corvette door panels are made up of many pieces, and they are not cheap to replace or repair. The base panels are not flat like most other door panels on any other model of car. These panels are complicated to fit, and if they are not attached properly, the door will not close without damaging the panel.

Understand that the door of a Corvette is made mostly out of fiberglass. The inside of the door has a window regulator, glass, and sometimes a few wires attached to the fiberglass. When removing, adjusting, or replacing items, the fiberglass can become fragile. Metal hardware, bolts, and screws are going to loosen and enlarge the mounting points and the next thing you know, you have a big mess.

Restoring the door panel and any other items takes time and a lot of finesse to avoid damaging the door structure. Remember to take your time and do not force parts together. They will fit if you have the patience to do the job right.

Removal

As with any other door panel, it is necessary to remove the window cranks, lock button, and armrest. Begin with the manual window crank. Insert a window crank removal tool under the base of the crank. If the crank was installed correctly, the tool should be placed in line with the knob on the crank to push the locking clip away, freeing the device from the car.

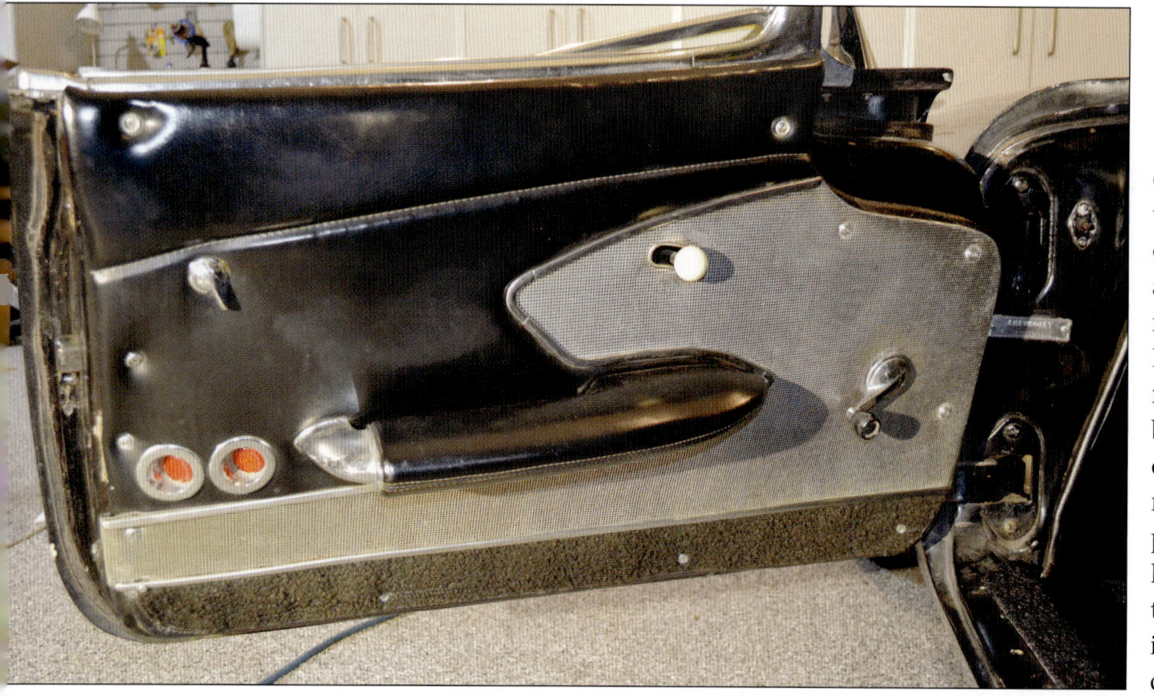

Our project features a 1959 Corvette roadster. This door panel has seen a previous recovery, and there are many nonstandard repairs that will need to be corrected to bring the upholstery back to its original condition. It will make a good case study on how to overcome problems.

Removing the Door Panel

1 A standard window crank removal tool is used to free the window crank from the door. The tool is wedged between the base of the crank and the protective escutcheon. A slight rotation of the tool helps guide it into position to release the retainer clip.

2 Because the lock knob is so small and the fastening clip is hard to access, a special pair of clip pliers is used to release the lock knob from the door panel. There are other methods that can be used to remove the knob, but this tool makes the process easy.

3 The interior space of the Corvette is very tight, and there is not enough room for the operation of standard door hardware. To open the door, a small round knob is attached to the release lever. The knob is simply unscrewed to take it off.

4 Trim screws are used to secure the door panel to the inside of the door, and they are removed with a Phillips screwdriver. Unfortunately, someone has added extra screws to the panel and damaged some of the stainless trim, which needs to be replaced.

5 *There are small hook features in the stainless door cap that retain the upper edge of the door panel. Removal of the door panel requires first lifting upward to clear the hooks and then pulling the panel away from the door.*

6 *After removing the door panel, it was evident that the armrests were not installed correctly. Instead of anchoring the armrest to the door, it was bolted to the panel. This explains why the armrest could not be removed in the traditional way.*

The lock knob on this corvette is held in place by a small retainer clip. To access the clip, a pair of clip pliers is needed. The clip can only be installed in one direction on the back of the knob. Reach in behind the lock knob opposite to the short arm. The clip can be released, and the knob will come off.

The next part to come off is the release lever knob. This part is simply unscrewed from the release lever shaft that protrudes from the center of the door panel. The last element that needs to be removed is the armrest. Three screws hold the armrest to the door. One is located in the lower region of the rear trim bracket, and the other two can be found under the forward section of the armrest. A Phillips screwdriver is used to remove the screws to free the armrest.

Before the door panel can be completely removed, the trim screws that are located around the perimeter of the panel must be extracted. These screws are generally oval-head Phillips screws with trim washers under them. With the proper screwdriver, carefully remove the screws and washers. When all the fasteners have been removed, the door panel can be lifted upward and off of the door.

Door Trim

There are many additional repairs that should be addressed while the door panel is off the car. One of these items are the window sweeps. Our project car has stainless trim that caps the door opening, and the window sweeps are attached to this trim. Remove the retainer screws holding the trim to the door to access the sweeps.

With all the worn parts removed from the door, a complete inventory of new replacement parts can be compiled so that an order can be placed. Quality reproduction pieces are available from many sources, and getting them takes a few phone calls.

Several trim screws are removed on the door glass opening trim. After the trim is removed from the door, the worn window sweeps can be accessed for replacement. New window sweeps help prevent the glass from becoming scratched.

Teardown

Salvaging the trim and other components of the door panel begins by placing the worn and damaged panel on the workbench for disassembly. Normally, the armrest is removed before the door panel can be taken off the car. A screwdriver and wrench are now used to remove the attached armrest.

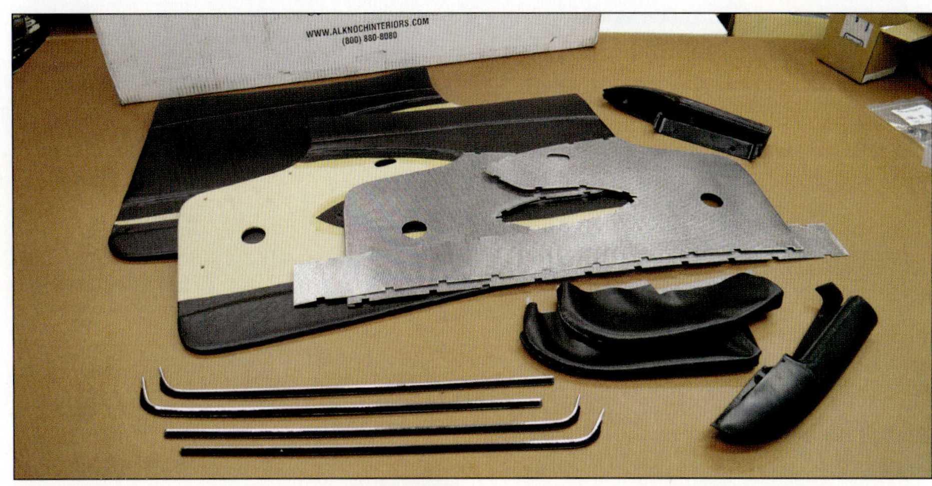

It is just like Christmas day when new parts arrive for your car. Reproduction door panels, trim panels, and armrests are a welcome sight. Soon they will be assembled, restoring the original appearance to the 1959 Corvette.

The window sweeps are attached to the inside of the stainless window opening trim pieces. With the door panel removed, the hidden retainer screws can be removed from the window opening trim so that the sweeps can be properly serviced.

Disassembling the Door Panel

1 *This door panel was restored many years ago by someone who probably wished that this book was available to help them. A lot of unnecessary damage has been sustained to the individual parts, and this will drive up the cost of the restoration.*

2 *The armrest was mounted directly to the door panel with lock nuts, and a wrench is needed to help free it. The attachment screws were also shortened and need to be replaced with new and correct attachment screws.*

3 *After the small retainer fastener is unscrewed from the retaining stud on the back side of the door reflectors, they can be removed. The reflector support bands need to be straightened and then reconditioned to remove the rust that has formed on the metal.*

4 *Someone has drilled a hole in the decorative trim, causing additional damage to the stainless trim. This is not an acceptable method of attaching trim or a door panel. New trim needs to be acquired if this cannot be repaired properly.*

5 *Small metal prongs are lifted from the back side of the door panel to release the stainless trim moldings that adorn the front of the door panel. Extreme care is taken while lifting the tabs so that they do not break off or damage the trim.*

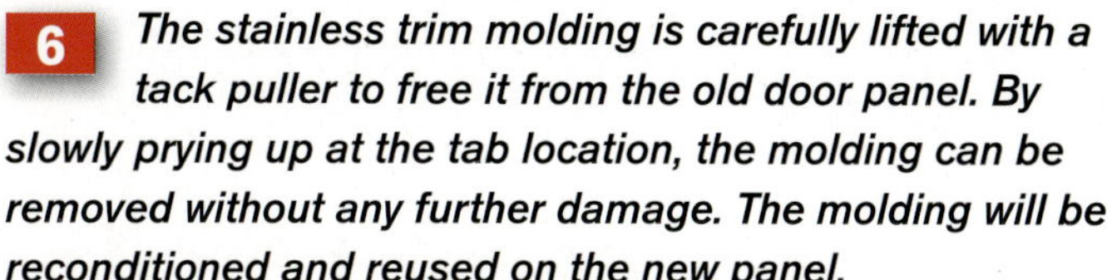

6 *The stainless trim molding is carefully lifted with a tack puller to free it from the old door panel. By slowly prying up at the tab location, the molding can be removed without any further damage. The molding will be reconditioned and reused on the new panel.*

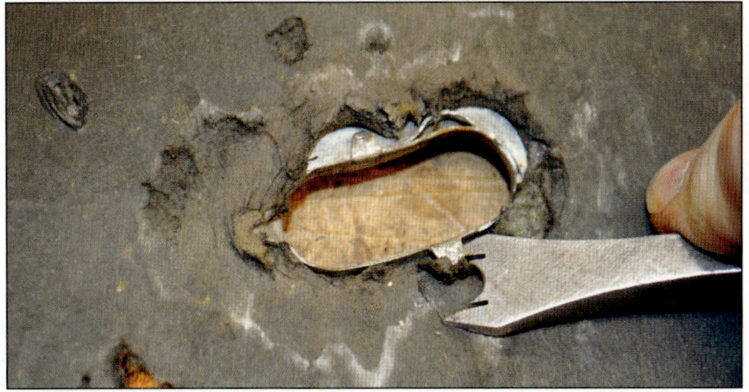

7 *There are more tabs to lift. The stainless-steel door pull has small tabs that hold it in place. Care is needed to lift the tabs without damaging the trim piece. Once removed from the door panel, the bezel can usually be straightened and reused.*

8 *Severe damage has occurred from the window crank handle rubbing on the decorative metal panel. This could have been prevented if a protective plastic bushing was installed behind the window crank. Damage like this cannot be repaired, and a new trim panel needs to be installed.*

Door reflectors are attached on the back side of the door panel with metal speed clips. The clips are unscrewed from the mounting stud on the reflector. After the clip is removed, the reflector and retaining band can be separated from the panel. The parts should be inspected to determine if they are viable for reconditioning.

Decorative stainless-steel trim is used to retain the metal trim panel to the surface of the panel board. The thin trim is attached with small metal tabs that pierce the door panel and are bent over on the back side of the panel board. Removal of the trim is done by lifting the tabs from the back of the panel. A tack lifter works well at getting under the fragile tabs without too much effort. The tab should be lifted just enough to allow the molding to be lifted off the front of the panel. It helps to lift the trim at the tab location. This reduces the strain on the trim and helps prevent the tab from any further damage.

Another part that has retainer tabs is the door-pull trim bezel. This piece is small and yet very tough due to the tight radius of the part. Getting under the tabs is not easy, as they are stiff. Needle-nose pliers can also be helpful to get the tabs raised enough to allow the part to be removed.

The last piece to be removed from the door panel is the decorative metal panel that covers the midsection. The metal panel is folded over the edge of the panel board. A 1-inch broad knife can be used to get under the front edge of the metal panel to raise it enough so that it can be removed. The small section at the rear needs to be lifted enough to clear the panel board. After the rear section is free, the metal can be slid forward to remove the trim. If the metal is in good condition, it can be reused on the new door panel.

Panel Assembly

Just about everything on our old door panel was unusable. The trim moldings can be fixed and then buffed to a driver-quality shine. New base panels were obtained along with new decorative metal panels. The stampings are very good, but some adjustment needs to be made to make them fit better.

Assembling the Panel

1 Most manufacturers do a pretty good job at creating accurate reproduction pieces, but do not assume that all reproduction parts will fit together properly. A new decorative metal panel is test-fitted to the new base door panel to verify that the finished assembly will look nice.

2 Take a close look at the fit of the decorative trim panel. It is obvious that a small adjustment will need to be made to obtain a perfect fit. Trimming a part to fit is better than one that is too small or is incorrect for the model and year you are working on.

3 Small slivers of material are carefully trimmed from the edge of the decorative metal trim panel until a perfect fit is achieved. Removing a minimal amount of metal at a time means there is less chance of making a mistake that could spoil the project.

4 Supporting the decorative metal panel while it is shaped around the edge of the panel board is vital to prevent unwanted kinks in the material. A wide body-filler spreader works well at supporting the metal while shaping it into position.

5 A dead-blow hammer is used to set the edge of the panel. The plastic mallet will not damage the thin metal as it is tapped onto the back side of the door panel. A small block of wood can also be used to secure the trim in place without scratching the decorative panel.

6 A flat jeweler's file is used to soften the surface around the opening of the window crank. Removing the burr on the edges of the stamped panel helps later when the window crank is installed. This action prevents damage to the window crank and helps it operate smoothly.

The first thing to look at is the fit of the metal to the panel. Dry fit the metal on the panel and look at the edges for any shortage or overreaching. The trim molding conceals and holds the edge of the metal panel to the surface of the door panel. If the metal is oversized, it can be trimmed with tin snips to prevent the raw edge from showing past the molding. A short-fitting panel can be adjusted by carefully reforming the front edge to allow the metal to reach farther onto the door panel. If pieces are misaligned or just do not fit together properly, contact the manufacturer before making any adjustments to the parts. If the part is cut or altered, it cannot be returned.

When you are satisfied with the fit of the trim panel, turn the panel facedown on the workbench so that it can be affixed to the panel board. The metal can be bent effectively with the aid of a body-filler spreader. The plastic spreader is wide and stiff enough to help shape the thin metal over the edge of the panel without scratching or denting it. You want to get the metal to fit as tight as possible.

To secure the metal, use a plastic hammer to tap the wraparound flat to the back side of the door panel. Do not try to bend the metal all at once, as this creates creases in the metal. Use short tapping strokes to secure the metal onto the panel board.

Turn the panel faceup and inspect the fit. There should not be any movement or rippling of the metal panel after it has been set. Now, look at the stamped openings in the metal panel. There might be a burr on the edges of the stampings left from the manufacturing process. This burr can be removed with a small flat file. Work the metal to the inside of the opening with short, deliberate strokes. Angle the file as flat as possible without scratching the pattern on the surface of the decorative panel.

Molding Installation

Reconditioning of the stainless moldings starts with the straightening of the fastener tabs. Flat-jaw pliers are used to realign the tabs. Broken tabs can be repaired by making new ones and soldering them to the back side of the molding. Small scratches can be polished out with a good sisal buffing wheel and emery compound.

Getting the best fit for the moldings is achieved when they are lined up with the profile of the decorative trim panel. A regulator is used to prepunch a hole in the cover material and panel board for each tab. This action prevents the tabs from

Cleaning, polishing, and straightening the stainless trim moldings is essential for the assembly of the new door panels. Bent prong fasteners are restored by flattening them with pliers to prepare them for reuse while broken or missing fasteners are replaced.

A little prep helps with the fitment of the stainless-steel moldings. Less stress is put on the molding fasteners when the cover material is prepunched to allow easy insertion into the door panel. Using the molding as a guide ensures that the new tab holes are made where they are needed.

From the back side of the door panel, the molding fastener tabs are tapped down with a tack hammer to secure the trim onto the door panel. These small metal pins break off easily, so a light touch is needed when flattening the fasteners.

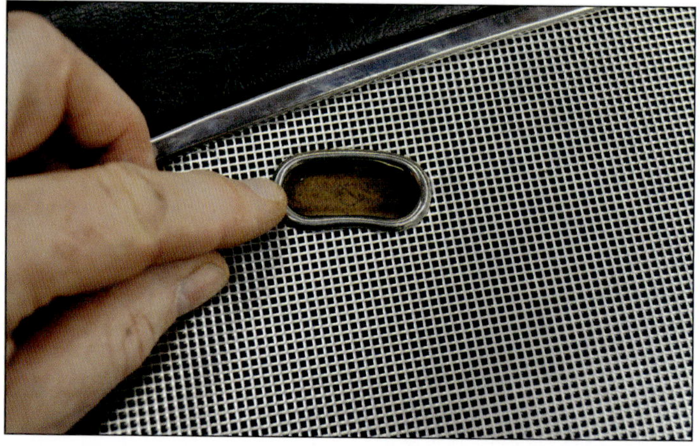

Many pieces make up the trim on the door panel. This door-pull bezel is not only decorative but also functional. Without the molding, the edges of the opening can become flared, and the sharp edges of the metal can be a hazard to your fingers.

To keep the door-pull trim bezel in place, the small retaining tabs are flattened against the back side of the panel board with a tack hammer. Support this small part from underneath during the installation to prevent damage to the stamped metal.

enough to allow the tab to fold over properly.

The last molding piece that needs to be set is the door-pull trim bezel. From the face of the door panel, set the bezel into the kidney bean–shaped hole in the metal trim panel. Turn the door panel facedown and support the bezel while tapping the locking tabs down and out to secure it to the panel.

Inspect the trim to verify that it has been locked tight to the surface of the door panel. Make any necessary adjustments to ensure that the trim fits correctly.

breaking as they are pushed through the door panel. After the moldings are set in place, they must be secured to keep them in place.

Turn the door panel facedown on the workbench and support the trim molding with a piece of 1/4-inch plywood. Use a tack hammer to bend the tabs over, securing them to the back of the panel board. The plywood is soft enough to prevent the molding from being crushed yet strong

Finishing Touches

Many practical adornments have been included on the door panel. One of these are the inner reflectors. These work as a low-tech warning device when the door is opened. The angular design of the reflector will catch the headlights of an oncoming car to alert the driver that there is an obstacle up ahead.

Final Assembly of the Door Panel

1 *A hobby knife is used to remove the cover material from the reflector mounting holes stamped into the panel board. The small blade of the knife works much better than a razor blade, and it is easier to control.*

2 *Small, angular-shaped metal retainer bands are used to hold the door reflectors from the back side of the door panel. The reflector is held tight to the retainer strap with a speed nut that is secured into place with the aid of pliers.*

3 *Mounting holes are made in the metal trim panel with a hole punch. The punch is placed in the prepunched hole in the panel board and then struck with a hammer while the door panel is supported with a cutting pad to prevent damage to the tool and panel.*

4 *Further modifications need to be made to the clean-cut hole before the door panel can be attached to the car. The panel opening must be dimpled to allow the retaining washer to sit flush with the surface of the metal panel.*

5 *Creating a proper dimple in the metal trim panel can be accomplished with some very simple objects. A wood screw and a small piece of wood that is hand crafted into a backer block can transform a panel to accept a flush washer.*

6 *Making a dimple in the metal trim panel takes a few blows from a tack hammer onto the head of a large wood screw. The result of this action creates a perfect recess in the door panel for the insertion of a flush washer.*

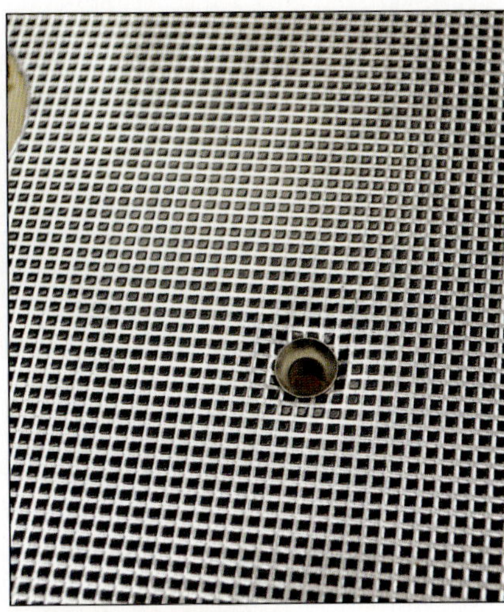

7 *A clean appearance is achieved when the flush washer is inserted into the dimpled recess of the door panel. Notice how the top edge of the washer sits even with the surface of the metal panel. An oval-head trim screw completes the installation.*

8 *The completed door panel assembly is now ready to be installed on the inner door of the car. Openings for the armrest will be made after the panel has been fitted to the car to ensure that they are in the correct location and concealed by the armrest base.*

Before the reflectors can be installed, the material concealing the mounting holes has to be removed. A hobby knife can follow the perimeter of the hole to cut away just the unwanted cover material from the panel without any mistakes.

The reflectors are set into the open holes from the front side of the door panel. Indexing or "clocking" the position of the reflector is important. When the door is opened, the surface of the reflector should be perpendicular to the car. The reflector is set in an angular casting, and when the deepest part is clocked to the rear of the door panel, the reflector will be in the proper position to catch the greatest amount of light when the door is open.

Turn the panel facedown on the workbench and place the retainer strap on the reflector base with the mounting post through the hole in the retainer. Twist the speed clip onto the mounting post to secure the reflector to the back side of the door panel. Pliers can help when tightening the speed nut.

Panel Flush Washers

The door panel will be attached to the door with oval-head trim screws. The cover material of the door panel is protected from the head of the trim screw with a flush washer. This small stainless piece of hardware is inserted into the door panel, and the trim screw is inserted through the fastener to hold the panel to the door. Before the door panel mount screw flush washers can be inserted into the door panel, the anchor holes need to be cleared.

Place the door panel facedown on the workbench and place a cutting pad directly under the fastener location. Use a hole punch and hammer to pierce the metal trim panel and the cover material on the face of the panel. The hole punch should be no larger than the size of the flush washer shaft, allowing the washer to fit snuggly into the open hole.

A small modification needs to be made to the face of the door panel so that the flared end of the washer sits properly into the door panel. To make this modification, dimple the newly cut hole in the metal trim panel. This is done with a #12 wood screw. The tapered head of the screw will provide enough relief to the metal, allowing the panel washer to become flush with the surface of the door panel.

Before dimpling the door panel, it must be supported from the back side to prevent damaging the metal. A small block of wood with a hole drilled though it will give enough support for this small task. Insert the wood screw through the hole in the door panel and then guide the shaft of the screw into the hole in the block of wood. Carefully tap on the head of the screw with a tack hammer to create the recessed dimple in the door panel. When the screw is removed, the flush washer can be inserted flush into the door panel. Recess the rest of the retainer holes to ready the panel for installation.

Armrest Preparation

New armrest covers give the old armrest a fresh appearance. Dismantle the armrest by removing the screws from the inner trim panel. Next, unscrew the tail piece from the armrest base. There are two screws

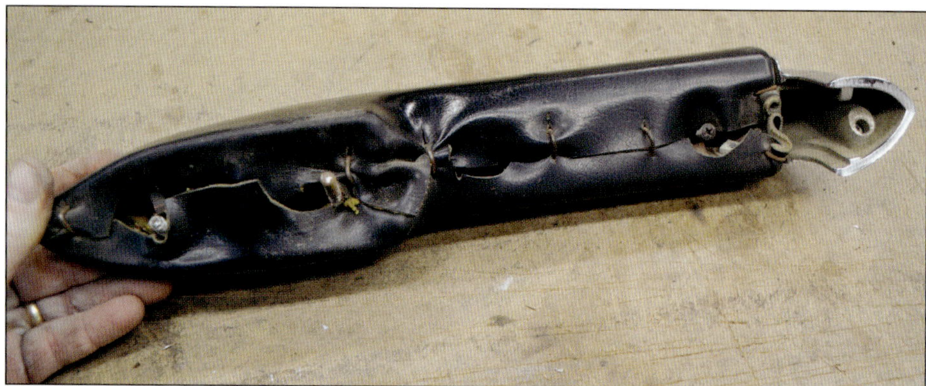

I find it hard to believe that someone actually used hog rings to attach the armrest cover material to the base. This technique is not acceptable, as it left the cover material loose and with several wrinkles. Other trim pieces are also missing.

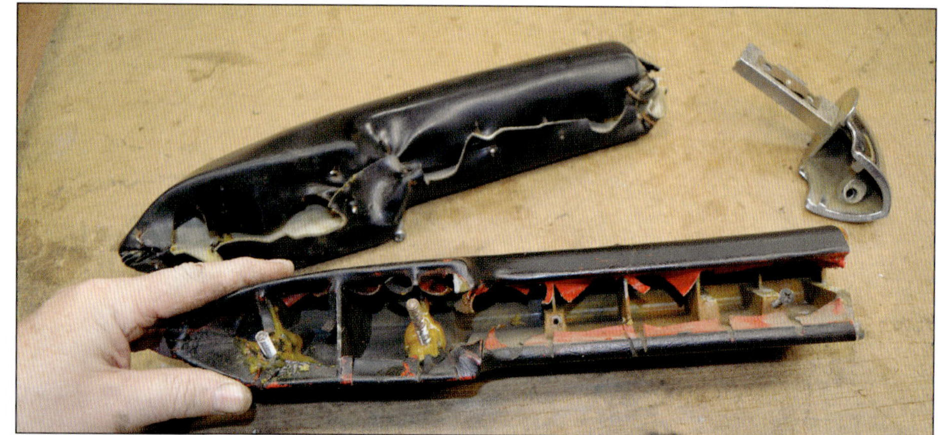

After the armrest cover was removed, I discovered that there was extensive damage to the armrest base. Hot glue was used to hold the mounting screws into the broken retainer holes of the armrest. The old cover material was also painted and then covered.

Years of tarnish and dirt have left the surface of the metal dull and unappealing. Fine steel wool is used to cut through oxidized film to clean the chrome finish on the armrest end cap. A coat of chrome polish helps preserve the newly acquired luster.

It may be necessary to refine the surface of the armrest base to help the new cover material fit and look better. A file can quickly remove the rough edges on the plastic base material, making it easier to sand the surface smooth.

to fit the new cover material. Flashing along the seams and edges from the casting process leaves sharp and unsightly bulges in the new cover material. Taking the sharp edges off the plastic will not only give the armrest a nicer appearance but also the new cover will install and fit better.

Use a file and sandpaper to make the surface smooth. When you are satisfied with the refinement of the new armrest base, the armrest cover material can be fit.

Cover Installation

If purchasing new armrest covers, some trimming needs to be done to help the cover fit and look better. Begin by turning the cover inside out to get better access to the seam allowance. Use scissors to reduce the seam allowance to about 1/8 inch. Do not trim too close or cut the stitches. The smaller amount of seam allowance material will cause less distortion when the cover is fitted to the armrest base.

that hold the chrome casting to the armrest. Remove the screws and separate the end cap.

Glue was used to hold the covering on the armrest base. Peel the cover material away from the armrest base and discard it. Inspect the base for cracks or other damage. If the armrest base is in good condition, it can be reused. Clean the remaining glue off the base with adhesive remover or lacquer thinner.

The chrome end cap should also be inspected for pitting or cracks. After a good cleaning, the cap can be polished to look like new. If any of the armrest components have damage or structural issues, they need to be replaced with a better part.

New reproduction armrest bases will need some sanding and refining to make them smooth enough

Installing the Armrest Base Cover

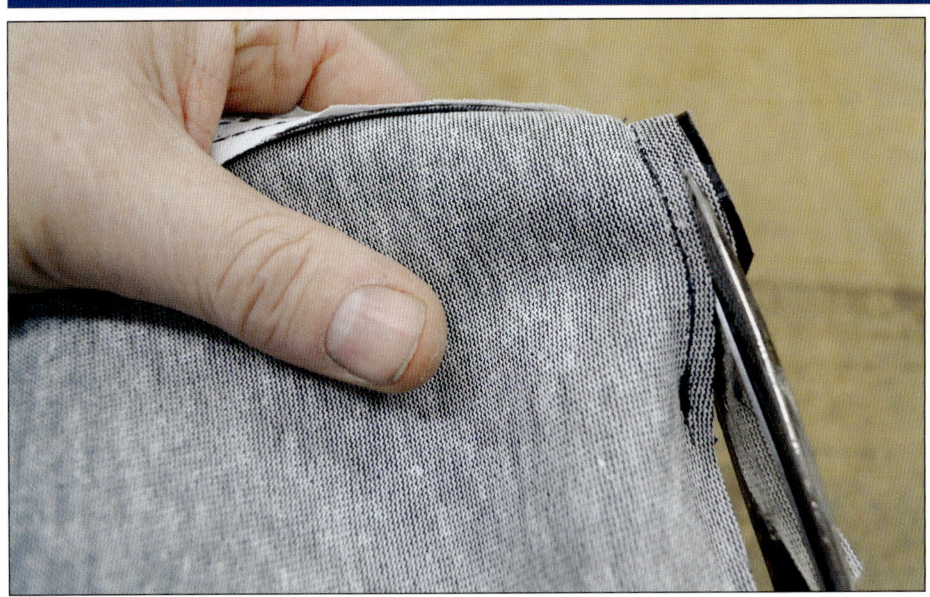

1 *For a better fit and finish of the armrest cover, scissors are used to trim off the excess material along the seam. It is important not to cut into the seam stiches while trimming, otherwise the seam will pop open and create more work.*

2 To prevent the new armrest cover from shifting position while it is in use, contact cement is brushed onto the end of the base. Keeping the seams aligned with the edges of the molded base gives the armrest a professional appearance.

3 The remainder of the seam allowance is arranged to flow in the same direction before the cover is installed on the armrest base. When the seam lies flat, it looks nicer than a seam with wrinkles and folds that cause lumps in the surface of the cover.

4 It puts less stress on the armrest cover during the fitting process when the back end is anchored first. Then, the cover can be slid forward over the tapered end. After the cover is in place, the centerline seam can be adjusted and smoothed.

5 A chip brush is used to apply contact cement to the inner surface of the armrest base and back side of the armrest cover material. For better results, work only a small section at a time with the glue.

6 To help the cover material fit smoothly over the contours of the armrest base, relief cuts are made to clear the structural supports on the inside of the base. Preventing bulk from forming makes the cover material easier to fit and adhere.

7 Neatness counts, even in the places that don't show. Removing the extra cover material from the corners and overlapping sections on the back side of the armrest base helps keep the armrest flush to the door panel when it is installed.

8 More gluing and stretching are needed to finish attaching the armrest cover material. Working the cover material in sections not only provides more control over the fit but it is also less messy, having less exposed glue to get on your fingers.

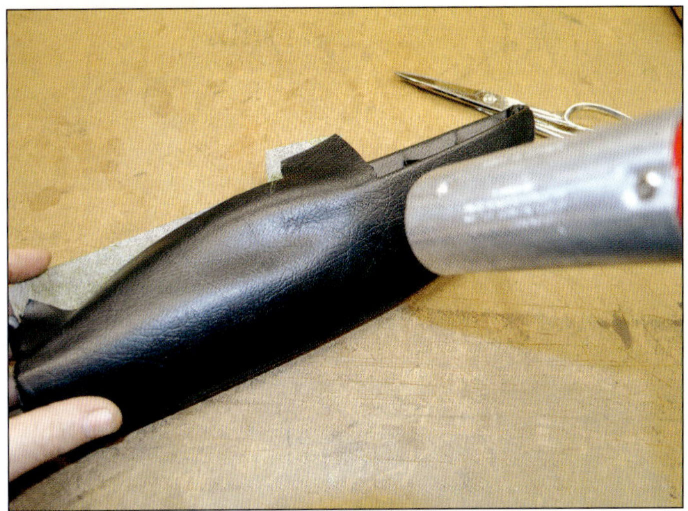

9 Getting the cover material to form around the inner curves of the armrest can be difficult unless the material is softened with heat. Warming the vinyl allows it to stretch and conform to the contours of the armrest base without tearing.

10 After the vinyl has been softened by warming it with a heat gun, a little pulling and stretching will help it conform to the armrest base. When the cover takes the desired shape, glue can be added to the back side of the vinyl and base.

11 Relief cuts can help the cover material wrap over the inside curve of the armrest base. Carefully placed small snips are made in the vinyl with scissors. Care is taken so that the material is not cut deep enough that the cuts are visible.

12 Getting the cover material to lay correctly on the inside curve of the armrest is difficult without making relief cuts. Notice the span that the vinyl takes after it has been fitted and glued onto the inside of the armrest base.

13 Before the end cap can be reinstalled on the armrest, some of the cover material is removed to allow the fitment of the chrome casting. Only the material covering the opening is cut out. The remainder of the material will be covered by the end cap.

14 *The end of the armrest cover has lost some of its tension due to the amount of material removed in preparation of adding the end cap. To prevent the cover material from moving, contact cement is brushed under the cover material to secure it in place.*

15 *Heat has been used to soften the cover material for the vinyl to be stretched into the recessed opening for the mounting screws. The back end of a large drill bit is used to help stretch the warm material into place.*

Contact cement needs to be brushed onto the seam and the edge of the armrest base to help keep the cover material from developing wrinkles from movement. Work the seam allowance as flat as possible before sliding the cover over the base. When fitting the cover, secure the back panel first and then carefully pull the material along the ridge of the base until it can be wrapped over the point.

Smooth out any bulges in the cover material before gluing the edges of the cover to the inside of the armrest base. Brushing the glue onto the cover and base is more efficient and much less messy than spraying. It also helps to only apply glue to one small section at a time. After the glue becomes dry to the touch, relief cuts can be made in the material to help it fit better. Keeping the bulk to a minimum makes the overall fit and appearance of the armrest more professional looking.

Adding Heat

The cover material was cut from a flat sheet of material, and it may take a little heat to relax the vinyl enough to wrap nicely around the curves of the base. Do not overheat the material, as this can create shiny spots on the surface of the vinyl. While the material is still warm, it can be formed to the armrest base, and when it cools, it will retain the shape. There is a limit to this process. If you overstretch the heated vinyl, it can damage the pattern or grain on the surface of the material.

It may be necessary to make a series of relief cuts to help ease the material around the inside curves. Begin with shallow cuts in the material. The cuts can always be made deeper, but do not allow the cut to show on the outside of the base. Ample glue should be evenly spread on the inner surface of the armrest base and back side of the cover material. When the material is pressed into the armrest base, excess bulk is trimmed away to prevent overlapping. Having less material and making the inside neat helps the inner trim panel fit better.

Additional trimming on the end panel is necessary to allow the chrome end cap to mate with the armrest base. Before the casting can be installed, more contact adhesive is added to the base and the edges of the back side of the vinyl cover material. When the cap piece is installed, it will help keep the cover material in place.

Form Fitting

Getting the vinyl cover material to conform to the shape of the retainer screw coves takes some heat and muscle. The head of the retainer screw is concealed inside the armrest base. These coves are located on the underside of the base and end cap. You could just cut a hole in the cover material to allow them through or ease the cover material into the opening.

When the vinyl is heated carefully, it can be formed to fit the screw receptacle. With the aid of a heat gun, the vinyl is warmed and then stretched into the screw sockets with the shaft of a drill bit. This process can take several applications of heat and stretching to achieve the desired result. If the material is overstretched, it will tear, and that is not the goal.

After the access holes have been formed, a small hole for the mounting screws can be made in the cover material. This will allow the hardware to pass without binding or grabbing the cover material.

Armrest Assembly

Now that the armrest base has a new cover, it is time to finish installing the final few pieces. The first item that is attached is the end cap. The long tang of the cap is inserted through the end section of the base and secured in place with two retainer screws.

The machine screws are inserted through the bottom of the armrest base and mate with the cap tang inside the base. A Phillips screwdriver is used to snug the screws, taking care not to overtighten them, which can cause the base to crack.

An inner trim panel is used to conceal the cut and glued edges of the cover material. Two oval-head sheet-metal screws are tightened with a Phillips screwdriver to hold the inner cover in place. The fit of the panel is just tight enough to help hold the cover material from moving, as it will give the armrest a finished feel when pulling the door.

A Phillips screwdriver is used to secure the retainer screws of the end cap after it has been fit into the armrest base. To prevent damage to the armrest base, the screws only need to be tightened enough to hold the cap in place.

An inner filler panel is secured to the armrest base to cover the raw, glued edges of the armrest cover material and end cap mounting tang. The filler panel also gives the armrest a more comfortable gripping surface when the door is pulled closed.

Panel Installation

There are a few things to pay close attention to when fitting the new door panel to the car. The first is to hook the door cap onto the tab on the inner trim panel. This keeps the top edge of the door panel tightly in place. The other is to center the door panel. Look at the front and rear edges of the door panel and verify that they are flush with or just inside the edge of the inner door.

When satisfied with the positioning of the door panel, use a regulator to locate the underlying screw hole in the upper corner of the panel. Insert an oval-head trim screw through the flush washer and snug the screw with a Phillips screwdriver. Do not overtighten the screw, as it can tear out the fiberglass. If this happens, the door panel needs to be removed so that a spot-repair plate can be riveted to the door and then a new screw hole can be drilled to hold the screw.

Secure the opposite upper corner in the same manner and double-check the fit of the panel. If the panel needs to be adjusted, loosen the screws and make any adjustments necessary to ensure that the door panel will not rub on the inner doorjamb. Continue adding trim screws around the perimeter of the door panel.

Installing a C1 Door Panel

1 *The door panel is suspended from a tab that fits into a small pocket located on the inside center of the door cap. It holds the top of the door panel tight to the inner door trim. Additional trim screws will be added to keep the door panel secured in place.*

2 *Finding the anchor holes for the trim screws is much easier when using a regulator. The small diameter of the regulator is less invasive and causes less damage compared to an ice pick. Once the screw hole is located, the trim screw can be inserted through the panel.*

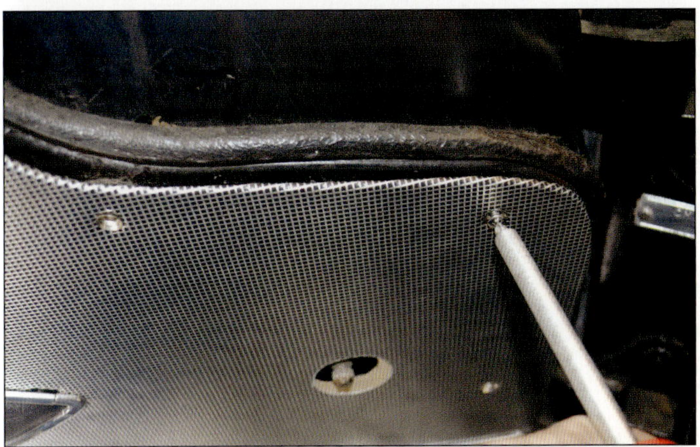

3 *To help keep the door panel centered, the corners are first secured with trim screws. By using fewer screws, the alignment of the door panel can be easily corrected to better fit the opening before the remaining screws are added.*

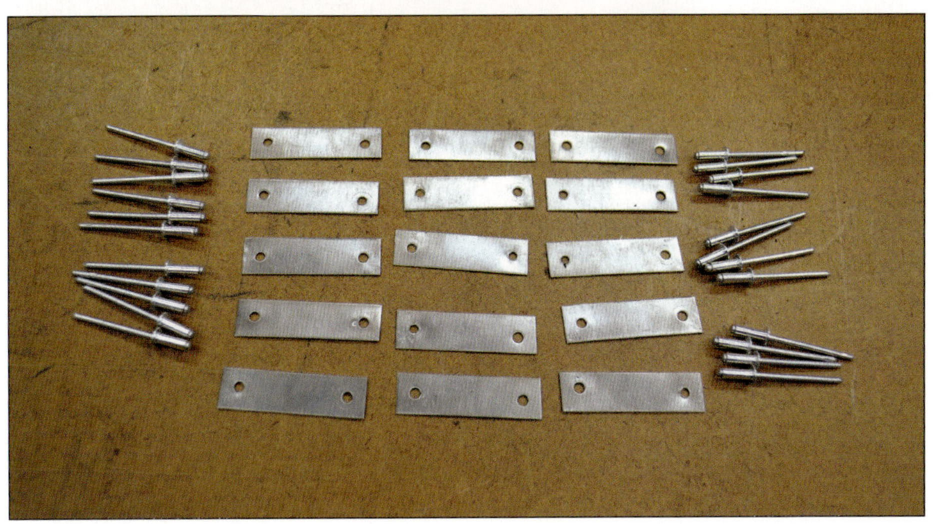

4 *Oversized anchor holes in fiberglass can be fixed permanently by adding a mount hole plate over the torn-out anchor point. After a plate has been riveted over the oversized hole, a new hole can be drilled into the metal to create a secure anchor point for the trim screw.*

Fit the Armrest

Before the armrest can be installed, the mounting holes need to be opened. Feel through the cover material on the door panel to locate the access holes in the panel board. Push a little harder to find the mounting screw anchors. A regulator can also be used to help locate the internal anchor.

The cover material should be removed to allow the mounting screw access to the anchor. Cut a small circle in the cover material to reveal the anchor points.

The armrest mounting screws can now be inserted through the armrest base. A #3 Phillips screwdriver is used to secure the armrest to the door. All the screws should be started before they are carefully tightened. This prevents the base from becoming cracked from over-tightening the screws.

Door Hardware

The door operation hardware is all that is left to complete the door panel installation. A slight bulge made by the lock actuator shaft should be visible in the cover material. A small circular section of the cover material needs to be removed to allow the fitment of the lock knob. Use scissors to cut through the material to expose the lock shaft.

Prepare the lock knob for installation by inserting the retaining clip into the retainer slot. To protect the cover material of the door panel, a nylon lock knob washer should be placed behind the knob when it is in service. Installation of the small lock knob is done by clocking the driver door lever portion of the knob at 9 o'clock and then pushing it onto the splined lock shaft.

The armrest anchor holes are located with the help of a regulator. After the anchor point has been determined, the cover material is then cut away to make way for the mounting screws to pass through the panel and into the door.

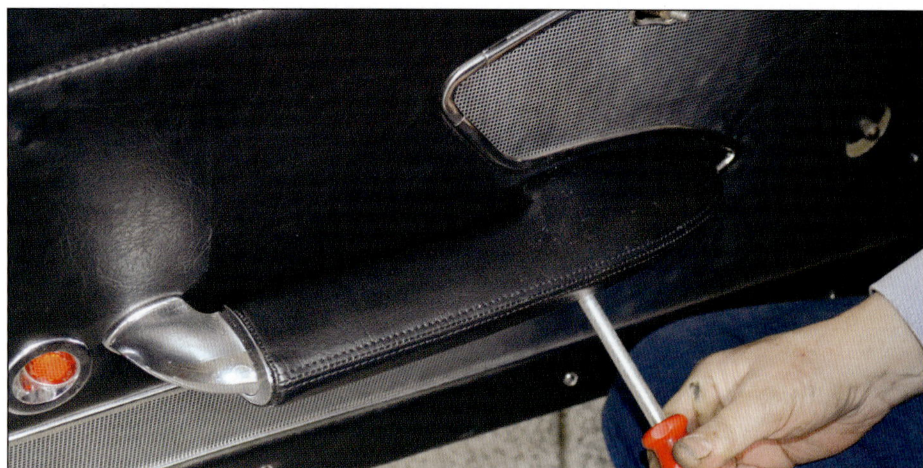

Securing the armrest to the door takes three long machine screws. The heads of these screws are specific in design to fit into the recessed openings in the armrest base. They require a #3 Phillips screwdriver to tighten them properly.

A small section of the door panel material has been cut out to gain access to the splined shaft of the lock actuator. Minimal cutting of the cover material is advised so that the rough edges will be concealed when the lock knob is installed.

A special nylon wear ring will be fitted underneath the lock knob to prevent the door panel material from abrasion when the knob is turned. To prevent the lock knob from popping off the lock shaft, a new retaining clip has been installed in the lock knob.

After carefully aligning the splines on the lock shaft with the internal splines on the lock knob post, the knob is simply pushed onto the post. When the lock knob is properly installed, the lever points toward the rear edge of the door panel.

A protective escutcheon will be used to prevent the window crank from wearing into the soft decorative aluminum trim panel. To ensure the window crank stays secure, a new retainer clip has been properly installed in the post of the crank.

Before the window crank is installed, the window was raised to the closed position. A nylon escutcheon is fitted behind the base of the crank, and then the device is pushed onto the regulator shaft. To give the driver a little more knee space, the window crank is positioned at 2 o'clock.

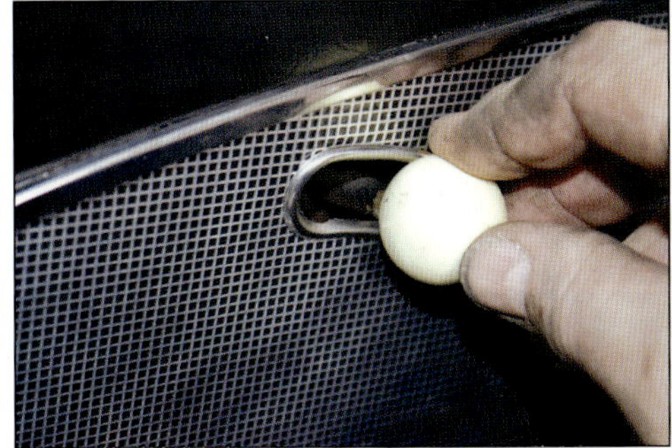

The small design of the door-release knob works well in the cramped cab of the 1959 Corvette. The installation of the new white knob is done by turning it clockwise onto the release lever shaft. When given a short pull, the door will open.

There is such a difference in the appearance of the finished door panel. Taking the time to observe the little details of preparing and installing the door panel is worth the effort.

With more than 47 years of very hard service, this door panel has definitely seen better days. The panel has already had an armrest repair and now the other applied upgrades are failing on the deluxe panel.

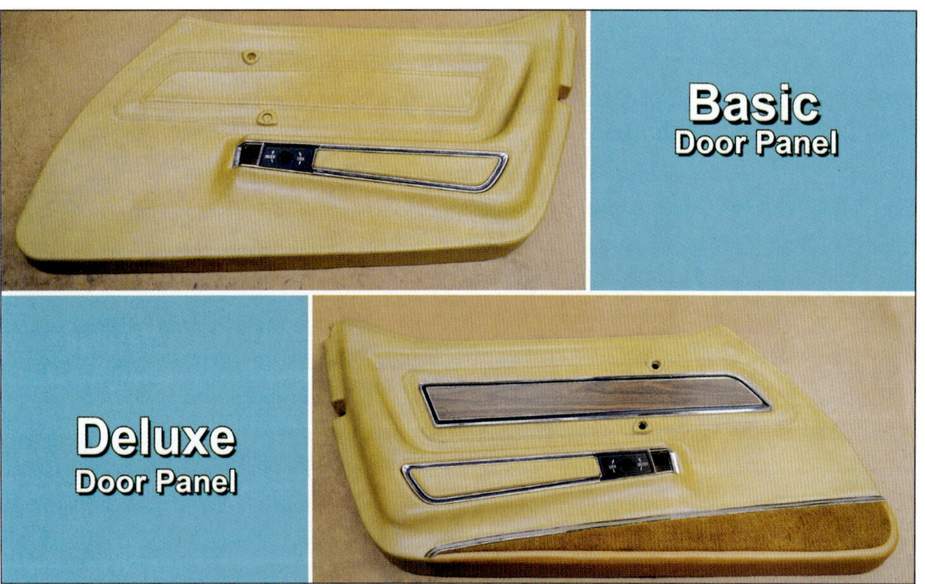

Even with its modular design, a basic door panel is practical, still very stylish, and what a difference the application of a piece of carpeting and a wood-grain panel can make to the appearance of the deluxe trim option.

Installation of the window crank is very similar to that of the lock knob. Before inserting the retainer clip, raise the window to the full up position. The retaining clip is installed by pushing it into the crank with the open end facing the lever. A plastic escutcheon is then placed between the crank and the door panel as it is pushed onto the window regulator shaft, clocking the lever at 2 o'clock. The clocking of the passenger-side hardware is 3 o'clock for the lock knob and 10 o'clock for the window crank.

Finally, the round door release knob is screwed onto the threaded shaft that protrudes through the release lever opening in the door panel. Check the function of all the hardware for binding and function before closing the door. Making any necessary adjustments to correct problems is much easier while the door is open than trying to get the door to open and operate properly after it has been closed.

C3 Door Panels

Replacing the door panel on a C3 Corvette is less complicated than those of the C1 and C2, but they still need to be fit with great care. The basic difference between these models is that everything is already attached or built into the C3 door panel, making it a modular design.

These third-generation door panels are thick and contoured, and they come in basic or deluxe options. Inset trim on the armrest is the same on both options. Carpet on the deluxe panel is keyed to the interior color. The wood trim panel was offered in walnut or teak from 1970 to 1976 and black in 1977.

Panel Removal

A #2 Phillips screwdriver is needed to remove the various screws holding components to the door. Begin by removing the door handle pull. There is a screw at the top and the bottom of the pull. Insert the screwdriver into the opening and make sure that it makes solid contact with the fastener head before turning. It is important not to round off the head of these screws, as they are deep inside the panel.

Next, remove the retainer screw and the washer at the front upper and rear upper corners of the panel. Each screw is fully exposed and should come out without difficulty. There are also retainer clips located on the front and the rear lower outsides of the panel. These each have a small screw that secures the lower portion of the

Removing a C3 Door Panel

1 *Bolted-on parts are also used to anchor other pieces securely in place. The door handle pull is a prime example of this. The two anchor screws that hold the handle as well as the door panel in place can be removed with a few turns of a screwdriver.*

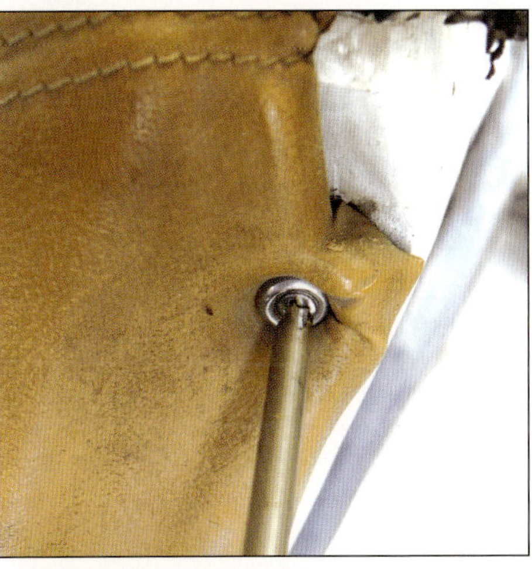

2 *Anchor screws located in the upper corners near the outer edges of the door panel bring stability to the panel by holding it close to the inner door. These are the only visible surface fasteners used on the door panel.*

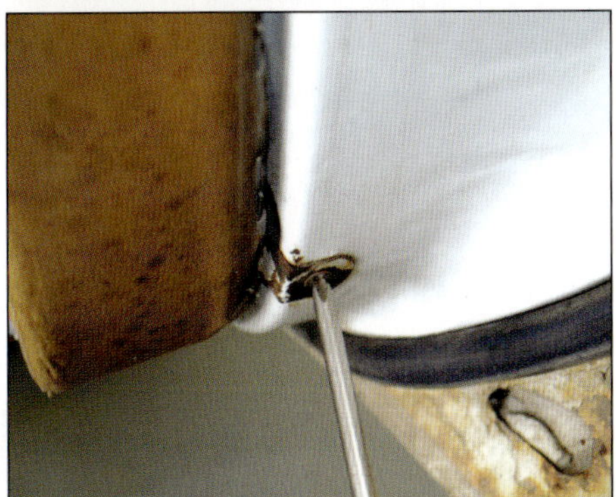

3 *Located at the lower outer corners of the C3 door panel are exterior retainer clips. It is unusual for the mounting hardware to be exposed like this, but they do an excellent job of keeping the door panel secured to the inner door.*

4 *Due to tight access, the removal of the lock knob can be difficult. A conventional window crank clip tool cannot always be used to release the knob. Getting behind the knob is easily done with a pliers-type clip remover.*

5 *Hidden behind the inner door release lever is an anchor screw that prevents the splined tail section of the cast handle from sliding out of the inner door-latch assembly. Accessing the spring-loaded mechanism is easier once the door panel has been removed.*

6 *After many years of use, this door panel has endured lots of abuse. It is now being removed to allow the placement of a new panel. Before a new panel is installed, all the internal components of the door can be checked to ensure many more trouble-free years of service.*

door to the car. Remove the screws.

Removing the lock knob requires a clip-removal tool. Behind the knob is a spring clip that keeps the knob from falling off. Slide the tool behind the base of the knob and push the clip out of its slot. The knob will release from the shaft of the lock actuator.

Cars that are equipped with manual cranked windows will need to remove the window crank from the regulator shaft. Place a clip removal tool under the base of the crank and push the retainer clip out of the slot in the handle. Remove the window crank and escutcheon.

There are small prongs that hold the window crank spacer to the panel, so it will most likely stay on the door panel and be removed later. If it does fall off, check that the retainer prongs are still viable. If they are damaged or missing, the spacer should be replaced.

Coming out of the front of the trim bezel is the inner door release handle. The handle is attached to the latch lock assembly with a small machine screw. There is no need to remove the handle unless it is damaged. If the inner handle is pitted, replace the part with a new one. To do this, lift the handle outward and remove the screw. It should then be possible to pull the handle forward to remove it from the inner casting.

On the back side of the panel, running along the outer edges, are dual-lock nylon fasteners. They hold the panel tight to the door and can be released with a panel-lifting tool. Insert the tool between the back of the panel and the door, and with a swift motion, pop the panel off the fasteners.

To remove the panel from the car, first pull the panel about 1 inch outward from the bottom and then lift it upward to clear the lip from the upper inner door. With the panel loose from the car, slide the panel forward to clear the inner door release handle. Be careful of the lower panel clips so that they do not scratch the paint.

Prep for Installation

Preassembled door panels require

very little preparation before they are ready to be installed on the car, but there are a few things that can be done to make the installation easier. Begin by opening the through holes for the door handle pull. Use a very sharp but small blade to remove the cover material inside the recessed opening. Also open the hole on the back side of the panel. This allows the handle to seat properly and the anchor screw to pass through without any obstruction.

Install the panel clips into the elongated holes on the front and rear edges of the panel. During the manufacturing process, the holes can clog with foam, and they will need to be cleared before the clip will fit properly. The upper mounting holes have a brass eyelet built into the back side of the panel that also needs to be cleared to allow the insertion of the trim screw and washer.

The panel is intentionally made without the through hole. To open the hole, use an upholstery regulator or a small awl to pierce the panel from the back side. After the opening is made, the panel is ready to hang on the door.

Panel Installation

Before the new door panel in installed, this is an excellent time to lubricate the window regulator and visually inspect the interior workings of the door. Take time to clean and repair any worn, broken, or missing parts. Although the door panel can always be removed later to perform some of these tasks, you run the risk of damaging the door panel during the removal and reinstallation process.

To make the door panel installation a bit easier, the window should be lowered to allow more room for

During the manufacturing process, some of the openings for the mounting screws remain blocked. This excess material should be removed from the door handle pull mounting points before the new door panel is applied to the car. Installation of the applied hardware becomes easier after these small modifications have been made to the panel.

Almost all door panels use blind or hidden fasteners to attach them to the car. The fiberglass structure of the door and design of the panel does not allow the use of traditional fasteners. Special clips were designed to secure the panel without being obvious.

the alignment and placement of the panel. Line up the inner release handle with the opening in the back side of the door panel and slide the panel inward, allowing the handle to go through the opening. It may help to place a regulator or a thin flat bar under the inner handle to help guide it through the panel opening. Be careful that the panel clips do not scratch the paint on the door as the panel is adjusted to fit.

The door panel should now be close to the inner door skin and squared up with the outer edges of the door. Lift upward on the door panel to allow the upper lip of the panel to fit over the top edge of the inner door skin. A panel-lifting tool may be needed to help the panel over the door skin.

Push down on the top of the door panel to capture the door skin under the panel lip. After the top of the door panel is set in place, make any adjustments necessary to square up the side of the panel. If the panel is lined up correctly, the door panel clips should fit on the outsides of the door edges.

Align the front and rear panel clips to the anchor points on the outer edges of the door and insert the correct trim screw into the panel clip. Tighten the screw with a screwdriver just enough to hold it firmly in place. Do not strip this anchor point.

Look along the edge of the door panel and inner door skin and verify that the dual-lock nylon fasteners are lined up. Then, tap the panel sharply with a soft mallet directly over each fastener to lock the panel to the inner skin of the door. Be careful not to scuff the door panel when doing this.

Use a regulator to align the panel

For fitment issues, the factory does not prepunch the mounting holes in the door panels. Making these openings is simple, and it actually makes for a better installation of the panel. Always use caution when working with sharp tools that poke through a panel.

o'clock or level position when the door is unlocked.

Insert the door handle pull screws into the recesses on the handle and then fit the handle to the door panel. Insert a #2 Phillips screwdriver into the recess and tighten each screw until it is snug. Do not overtighten the retainer screws of the pull, as they can break through the retainer loop. If that happens, remove the door panel to extract the screw and begin the installation all over again.

Wipe down the door panel with a soft microfiber towel to remove any residual fingerprints or installation smudges that may have accumulated on the panel. Slowly close the door and check the fit of the new door panel. The door should close without the panel rubbing or binding on the door opening. If you encounter any fitment issues, correct them before the door is put into service.

with the upper trim screw anchor holes. Insert the trim screw and washer and secure the panel to the door. Do not overtighten the screw. The surface of the panel skin should deflect slightly but not dimple from the trim screw. Too much pressure from the trim screw causes the door panel skin to prematurely crack. The

door panel should now be securely fastened to the door, and the final trim can be added.

A lock escutcheon is fit into the lock knob recess on the lock bezel. Install the spring clip into the slot of the lock knob and push the lock knob onto the knurled shaft. The lock knob should be clocked in a 9

Installing a C3 Door Panel

1 *Sometimes three hands are needed to get a panel to fit. Guiding the inner release handle through the door panel opening with a regulator will help get the door panel into position with less effort. Having a free hand allows you to concentrate on safely setting the heavy panel.*

2 *Although adding color is not necessary, painting the lower door panel clips to match the door will help them to disappear once they are installed. It's these little things that make a simple installation look much better. Even the trim screws can be touched up to blend in.*

3 Additional anchor screws are used near the upper corners of the door panel to keep it from shifting. A secure panel is less prone to damage, and it looks nicer to have the panel fit snugly against the inner door. A loose door panel can rub in the door opening and start to show signs of wear.

4 Some components, such as this nylon lock escutcheon, are used to protect other parts from damage and wearing out with use. They also cut down on squeaks and make the removal of the part a little easier. Many times, these protective components are forgotten during the reinstallation.

5 Fine-threaded machine screws are used to hold the door handle pull securely to the door. The fine threads of the screw are less likely to work themselves loose over time, and they do a great job of keeping the door handle in place.

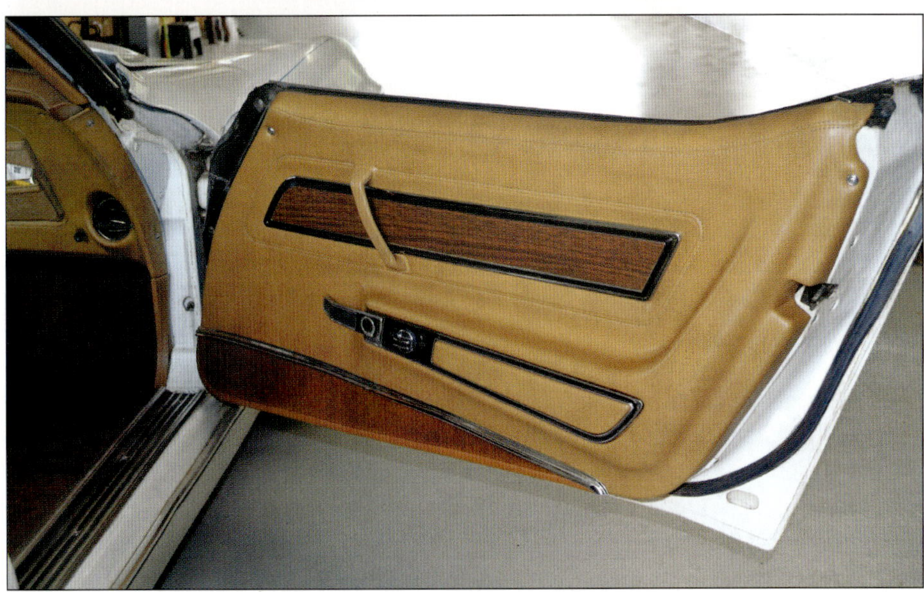

6 What a transformation the new door panel makes to the interior. This is one of the quickest upgrades that can be made to restore the original beauty back to the car. Now that the panel is securely in place, it will bring many more miles of comfort and enjoyment for years to come.

Panel Conversion

Upgrading the interior of your Corvette can be done with a few additional parts and a little effort. Transforming the basic door panels into the deluxe model can be done in a few hours for a lot less than the cost of new panels. To do that, order an insert panel set and door panel carpet with the vinyl trim strip to match the color of the existing panel and the lower diecast trim moldings.

C3 Panel Upgrade Conversion

1 *Using the actual trim panel as a guide to make indentations in the surface of the door panel will provide the most accurate positioning for the placement for the anchor holes. This method is quicker than measuring and will show exactly where to drill.*

2 *Small relief cuts are made along the curved section of the sewn-on vinyl trim to help the material lay flat. After the carpet strip is glued in place, the vinyl binding is pulled over the edge of the panel without the worry of wrinkles forming.*

3 *To prevent a lot of glue mess, masking tape is used to hold the carpet strip temporarily in place along the lower edge of the door panel. It is important to get an accurate placement of the carpet to ensure the proper fitment of the chrome trim strip over the edge of the carpet.*

4 *Masking tape is used to protect the surface of the door panel before a reference guideline is drawn to indicate the top edge of the carpet strip. This guideline is used for the positioning of the trim molding that conceals the raw edge of the carpet.*

5 *The posts of the trim molding should intersect with the guideline on the masking tape to accurately show where the anchor holes are to be made. Dimples are made into the tape by pressing down lightly over the anchor posts of the trim molding.*

6 *Check and double-check the fitment of the trim panels before making any holes in the door panel. A new high-speed drill bit should be used to prevent any unexpected walking or tear-out from a worn or dull tool.*

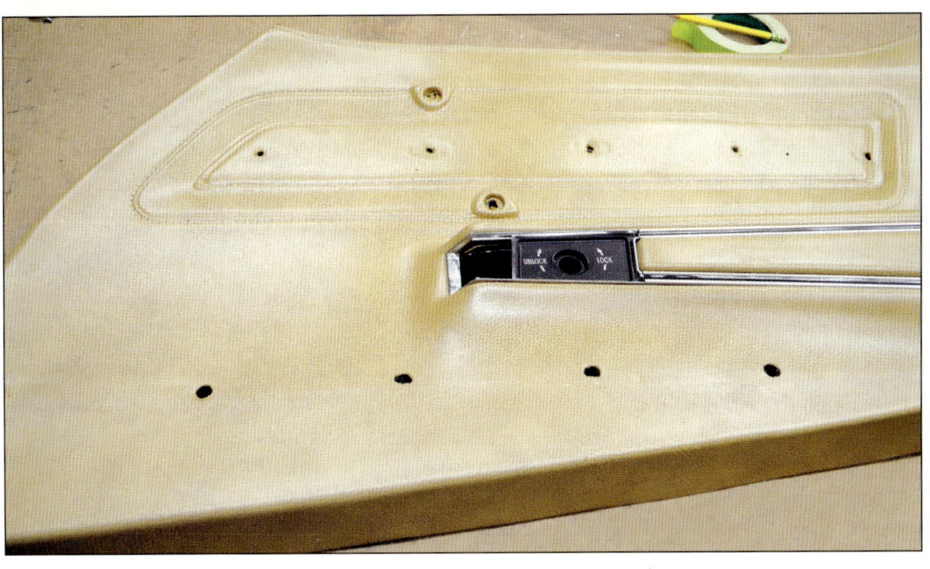

7 *At first thought, it might be a little intimidating to deliberately make holes in a door panel, but with all the planning and precautions, you should have no problems getting your trim to cover and fit properly. Remember to take things slow and be very careful with power tools.*

Mounting holes are needed in the door panel to allow for the fitment of the insert panel. Before the holes can be made, you must know where to make them. This is done by placing the trim panel in position over the upper embossed area of the door panel and applying even, downward pressure on the trim panel to leave an imprint of the anchor posts in the surface of the panel skin. Only dimple the skin; do not pierce it. If too much pressure is applied, there is a risk of cracking the casting or damaging the door panel. The through holes will be made after the other trim is positioned and fit.

Deluxe panels also have a carpeted section that runs along the bottom of the panel. The carpet matches the interior carpet, and it is capped off at the top edge by a decorative, chrome-plated trim piece. This trim is fit to the door panel in a similar way to the upper trim panel.

To find the location of the lower trim, the carpet must be fit properly.

Prepare the carpet section by making small relief cuts in the vinyl around the curve of the carpet. This helps the vinyl wrap smoothly around the front of the panel. Be careful when making the cuts to not cut the stitching.

Position the edge of the carpet flush with the outer edge of the door panel and use masking tape to hold the sewn edge in place. It is not recommended to use glue at this time. Pull the vinyl material around the edge of the panel to check the fit. Run another piece of masking tape under the top edge of the carpet and then use a pencil to mark the location of the top edge of the carpet onto the tape.

To conceal the raw edge of the carpet, the chrome trim must be over the edge of the carpet with the anchor posts of the trim on the pencil line. This ensures the center point of the trim. The trim panel should cover the cut edge of the carpet without extending past the front edge or

the lower edge of the panel. When positioned correctly, press down on the trim with enough pressure to dimple the masking tape with the anchor posts. Do not pierce the panel with the trim. Remove the trim and the carpet from the panel, leaving only the upper masking tape with the pencil line.

A 3/8-inch drill bit will be needed to make the through holes on the door panel to allow the trim pieces to sit flush along the surface of the panel. Be very careful while using a power drill for this operation. Place a scrap piece of plywood under the door panel to prevent damage to the surface of your workbench from the drill bit. Position the tip of the drill bit in the center of a dimple and begin drilling slowly with an even downward pressure on the drill bit. Keep the drill bit vertical to the surface at all times. If the drill bit gets away from you, it will ruin the door panel.

Keep checking the fit of the trim pieces and make small adjustments

All panel fasteners should be started with your fingers to prevent any cross threading. Small machine screws can jam easily and ruin trim pieces if you are not careful. Use a manual screwdriver to tighten the screws until they are snug and not dimpling the panel.

Always protect your work surface with cardboard before spraying glue. This protects the parts from excess glue and allows you to get an even edge-to-edge coat on the parts. Observe safety precautions and follow the manufacturer's directions on how to properly apply the adhesive.

to allow the parts to lay flat against the panel surface. Remove the masking tape and any debris from the surface of the panel before installing the trim pieces permanently.

Attaching the Trim

Cover the surface of the workbench with a soft towel to protect the door panel while installing the new trim pieces. Apply the upper insert anchor posts into the holes on the panel and then turn the assembly upside down on the workbench.

Insert the machine screw through the anchor washer and then carefully start threading the screw into the anchor post just a few turns. Do not tighten the screws until they are all in place. This ensures that the panel has been positioned and anchored securely.

After all the screws have been placed, turn the panel over and check the fit of the insert. If you are satisfied with the positioning, carefully tighten the screws to secure the panel in place. Do not overtighten the screws. The casting is made of a soft metal, and the anchor post can be damaged by cross-threading or pulling out the threads with too much pressure.

Glue must be applied to the carpet section before it can be installed. Cover the work area with cardboard to prevent overspray from getting onto the workbench. Clean the lower surface of the door panel with a degreasing solvent to help the glue stick. Spray the back side of the carpet section and the lower door panel area with an even coat of contact cement. Allow the contact cement to get tacky before setting the carpet in place on the door panel.

When the glue is dry to the touch, fit the carpet to the panel.

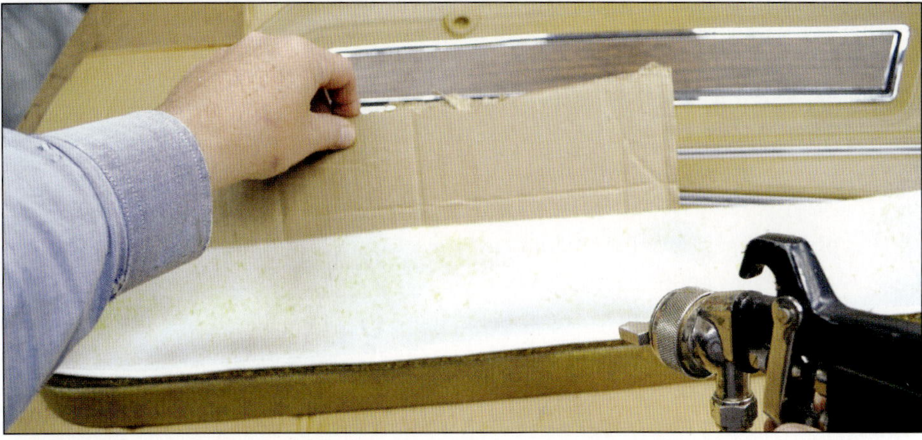

Overspraying of contact cement can be prevented by using a scrap piece of cardboard behind the edge of the vinyl trim. This helps keep the cleanup to a minimum and provides a neater installation of the carpet strip.

A nice row of staples is added to the back side of the panel to keep the carpet binding from coming loose. Wrinkles are removed along the inside curve by pulling on the vinyl just enough to help the material lay smoothly against the bottom edge of the door panel.

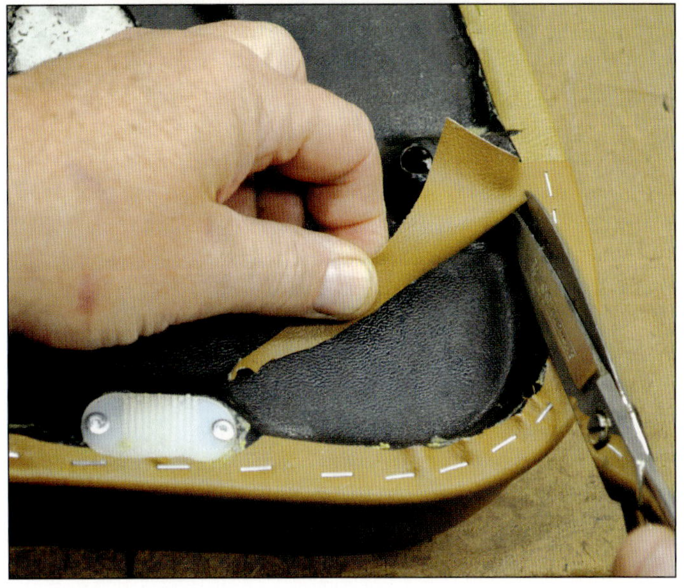

A final trimming of the carpet binding completes the installation of the carpet strip. Removing the excess material not only makes the job look nicer but is also a necessary step to ensure a good fit along the bottom edge of the panel.

Make sure that the outer edges of the carpet are flush with the outer edges of the door panel before working the carpet into the glue. Let the piece set for a few minutes before turning the vinyl edging.

Apply a light coat of contact cement to the back of the vinyl trim and the lower edge of the door panel. A small piece of cardboard can be used as a glue shield to prevent overspray from getting onto the door panel. Keep the glued surfaces from touching each other until you are ready to finish the assembly.

To prevent the vinyl trim from catching in the glue and wrinkling, pull upward and then down and around the lower edge of the door panel. The vinyl edging must lay tight and smooth along the edge of the carpet before finishing the edges.

If wrinkles appear, lift the vinyl from the center point of the wrinkle, just enough to pull the wrinkle out. Then, work the material outward in both directions, smoothing the vinyl as you go.

Turn the panel upside down and finish the edges of the carpet by pulling the vinyl over the bottom edge of the panel. Staple the vinyl to the back edge of the door panel to keep it in place. Add staples in a continuous line. Do not overlap the staples, as this will not allow the panel to sit flush against the inner door.

When the stapling is finished, the vinyl can be trimmed to the inside edge of the door panel. Trim the vinyl away from the dual-lock nylon fasteners. They must be clear of any other material to mate properly with the inner door.

Turn the panel faceup on the bench and trim away any carpet that may be over the trim anchor holes. Do not trim too much of the carpet.

A small amount of the carpet has been removed from over the anchor post hole in the door panel. This simple action helps the trim molding fit properly over the top edge of the applied carpet strip, concealing the raw edge from view.

After the door trim has been fit, a final tightening of the retainer hardware is made. This ensures that the trim will stay in place and properly cover the raw edge of the newly added carpet strip along the bottom of the door panel.

A few careful taps from a tack hammer are all it takes to reshape the anchor washer, allowing it to fit the inner contour of the door panel. By reshaping the washer, the door panel fits better on the car and does not interfere with the other components that the door panel is designed to conceal.

You only want to allow the post to get through and still have the trim molding conceal the cut edge of the carpet.

Insert the anchor posts of the trim molding into the door panel and then turn the panel facedown on the workbench. Apply the machine screws and washers just like you did for the upper trim panel. Check the positioning and fit of the trim before the final tightening.

These simple upgrades have turned a basic door panel into a deluxe panel in just a few hours. Inspect the door panel for any discrepancies and adjust as necessary. Wipe down the panel to remove any smudges and fingerprints prior to installation.

Armrest Repair

A common problem with the modular design of the C3 door panel is the armrest area. This portion of the panel is prone to the most wear and damage. Since the armrest is not removable, it cannot easily be replaced unless a whole new door panel is installed. This fix can become a costly repair if the rest of the door panel is not worn or damaged.

To address this issue, a replacement panel was developed to overlay the damaged area, extending the life of the door panel. This repair is a quick and easy way to dress up the door panel. An armrest patch panel kit can be ordered for 1968 to 1977 C3s from your preferred vendor in the matching color of your door panel.

To get a good idea of how the panel will sit on the door panel, pre-fit the new patch panel to the door. Double-faced panel tape is used to attach the patch panel to the exist-

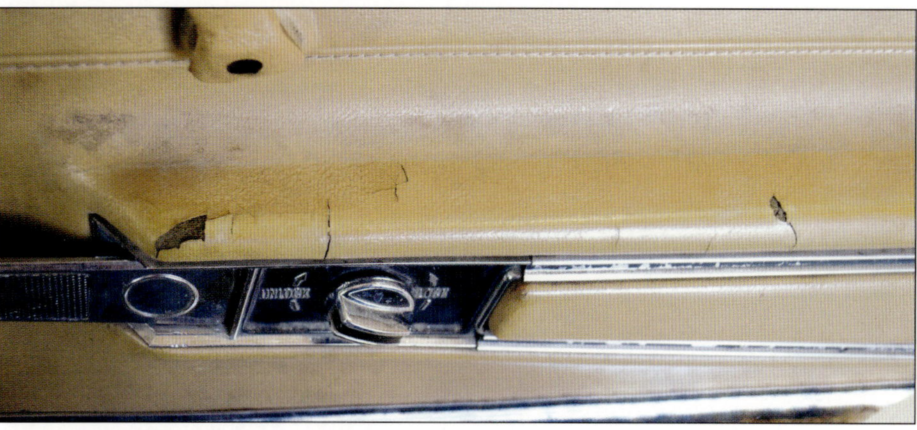

What a shame that the armrest area of this door panel is in such rough condition compared to the rest of the door panel. A total replacement of the door panel can be an expensive solution, but to get a few more years out of the panel, a repair panel can be fit to cover the damaged area.

After a good cleaning, a new patch panel has been installed over the damaged portion of the door panel. The new piece is color matched to the original panel for a neat and tidy appearance, saving the owner a lot of money and adding more life to the panel.

ing door. Do not remove the protective paper from the adhesive strips at this time; just set the panel on the door and see how it will fit the existing panel.

To get a good install, thoroughly clean the door panel before attaching the panel. Cleaning the surface can be done with any good vinyl cleaner and a soft cloth rag. After the surface has been cleaned, use an alcohol wipe to further degrease the armrest surface and then let the door panel air dry. Do not touch the area with your fingers after it has been cleaned.

Remove the protective paper from the adhesive strips on the back side of the patch panel and fit the patch panel to the door. Press down on the surface of the patch panel to ensure that the adhesive tape has made a good bond.

CARPET

A common feature of all early C1, C2, and C3 Corvette flooring is that the carpet sets are composed of multiple pieces. Because the interior contours of the Corvette are complex and small, the two-seat design makes the installation of the carpet somewhat of a challenge. Since the carpet set is made up of small segments, fitting the pieces is not as cumbersome as you may imagine. Arranging them in the correct order is the key to achieving a tailored look.

Carpet sets can be obtained from any supplier of Corvette parts. Because the Corvette body is made of fiberglass, heat transfer and noise are a common problem. To overcome this issue, the original factory carpet set was made with a rubber backing. Not all carpet sets are offered with the rubber-back choice, so if you desire that option, you must ask for it and be prepared to pay a higher price.

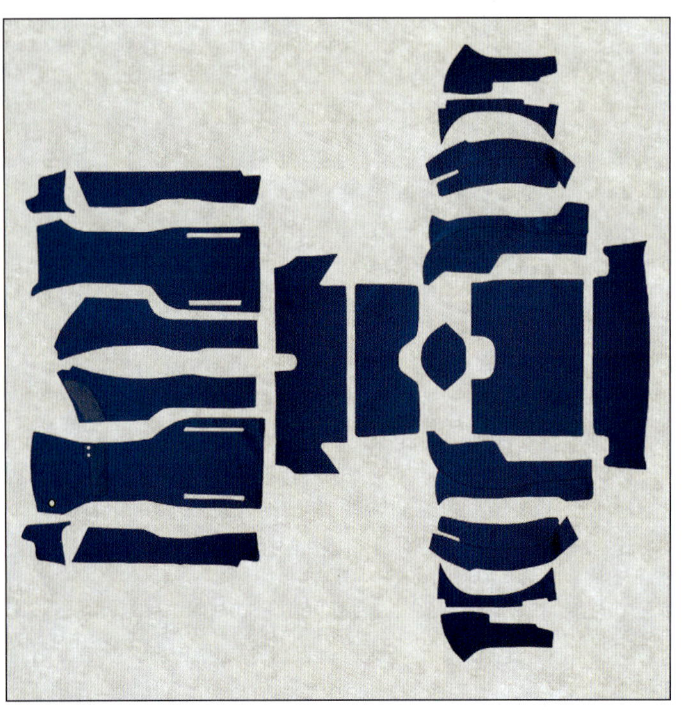

When laid out on the garage floor, a Corvette carpet set looks like a giant jigsaw puzzle. The small pieces are much easier to install in the confined areas than a much larger molded section of carpet. Once the pieces are installed in the car, they blend together.

Teardown

This project features a 1964 Corvette roadster with remnants of the original carpet. Before the new carpet set can be installed, all of the old carpet must be removed. The first items to remove are the sill plates. These are attached to the lower door opening with screws.

Removal of the screws requires a Phillips screwdriver to loosen the oval-head trim screws. If the sill plates are in good condition, they can be reused. Worn or damaged parts should be replaced with new pieces.

The next step is to remove the seats. The Corvette seat is fastened to a seat track that is bolted to the floor of the car. I like to use a 1/2-inch box wrench to loosen the mounting bolts. The wrench is able to get into the tight space better than a socket, and it will only take a few turns to remove the anchor bolt.

Begin by adjusting the seat all the way to the rear to expose the front anchor bolts. There should only be one bolt on the front of each seat rack to remove. After the bolts have been extracted, the seat can be pulled forward and then lifted out of the car.

After many years of use, some of the original damaged carpet has already been removed. Restoring the carpet set in this roadster not only makes the car look better but also helps with excessive noise and heat issues common to the Corvette.

Fading from the sun, mold due to exposure, and wear from years of neglect and abuse make this 1964 Corvette soft top the perfect project car for a carpet replacement. A new carpet set will completely transform the interior back to its original glory.

Located at the base of the door opening are the sill plates. These decorative pieces cover the raw outer edge of the carpet and are the first parts that need to be removed before the new carpet set can be installed.

With the seat moved back, the bolts that secure the seat tracks to the floor are exposed so they can be removed. Due to the limited access, a 1/2-inch wrench is used to extract the bolt, allowing the seat to be taken out of the car.

Early models may have a lift-out lower cushion that needs to be removed before the seat frame bolts can be accessed. Later models (C3) will have anchor bolts on the front and rear of the seat tracks.

It is not uncommon for some of the bolts to either break off during the removal process or for the anchor plate that they thread into to come loose and spin under the floor of the car. These can be fixed later after the seat has been removed.

Our 1964 roadster has rear anchor loops that are bolted to the floor. These can be removed and reconditioned if desired. If the anchor bolts are frozen or difficult to loosen, leave them in place to prevent any additional repairs. If a bolt does break off, it should then be removed and repaired correctly before proceeding.

Trim Panel Removal

Many of the interior trim panels and components have to be removed so that the front flooring sections can be completely cleaned before the new carpet is installed. Begin by extracting the screws that hold the gas pedal to the floor. Use a #3 Phillips screwdriver to loosen the screws, and once they are free, bag and tag the pieces so that they can be reinstalled later.

Next, remove the kick panels and wind lace trim. There is a metal retainer along the front edge of the kick panel and several other screws with small washers that hold the perimeter of the panel in place. The screws can be easily removed with a #2 Phillips screwdriver. Save the hardware.

Before the center armrest can be removed, the console plate trim screws must be taken out to gain access to the underlying armrest

Because of the limited space inside the passenger compartment, the C2 Corvette has an anchor loop that the rear portion of the seat track slides into. This unique feature is bolted to the floor and can only be accessed after the seat has been removed.

Removing the gas pedal makes installation of the new carpet much easier and yields a better result than trying to work around it. After the anchor screws are removed, the pedal and carpet can be lifted out of the car.

Decorative trim screws hold the kick panels and wind lace retainer trim to the inner panel of the car. A screwdriver is used to remove the panel and the trim so that new carpeted kick panels can be installed.

Hidden under the center console plate is a bolt that holds the center armrest in place. Trim screws are removed from the trim panel so that it can be lifted enough to allow access for the removal of the retainer bolt.

Complete removal of the center console plate is not necessary to expose the hidden armrest bolt. After the retainer screws have been removed, the console panel just needs to be lifted enough to remove the armrest bolt.

While the center console plate is raised, reaching the armrest anchor bolt is easy with a socket attached to a ratchet and long socket extension. This would be a real knuckle buster if you used a box-end wrench.

retainer bolt. Remove the Phillips-head screws from the perimeter of the console plate and set them aside.

The console plate does not need to be removed from the car; it just needs to be lifted enough to get at the bolt holding the armrest in place. Use a 3/8-inch socket to loosen the retainer bolt and then set it aside. The armrest can now be moved to the side to clear the console plate and then be lifted from the car. Once removed, it is an ideal time to re-cover the armrest before it gets reinstalled.

Seat Belts

Secured to the rear inner corners of the cab are the seat belts. Due to the limited space inside the car, a socket cap bolt is used to anchor the ends of the seat belts to the car. Removing the anchor bolt requires a hex socket and a ratchet wrench.

Later C3 models used a retractable seat belt that was bolted to the floor. These anchor bolts are often seized into the metal anchor plates and tend to dislodge the plate when the bolts are extracted. If this happens, you need to replace the anchor plates with new ones and install them to factory specifications to ensure that they are safe and will not tear out.

C3 hardtop models also had shoulder belts that are attached in the rear compartment. Remove these the same way before taking out the carpet.

Quarter Trim Removal

On the inside rear of the cab are decorative trim panels that finish the lower B-pillar and doorjamb. These panels are also made of fiberglass and are held in place by two screws along the trailing edge and a small bolt located at the bottom of the panel. To

---

free the panel from the car, loosen the screws with a Phillips screwdriver and then use a 3/8-inch socket to remove the bolt from the bottom of the panel.

After the fasteners have been removed, the trim panel can then be lifted from the car by first pulling upward and then tilting the panel forward to clear it from the doorjamb. After the panel is removed, it can be cleaned and repainted if necessary.

Now that all the interior trim and components that obstructed the removal of the carpet have been removed, the remnants of the carpet can be pulled out of the car and discarded. Start with the large piece that covers the main floor section.

Pull up a corner and work the carpet loose by peeling it away from the flooring. Do the same with the carpet that is attached to the transmission tunnel and then the carpet on the inner door threshold.

Removing the seat belts from the car requires a hex socket wrench to extract the low-profile anchors holding them securely in place. Rust and debris often make these bolts very difficult to remove without damaging the bolt or anchor plate.

Several trim fasteners are used to hold the decorative fiberglass B-pillar cover panel to the interior of the car. A socket is used to remove the small bolt holding the lower portion of the trim panel to the car.

Before the pillar cover can be removed, a screwdriver is used to loosen the two remaining trim screws located on the rear apron of the trim panel. Once the screws are removed, the decorative panel can be taken out of the car.

Removing the B-pillar cover panel takes some finesse to free it from the car without damaging the fragile fiberglass. A gentle rocking motion allows the cover to be lifted from the car without cracking the panel.

Rear Compartment

Behind the trunk partition are the inner rear wheel tubs and storage compartment of the car. This era of Corvettes did not have an actual trunk, and the space was generally used for luggage and parcels that needed to be transported. There are many individual pieces of carpet that line the inside of the rear compartment. Each of these will need to be removed before the new carpet set can be installed. There is also a specific order that needs to be followed to ensure that the pieces fit correctly.

Located in the front of the space is the jack storage compartment. A simple compartment cover is used to conceal the contents of the deep bin. As the Corvette evolved, this compartment was divided into sections for the battery, a storage area, and a lockable center glove box.

To remove the compartment cover, use the finger pull that is located in the cover. There are no physical fasteners holding the cover in place, and it will just lift up. The carpet on the cover board needs to be replaced, so we will set aside the cover for now.

The main rear deck section of the carpet is removed next. This section of carpet is bound around its edges, and it conceals all of the raw edges of the other carpet pieces. Begin removal of the main section by lifting a corner and peeling it away from the floor of the compartment. After the piece has been removed, it can then be discarded.

Each wheel tub is covered with several individual pieces of carpet. Peel back the top section of carpet from the top of the rear wheel tub. This piece covers the inner edge of the wheel tub and the side of the compartment. Repeat this action on the other side of the compartment.

Corvettes with T-tops may also have footman loops screwed to the tops of the wheel tubs. These are used to secure the top panels with cinch straps when the panels are removed from the car. A Phillips screwdriver is needed to remove the screws that hold the footman loops in place before taking out the carpet.

The wheel tub midsection is made of two pieces of bound carpet. This section is designed to lay flat against the inner panel as it wraps around the contour of the wheel tub. Grab a corner and pull back on the carpet section to remove it from the wheel tub.

The lower carpet section of the wheel tub also has two sections of carpet sewn together, similar to the midsection but a little larger. Removal of this carpet piece is just like the last, just grab a corner and pull it up and away from the car.

Removing the Rear Component Carpet and Covers

1 *The best way to describe the storage compartment lid on the C2 Corvette is simple yet functional. Built without hinges or latches, friction is used to keep the cover in place before it is removed with a single-finger grab hole.*

2 Removal of the large carpet section that covers the center decking area of the rear compartment starts by lifting the bound edge of the material and pulling the worn and faded carpet away from the car. This action reveals the edges of the other carpet sections.

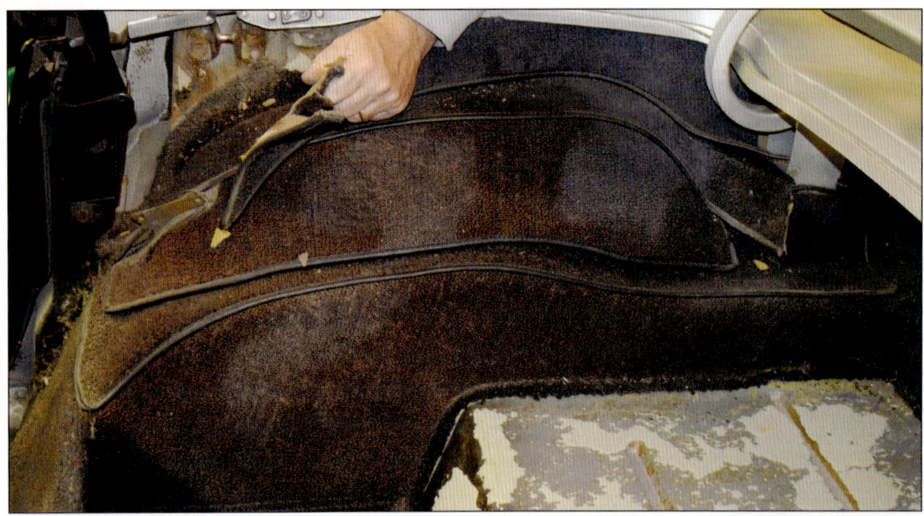

3 Layers of individual carpet sections need to be removed from the wheel tubs to prepare for the installation of the new carpet set. The upper vertical section is the first to be peeled away from under the lip of the decklid.

4 On top of the wheel tub is a dual section of carpet that is specifically designed to fit the curve of the inner body. Once the piece is peeled back and removed from the top of the wheel tub, the lower section can be easily accessed.

5 Another compound section of carpet is pulled back and removed from the lower section of the wheel tub. During the extraction of this carpet section, some of the original rubber backing has become detached and needs to be removed later.

Base Section Carpet Removal

At the bottom of the carpet layers are the foundation pieces. These were installed first, and the other sections were built upon them, each concealing the edges of the previous layer of carpet. The trunk partition is covered with a large section of carpet that begins at the floor line of the cab and moves up and wraps over the top edge of the partition, finishing along the rear deck floor line. Loosen a corner and begin to peel the carpeting off the partition and then discard the worn piece of carpet.

Next, remove the oddly shaped piece of carpet that covers the semi-round differential panel. Lift up on the edge of the carpet and peel it off the floor.

The last piece of carpet to be removed is attached to the rear wall deep inside the rear compartment. Later models may have a rear compartment light attached to the rear wall. This needs to be removed before the carpet can be taken out. Accessing the mounting screws can be done by popping off the lens of the light and removing the bulb. The screws can now be removed with a #2 Phillips screwdriver.

Removing the rear carpet section is just like the others. Start by working a corner loose and pulling the carpet away from the car. This piece of carpet can also be discarded.

Clean Up

When the old carpet was removed, remnants of the rubber backing were left behind. This residue must be cleaned off the surface of the floor before new carpet can be installed. It is not advised to use any chemical- or solvent-based cleaners to remove the adhesive from the surface of the

One of the larger pieces that make up the base layers of carpet in the Corvette is covering the vertical trunk partition. This worn and faded carpet section is removed by peeling it loose from the face and the back side of the partition.

Although this carpet section is small, it's the center point of the rear compartment, and it covers the differential panel well. Age and the elements have taken their toll on the carpet due to the amount of rubber carpet backing left behind during removal.

Reach deep into the rear compartment to remove the final vertical rear section of carpet. Fortunately for us, there isn't a dome light to remove. Lifting the top and rear deck cover on this convertible makes access much easier.

fiberglass. Harsh chemicals can damage the fiberglass and cause it to soften.

The best method for removing the old stuck-on pieces of rubber is scraping it off the interior surface with a stiff-blade putty knife. Care must be taken to prevent gouging the fiberglass with the broad knife. Even pressure is all that is needed to loosen the residue. Wear a dust mask to prevent any accidental breathing of the debris while scraping.

A vacuum cleaner works well to pick up the loose debris as it is removed. The fine dust that remains can be removed with a damp rag. After the surface has been cleaned, new carpet pad and carpet can be installed.

Carpet Pad

The conventional style of Corvette carpet is made with a dense rubber backing. The rubber backing works well as a pad and helps control heat and sound from entering the car. The downside of rubber comes from drying out and crumbling due to exposure and aging.

I have always preferred working with the traditional jute pad. It is easy to work with and holds up well. The cost difference between the rubber and jute can be a factor to some car owners, although there are only marginal differences in overall performance.

Now is the perfect time to make any repairs that may be needed to the floor while the old carpet is out and the floor is clean. It is also a good idea to chase the threads of all the anchor points with the proper tap to ensure that the gas pedal, seat, and belt bolts go in without binding.

Before any of the new carpet set can be installed, the floor surface requires a thorough scraping. Then, vacuum all the old carpet padding remnants. Proper preparation ensures that the glue will bond the new carpet pad securely to the car.

Having a smooth and clean surface to apply the carpet yields a much better-looking carpet installation than a quick vacuuming. Removing the lumps and bumps takes a lot of time and is well worth the effort that you put in as preparation for new carpet.

Installing a Jute Pad onto the Main Deck

1 Here, the padding is dry fit to verify coverage and fitment. You can clearly see that the jute carpet pad comes up short in many areas. It is best to maximize the precut pad and then fill in the empty places with additional pad from an auto trim supplier.

2 Adjusting the fit of the padding is done with a pair of heavy-duty scissors. Trimming the pad to fit the contours of the floor allows the carpet to be installed without bulges and still obtains the maximum sound and heat reduction inside the car.

3 An even coat of contact cement is sprayed onto both the floor and the back side of the carpet pad. To help the installation, glue is applied in small sections to make the material less difficult to work with, which reduces the number of wrinkles.

4 The main deck pad has been trimmed to fit and glued to the floor of the rear compartment. The excess material is used to fill other gaps while additional jute pad material was added to cover the rear vertical wall of the compartment.

Precut Pad

Many carpet sets come with the padding already attached to the back side of the carpet. This does not always make for an easy installation due to wrinkles caused by a poorly attached pad. The solution is to order the carpet set with the padding loose.

The loose pad supplied by the carpet manufacturer is often crudely patterned and does not give complete coverage of the floor. It is advised that you dry fit the pad and trim it to fit properly before gluing it in place. To make up the deficit left by the lack of coverage, additional yardage of jute padding can be obtained at any upholstery supplier and cut to fit the voids.

For the best finished carpet results, the new pad should be glued to the floor. An even coat of contact adhesive should be applied to both surfaces before setting the pad in place. Be careful to eliminate any wrinkles in the pad as it is fit to the floor. Applying the carpet pad to cover 100 percent of the floor surface provides better sound and heat control as well as a solid base for the new carpet set.

New Carpet

Begin by laying out the contents of the box on the floor to get an idea of what the carpet set looks like. It is very important to install the carpet in the correct order to prevent damage from removing a misplaced section. It also helps to dry fit the carpet section and make any necessary alterations to the piece before it is glued in place.

The rear compartment wall is the first area to be covered with carpet. Once you have an idea of the fit, apply a small band of glue to the

Included with most carpet sets is an instruction sheet that has a diagram of the carpet along with a few tips on how to install it. This can be a helpful resource if you get confused on the orientation of the individual pieces.

It is easy for a section of carpet this size to develop wrinkles or become misaligned during the installation process. Avoiding these issues can be accomplished by gluing only a small portion or the carpet at a time so that alterations can be made.

To help conceal the pad from showing at the carpet joints, 1 inch of the rear compartment wall carpet has been allotted to spill out onto the main deck. To relax the carpet so that it will not develop wrinkles along the fold, small relief cuts can be made in the carpet.

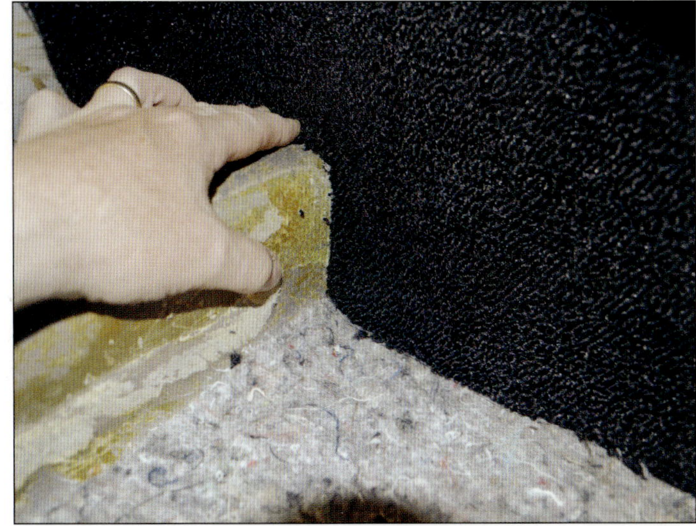

Contours and sharp angles can be a problem when trying to get the carpet to lay flat around the obstacle. Relieving the tension at the corners by making a small cut in the carpet helps the material wrap around irregularity without puckering.

A simple snip with sharp scissors allows the carpet to open just enough so that the rear wire harness can pass though the carpet without being detected. Small cuts like this make all the difference in the final appearance of the carpet.

back of the carpet and the mating surface of the pad to get the piece started. This allows adjustments to be made while the section is aligned with minimal error.

To prevent any gaps in coverage, it is best to have at least 1 inch of carpet to lay along the floor. This allows the final decking to butt up against the vertical rise in the carpet without having any of the underlying pad show. The same margin of carpet is worked over the riser of the wheel tub. Small cuts are made in the corners of the carpet to allow the material to follow the contour of the floor without bunching up and causing a wrinkle in the carpet.

Additional relief cuts are made in the carpet to accommodate the wire harness that runs to the rear lights and decklid springs. Adding glue a few inches at a time while working the carpet gives you better control and results in a nicer fit.

Rear Compartment

Check the fit of the center base carpet section before applying glue to the surface of the carpet pad and the back side of the carpet section. Glue should be applied by spraying an even coating on the pad and the lip of the storage compartment. Use a small piece of cardboard as a guard to prevent overspray from getting all over the storage compartment.

To get the best glue coverage on the carpet, place it facedown on a piece of cardboard and spray the back with an even coat of contact cement. Pay close attention to get enough glue on the outer edges of the carpet panel. This ensures that it will adhere securely to the lip of the storage compartment.

After the glue has reached a dry tack state, position the carpet so that it

Here, the rear carpet section has been properly installed. A lot of effort has been made to make sure that all the wrinkles and puckers have been eliminated. This kind of attention to detail gives your project a professional appearance.

will completely cover the area and the compartment lip. The compartment edge of the carpet can be trimmed to fit around the lip once the glue has set and the carpet settles in place.

Both sides of the rear compartment need to be covered with new carpet pad. The new pad should be applied to the wheel tubs to soften the carpet and deaden road noise. Cut and fit the new carpet pad so that it will fit tight and allow the carpet sections to lay smooth.

An inner wire harness may run to the rear along the bottom of the wheel tub. The pad should not cover the wire, as this will create a lump in the installed carpet section. Butt the carpet pad up to each side of the wire so it sits snug in the void, making a channel along the base of the wheel tub. When the carpet is installed, it will cover the wire and make a smooth upward transition that protects the wire and lets the carpet look smooth and natural.

The jute pad material should be cut large enough to cover the wheel tub. Spray contact cement onto the surface of the wheel tub and the back of the carpet padding. Square up the lower edge of the pad and apply it to the wheel tub. Make sure the material runs along the bottom of the wheel tub without covering the lip of the storage compartment. Do not allow the pad material to lay on the lip of the compartment, as this will cause a problem with the fit of the compartment cover.

Make relief cuts in the pad to help it contour to the shape of the interior panels. The object here is to get the pad as smooth as possible. The pad may not look pretty, and that is fine because the new carpet section will cover over the padding. The carpet must be applied wrinkle free to look

An even coating of glue has been applied to the carpet pad and allowed to get tacky before the new section of carpet is fitted. If the glue is too wet, the new carpet piece will not adhere properly and can lift away from the pad.

Most base layers of carpet are cut a little larger than necessary to ensure complete coverage. After fitting the piece and allowing the glue to set, the visible edges need to be trimmed flush with the lip of the storage compartment.

Carpet padding is fit and then glued in place along the lower edge of the wheel tub. To get the compartment cover to fit properly, care must be taken to prevent the pad from being applied to the horizontal surface of the storage compartment.

During installation, the jute padding can be stretched and shaped to fit the interior curves of the car body with very little effort. Excess material can be reduced by trimming the bulk with scissors.

good. Do not install the carpet pad to the upper wheel tub at this time. The padding will be added after the lower carpet section is in place.

Trunk Partition

Although it is not necessary, I like to add carpet pad to the trunk partition. This softens the thin panel and helps the carpet wrap over the top edge, making the transition from the cab to the rear section a little more comfortable when reaching into the back of the car.

Applying the new carpet section to the partition is similar to that of the rear compartment wall. Begin by spraying glue to just the lower area of the partition and carpet backing to get the section aligned. There should be at least 1 inch of carpet flat on the floor before the material begins its vertical rise up and over the partition.

Relief cuts can be made around the transmission tunnel to help reduce any wrinkles or puckers from forming in the carpet. Working the carpet piece 3 to 4 inches at a time is easier than trying to glue and apply it all at once.

After the main section of the carpet has been set, the upper edges can be tucked in place with a headliner tuck tool. Glue should be applied to the pad and the back side of the carpet and allowed to tack before it is tucked in place.

If the carpet is too long, some trimming may be necessary to allow it to fit into the tight space at the upper inside corners. Continue to glue and secure the carpet down the back side of the partition until it flows to the lip edge of the recessed compartment. When the carpet has reached full adhesion, it can be trimmed flush along the edge of the storage compartment.

Many irregularities and unwanted surface imperfections can be smoothed out and hidden by applying a layer of jute padding to the inner surface of the car. Once the carpet pad has been fit and trimmed, the new carpet section can be installed.

A layer of carpet padding has been added to the metal surface of the trunk partition to help soften the feel and appearance of the carpet. Doing this also provides a better bonding surface, making the installation of the carpet much faster.

A tucking tool is used to help with the final finishing of the carpet along the outer top edges of the partition panel. Using your fingers to do this task can be difficult, as it is a tight fit for the thick and stiff carpet to settle into.

After a lot of trimming and tucking, the large carpet section has been installed on the trunk partition panel. This foundation piece is wrinkle free and ready for the rest of the carpet pieces to be installed.

Wheel Tubs

There are three sections of carpet that cover the rear wheel tubs. Each section should be dry fit and checked for any adjustments before any trimming or glue is applied. Start the installation with the larger lower two-piece section first. The front bound edge of this carpet section should extend from the back side of the partition to the rear wall of the trunk compartment.

Make sure that the bottom of the carpet covers the lip of the storage compartment and extends about 1 inch onto the floor of the main deck. When fit correctly, the seam of the lower section follows the contour ridge of the trunk compartment.

When gluing the upper edge, at least 1 inch of material needs to flow up onto the wheel tub. Also, pay attention when covering the wire harness on the driver's side so that the carpet lays smooth and without any wrinkles or distortion. Make any adjustments at this time in the fit before you begin to apply glue to the mating surfaces.

Finishing the fit of this section requires a few relief cuts to make the carpet lay flat along the contours of the interior. After the lower edge has set, it can be trimmed flush with the lip edge of the storage compartment.

Carpeting the Wheel Tub

1 *This lower wheel tub section of carpet is the most difficult of all the sections to fit due to the many tiny details needed to make it fit correctly. When finished, the carpet provides a foundation for the rest of the rear compartment section to build on.*

2 After all the trimming has been completed, the lower portion of the wheel tub carpet is finished with sharp and clean transitional lines. This detail allows just enough friction for the storage compartment cover to fit perfectly in place.

3 Before the middle section of wheel tub carpet is installed, a layer of jute carpet padding has been added adjacent to the previously installed carpet section. The pad helps smooth the surface of the wheel tub and provides a smooth transition for the new carpet section.

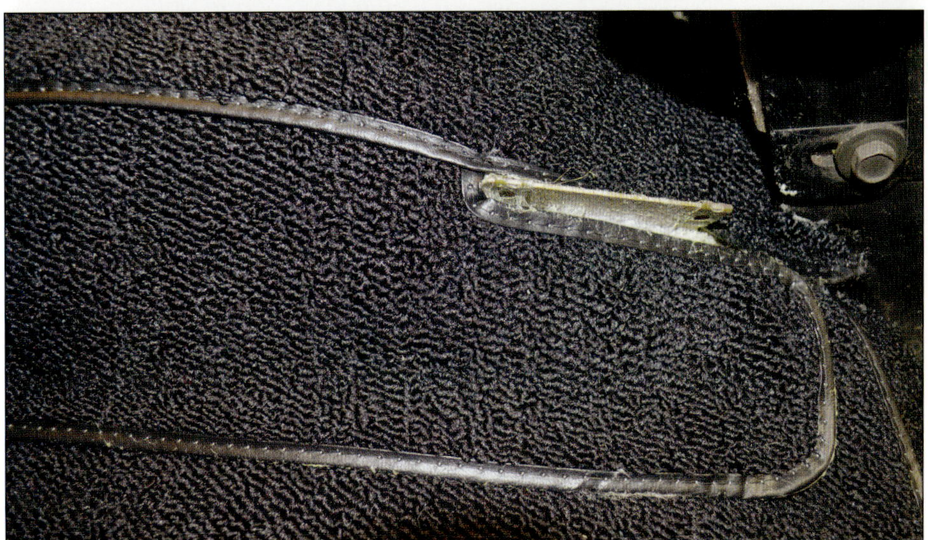

4 Prefitting the carpet section provides a better idea of how the finished installation should look. Applying just the right amount of glue to the edges along the back side of the carpet makes it stay in the correct position.

5 Notice how the bound rear edge of the middle carpet section lines up to the edge of the decklid spring bracket and lays across the rear of the wheel tub. These are the neatness details that make the carpet installation look more professional.

6 *The bound carpet edges of the middle section lay straight and smooth along the lower section and the center contour of the wheel tub. To achieve this look, pull a little on the seam when setting it in position to keep the binding tight and flat.*

7 *In preparation for the installation of the upper section of carpet, an even coat of glue is sprayed onto the vertical section of the wheel tub. To prevent overspray onto the lower carpet sections and body panels, a cardboard glue guard was used.*

8 *After the upper section of carpet was positioned and then smoothed against the vertical section of the wheel tub, scissors were used to cut a tab in the carpet. This allowed the carpet to lay flat on both sides of the rear deck latch.*

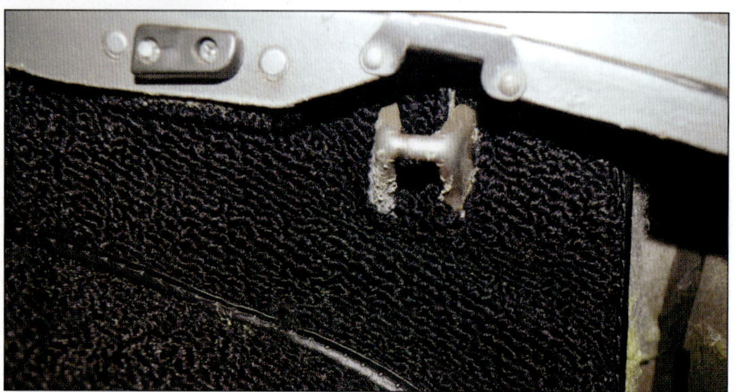

9 *Additional trimming was done to the relief tab to make the carpet look better. By removing just enough material to clear the thickness of the bracket supports, the remaining material could be repositioned under the latch bracket for a finished appearance.*

Middle Section

Now, the carpet pad can be added to the wheel tub. To prevent a bulge in the middle section, the carpet pad will butt up against the upper edge of the already installed lower carpet section and end just under the decklid rail.

Spray glue on the padding and the interior surface. Allow the glue to tack before setting the pad in place. Trim the pad to fit and smooth it around the trim panel bracket and decklid latch.

Dry fit the middle carpet section and adjust it for a proper fit. This is done by positioning the carpet section to straddle the trim panel bracket. The carpet section should contour over the wheel tub with the lower bound edge just touching the lower carpet section. When properly positioned, the seam of the middle section conforms to the contour of the wheel tub and lines up with the rear decklid spring bracket.

Remove the carpet section and spray an even coat of glue to the back side of the carpet with enough glue on the lower bound edge to ensure a good bond. Use a piece of cardboard as a glue guard to prevent unwanted spatter when spraying glue onto the wheel tub. Refit the carpet section when the glue gets tacky by pressing it into place.

To finish off the wheel tub, the cap piece will cover the upper raw edge of the middle section and tuck under the decklid rail. Spray glue onto the back side of the cap section of carpet and the vertical surface of the tub. Position the carpet section by centering it on the tub wall and set it into the glue with the lower bound edge fit tightly against the middle section.

Tuck the upper edge of the carpet section under the lid rail to conceal the raw edge of the carpet. Small relief cuts need to be made in the carpet for it to lay smoothly around the decklid latch bracket. A small amount of the carpet then needs to be removed on the edges of the carpet flap so that it can be tucked into the bracket, allowing for a smooth look.

Rear Deck

To complete the rear compartment, a large section of bound carpet will be applied over the center deck

To prepare the rear deck surface for the installation of the new carpet section, an even coating of contact cement is sprayed onto the carpet pad. A cardboard glue shield is used to prevent accidental overspray from getting onto the already installed carpet pieces.

Notice how the bound edges of the rear deck carpet section butt up tightly to the other carpet pieces to conceal their raw edges and the carpet padding below. After a little steam to relax the box wrinkles and some trimming along the front edge, this area of the carpet is complete.

---

carpet pad. Fist, dry fit the section to verify the positioning. It must cover the lower edges of the previously installed sections and finish along the rear lip of the storage compartment.

To secure the decking carpet, glue is sprayed on the back side of the decking and the surface of the carpet pad. Care must be used to prevent any wrinkles in the carpet as it is smoothed into place. Work the carpet from the rear bound edge forward and finish by trimming the front edges flush with the opening of the storage compartment.

Compartment Lid

If the base material of the rear compartment lid is not warped or damaged, it can be reconditioned and then reinstalled in the car. New reproduction compartment lids and components are also available to replace cracked or damaged pieces.

Carpeting the Compartment Lid

1 After many years of use and abuse, the removable rear storage compartment lid is showing signs of its age. With a little effort, and the availability of all-new modern materials, it will be easy to restore this simple device to its original glory.

2 Some small irregularities were found when the new base was compared to the original. After carefully marking the differences on the new material, the excess material can be removed with a little sanding to improve the profile of the compartment lid.

3 Some modification is needed to make the new materials work together. The premade hole in the cover is too small for the metal finger pull ring. Only a few strokes with a half round file are needed to enlarge the opening, giving a perfect fit.

4 *Contact cement is sprayed onto the back side of the compartment cover carpet. Cardboard has been laid down prior to gluing to protect the surface of the workbench from overspray as the outer edges are sprayed during the gluing process.*

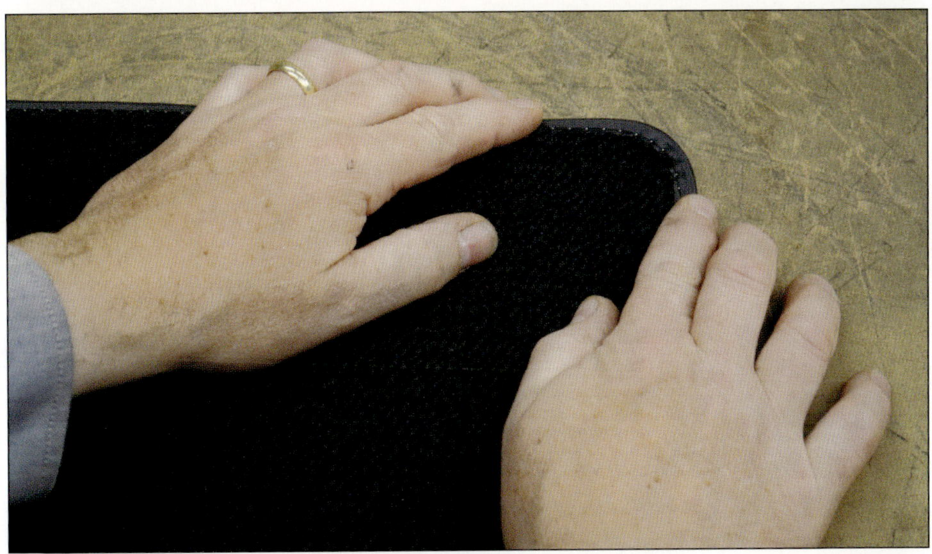

5 *During the installation of the storage lid carpet section, a little extra stretching may be needed to help the carpet reach the outer edges of the cover board. It is vital to keep the carpet smooth and wrinkle free as the carpet is worked to the edges.*

6 *The newly installed carpet on the compartment lid has covered over the finger grab hole. Removing this small amount of carpet from the hole was done by using a sawing motion and a razor blade.*

7 *After the metal finger pull ring was inserted into the opening on the compartment cover, it was turned over to gain access to the locking tabs. A tack hammer is used to bend the tabs over, which prevents the ring from coming loose.*

8 *Before the new jacking instruction decal can be positioned and applied to the back side of the storage compartment cover, the protective paper is partially removed from the back of the decal to reveal some of the adhesive.*

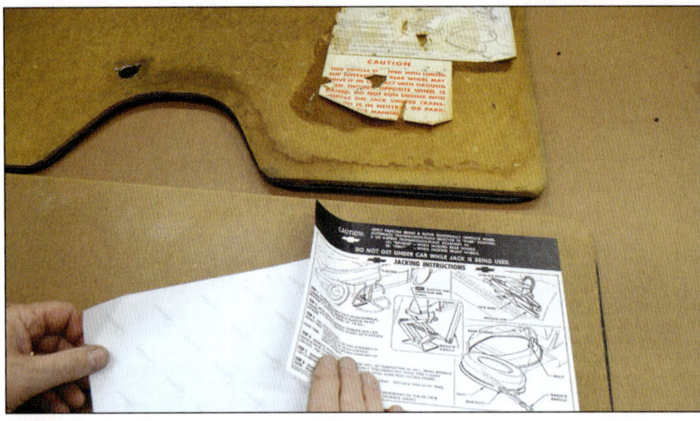

9 *Using the old compartment cover as a reference guide for the placement of the new jacking decals takes a lot of the guesswork out of the installation. Care must be taken to ensure that the decal is applied squarely and without any wrinkles or bubbles.*

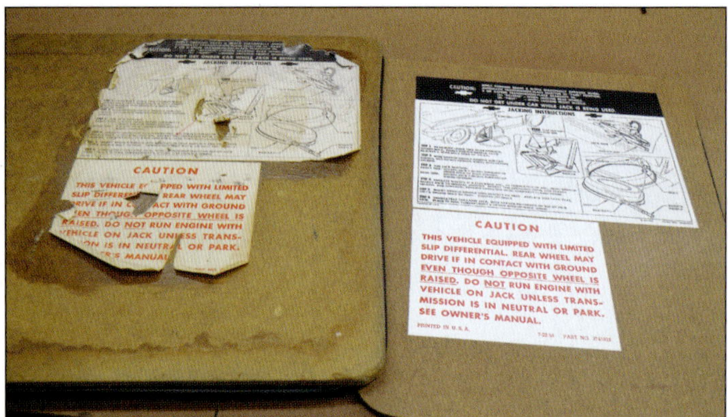

10 *What a difference in the appearance between the old compartment cover and the new one. It was a wise choice to freshen up the carpet installation with all new components. This project will look just like it did in 1964 when it was new.*

11 *Our new storage compartment cover fits perfectly in place without any latches. Gaining access to the underlying storage compartment is done by simply lifting the compartment cover up and away by means of a single-finger grab hole.*

Prep for Restoration

Reconditioning the original lid will require stripping off the old materials, exposing the base, which is made of 1/4-inch Masonite press board. Begin by turning the lid face-down on your workbench and prying up on the retaining tabs of the finger pull ring.

Remove the ring from the panel and inspect the metal for rust or other damage. If the ring and tabs are found to be in good condition, they can be reused, otherwise plan to replace them.

Next, use a broad knife scraper to help lift the old carpet from the surface of the panel. Carefully scrape the old glue off the Masonite and try not to gouge the material. Apply lacquer thinner or another type of adhesive remover to a rag and clean the surface of old glue and contaminants. This leaves the panel ready for new carpet.

New Materials

In the event that an original compartment cover panel is not useable, replacing it with a new one is a good option. To verify the parts are compatible, place the old cover on top of the new piece and compare the old base panel with the new one.

Use a pencil to mark any dimensional changes that may need to be made. To prevent excessive damage and tear out to the Masonite, I recommend the use of a file or a handheld belt sander to work the edges of the panel.

Also check the size and fit of the finger pull. If the existing hole is too tight, a half-round file will help enlarge the opening just enough to allow the metal ring to slide easily into place. If the hole is a little too large, the metal ring can be wrapped with tape to help it fit better. The retaining tabs on the finger pull will keep it in place, but the tape will keep it centered in the hole.

Covering the Lid

Dry fit the new carpet section to verify the fit to the compartment lid before applying glue to the pieces. The carpet should have a bound edge. If it hangs over the edges of the base a little, that is considered okay and is better than being short.

Spray an even coating of glue to the back side of the carpet section and to the surface of the compartment lid. Align the pieces and smooth out the carpet to eliminate any wrinkles. Work the edges of the carpet to cover the entire surface of the lid. After the carpet is positioned and the glue has set, the finger pull can be installed.

Before the finger pull ring can be installed, the carpet covering over the finger pull hole in the lid must be cut away. To make a clean cut, use a razor blade to remove the carpet by following around the edge of the finger hole. Be careful when cutting the carpet not to snag or pull out a row of the carpet loops. There is nothing special that needs to be done to the raw edges of the hole, as they will be concealed by the finger pull ring.

Insert the finger pull ring into the panel and then place the panel face-down on the workbench. The bottom edge of the finger ring should be flush with the underside of the compartment panel. To secure the metal ring to the panel, the locking tabs need to be bent over onto the panel. Gently tap the tabs over with a tack hammer. The tabs should lay flat on the under surface of the cover.

Decals

They say that the devil is in the details, so go all out and get a new set of jacking instructions to replace the torn and wrinkled originals. These decals are an exact reproduction of the original and dress up the underside of the compartment cover.

Before applying the new decals, first dry fit the decal to the proper location. Make sure that the surface is free of any grease or dirt that can prevent the decal from adhering properly to the surface of the cover.

The decals are made of a peel-and-stick paper and do not require any water to apply. Simply lift up on the corner of the backing paper to expose a small portion of the adhesive on the decal. Position the decal onto the back side of the cover and press the decal firmly onto the panel. Smooth the decal on without leaving any bubbles or wrinkles in the paper as you continue to pull the backing paper way from the decal.

After the decals have been applied, the compartment cover can be installed in the rear section of the car. The cover relies on friction to keep it securely in place, as it does not have any physical fasteners or retainers.

Later-model Corvettes that are equipped with a multicompartment lid have a plastic perimeter cover frame to conceal the raw carpet edges of the compartment doors. These are held in place by small wood screws and are then hinged to a larger compartment frame that is screwed to the perimeter of the storage compartment.

Front Pad

Installation of the new carpet is the same on both sides of the cab section of the Corvette with one variation: the driver's side has a gas pedal and the passenger's side does

Upon dry fitting the jute carpet pad that was supplied with our carpet set, we can clearly see that there just is not enough of the pad material to cover the entire floor area of the cab. More jute pad can be purchased from a local supplier to finish this installation.

For more comfort and better heat and sound insulation, the carpet pad is glued to the floor with only small cutouts for the seat mounts and gas pedal clearance. The omitted areas are necessary for the proper fit and installation of the interior pieces.

Jute carpet padding is applied to the floor all the way up to the firewall in the cab. The pad is not normally glued directly to the floor under the pedals or around the headlight dimmer switch. This allows lifting of the carpet and pad to service worn parts or wires.

not. The supplied carpet pad may not cover the entire floor area. Additional carpet padding may be desired to achieve a better sound and heat barrier.

Bulk yardage of 1/2-inch automotive jute carpet pad was obtained to get the complete coverage desired for our installation. Contact cement will be applied to the pad and floor to secure the jute in place, preventing future bunching and shifting of the carpet.

Small pieces are cut from the pad to expose the mounting points for the seat tracks and gas pedal. Removing the bulky material from these areas will make the anchors easier to access and get a better fit when doing the final installation of the seat and gas pedal. Cutting the pad away from the exposed bolt heads also helps the new carpet look smoother, since it flows over the obstructions without unsightly bulges.

Vertical Panels

Installation of the vertical transmission tunnel and outer side panel carpet sections need to be in position before the main carpet section can be installed. Layering the carpet section in this manner will cover the unfinished lower edges of the vertical carpet pieces with the main section of carpet, which has bound or finished edges that will butt up to the preinstalled sections.

Start by dry fitting the inner transmission tunnel section to give you an idea of where the outer margins of the carpet will finish, but do not make any relief cuts at this time. The top edge of the carpet tucks under the center console trim and is then glued to the top of the tunnel under the center armrest pad. You also need to allow at least 1 inch of carpet to be horizontal to the tunnel along the floor. The bound rear edge of this section butts up tightly to the trunk partition.

After the orientation of the carpet panel is figured out, lay the section on the floor of the car and spray an even coat of glue onto the back side of the carpet section and on the vertical surface of the transmission tunnel. It may help to use masking tape or a glue shield to protect the console trim when spraying glue along the transmission tunnel.

Set the carpet by starting at the rear bound edge and work forward. Remember to check the margins as you go. Once the carpet section is in place, smooth out the lower edge along the floor. Next, tuck the upper edge of the carpet under the center console trim. This can be done with your fingers, but a tucking tool makes the task much easier.

Small relief cuts help the carpet form around the console anchor points. A small relief cut may be necessary to help the carpet transition along the top of the transmission tunnel. The forward edge of the carpet finishes along the firewall with a small margin that will eventually be covered by the main section of carpet.

Follow the same steps to fit and apply the outer vertical carpet section. After the section is glued in position, make relief cuts where necessary to allow the carpet to flow smoothly and wrinkle free.

Carpeting the Transmission Tunnel

1 *The finished position of this carpet section has already been determined, and contact cement is now being applied to hold it in place. During the installation of the vertical panel, a lot of tucking along with many relief cuts will be made to help the carpet contour to the transmission tunnel.*

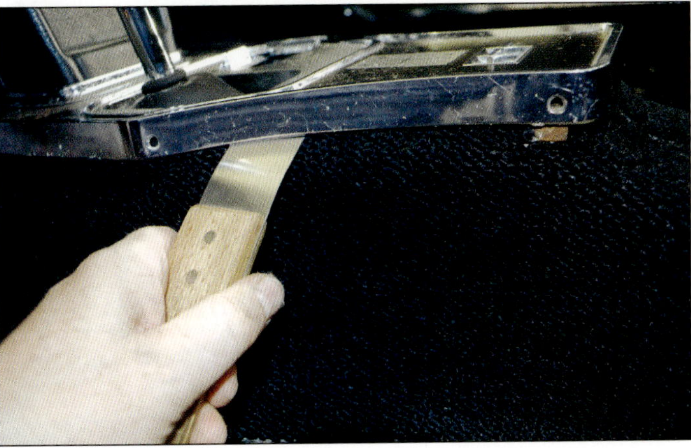

2 *This heavy blade tucking tool works great at getting the edge of the carpet into the tight space under the console trim. Small cuts were made to allow the carpet to conform neatly around the console trim-mounting brackets.*

3 *Careful trimming is done to the carpet along the painted doorjamb and threshold area. After trimming, a hot soldering iron is used along the cut edge of the carpet to melt the fibers, which will prevent any fraying of the carpet yarns.*

4 *When the finished carpet sections are properly in place, the margins should not cause any lumps along the edges of the next layer of carpet. This extra material prevents any gaps in coverage when the main section of carpet gets installed.*

Main Carpet

Getting the main carpet section to fit on the driver's side is a little challenging. The heel pad must be in perfect alignment to allow the reinstallation of the gas pedal. Preparing for this is not difficult, but it is rather tedious.

To ensure the proper alignment, locate the gas pedal anchor points through the heel pad with an awl or upholsterer's regulator. Leave the alignment tool in place and adjust the carpet to fit the rest of the floor area.

When you are satisfied with the fit, carefully fold back the front section of the carpet to expose the underlying pad. Spray glue onto the back side of the heel-pad area and

With a little help from an upholsterer's regulator, the anchors for the gas-pedal bolts can easily be found through the heel pad in the carpet. When the tool is left in place, correcting the position of the carpet section is much simpler.

the mating area on the floor. When the glue has flashed, reposition the carpet as before.

Check the clearance for the gas-pedal anchor points before pressing the carpet into its permanent position. It is important not to disturb the position of the heel pad, so allow the glue to set before applying more glue to secure the rest of the carpet section.

After the carpet has been fit, the gas pedal can be installed. Insert the correct screws though the base of the rubber pedal and be cautious so that the screws do not get cross-threaded in the floor anchors.

Dimmer Switch Grommet

Fitting the grommet for the dimmer switch is the same as any other carpet installation. Always use caution when cutting the hole in the carpet. Start out with the smallest initial cut possible and then enlarge it to be as accurate as possible without making it oblong or offset.

Use this same philosophy for the seat track anchors. Locate the anchor in the floor with an upholsterer's regulator and then use a 40-watt pencil-type soldering iron to create the hole through the carpet. Cut the carpet as close to the rear track anchors as possible so that the carpet sits flat and smooth around the bracket.

Installing Seat Belts

A hole needs to be made in the rear corners of the cab compartment to allow the seat belt anchor bolt through. The best way to make the through hole is with a 40-watt pencil-type soldering iron. Use a regulator to locate the anchor point and

During the beginning stage of the front carpet installation, only a small section of the front carpet is glued to help prevent a positioning error. After the alignment has been established, the balance of the carpet section is glued in place.

Before a hole is cut for the grommet, the carpet is folded alongside the dimmer switch to reference the exact size and position of the switch. Adjustments can be made to make the carpet fit without being distorted. After the fit has been adjusted, a decorative grommet can be installed.

A hot soldering iron is used to make an access hole in the carpet for the seat belt anchor bolt. The results of this method are a quick and easy way to get into a tight location while creating an opening that the carpet fibers will not get snarled with the threads of the bolt.

then use the preheated solder iron to penetrate the carpet. The hot solder iron will make a perfect hole that not only will allow the bolt to easily pass through but also prevent the fibers from being snagged by the turning of the anchor bolt.

Attaching the seat belt to the car requires a hex socket wrench to tighten the cap bolt securely to the car. You should also use a torque wrench to check that the bolt has reached at least 30 ft-lbs of torque for safety.

Armrest Pad

There is a single armrest pad that sits on top of the transmission tunnel that conceals the raw upper edges of the carpet and is also shared by both passengers. To keep the pad from moving, the armrest is secured in place with a small pin at the rear of the pad along with a flat tab and small bolt in the front.

The small pin at the rear is inserted into a retaining hole located just above the center point of the transmission tunnel. This anchor hole can be opened by burning through the carpet on the trunk compartment divider with a 40-watt pencil-type soldering iron. Insert the pin into the retainer hole and then center the armrest pad on the transmission tunnel. The flat tab should be under the console trim panel.

Secure the front of the armrest in place by inserting the small retainer bolt through the slot in the flat tab and tighten it with a socket. Lower the center console trim and secure it in place with the correct oval-head trim screws. Locate the anchor points for the screws with a regulator and do not overtighten the screws.

Because of the limited space in the cab of the Corvette, a socket cap bolt is used instead of a tradi-tional seat belt bolt. The slimmer profile of the hex socket works well to secure the seat belt to the inner corners of the floor.

This center armrest anchoring setup couldn't be any sim-pler. To prevent any side-to-side move-ment of the armrest, the pin protruding from the rear of the unit is inserted into a small hole in the lower center of the trunk partition.

A socket and exten-sion are used to reach the small armrest retainer bolt located under the console trim plate. After tightening the armrest bolt, the trim plate will be fitted and then secured to the car with the correct trim screws.

Trim Panels

Located in front of the door are the kick panels. Decorative trim screws with attached washers are used to fasten the panels and wind lace retainer to the car. A regulator is used to locate the position of the underlying screw holes through the panel.

A metal retainer is used along the front edge of the panel to lock the wind lace in position. Tuck the wind lace behind the leading edge of the kick panel and position the retainer along the sew line of the wind lace.

Insert the regulator through all the components to clear a passage for the retainer screw. Insert the screw into the opening and tighten the screw just enough to keep the parts from shifting. When all of the trim screws are in place, they can be tightened by snugging them with a Phillips screwdriver.

Reinstall the rear B-pillar trim panels and secure them in place with the correct trim hardware.

Finishing

Reinstall the seats and secure them to the floor with the proper bolts and washers. Fit the sill plates over the threshold of the door opening and the top edge of the carpet. Secure the plates with the correct screws.

C3 Carpet

In 1968, a new Stingray design was added to create the next-generation, or C3, Corvette. In addition to a whole new bodystyle, the T-top roof option was added. On a whim, the roof panels could be removed, transforming the coupe into an open-roof cruiser.

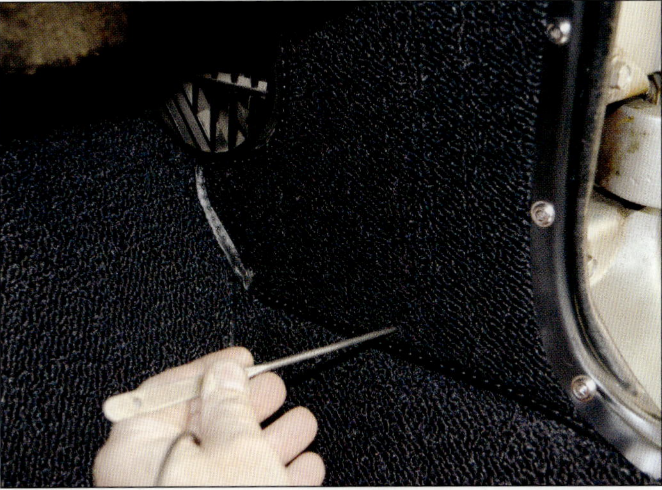

New kick panels are installed to finish off the area in front of the door opening. Several trim screws are used to secure the panel to the interior of the car. Before the screws can be inserted, the foundation hole is located with an upholsterer's regulator.

What a difference a little sanding and some fresh satin paint can do to the appearance of the original rear trim panels. After the reconditioning process was completed, the panels were installed to conceal the convertible top anchor points.

With the installation of the seats and sill plates, the carpet installation is now complete. This restoration has transformed the interior into what looks like a new car. With periodic vacuuming and care, the new carpet set will last for another 40 years.

Storage of the panels was typically an issue, but with minimal effort they could be secured in the cargo space with tiedown straps that clipped to footman loops. This system kept the panels safe while the car was moving.

During the process of replacing the carpet, removal of the footman loops can be a challenge. Due to the location of the footman loops on the top side of the inner fender, rust can fuse the small machine screws with the anchor plate on the underside of the car. During removal of the screws, they usually break off, making for a difficult repair. The simple solution is to remove just the carpet and padding without disturbing the loops and cleaning the area in preparation for the new carpet.

New padding and carpet can then be installed directly over the footman loop, and later they can be exposed by cutting a small slot in the surface of the carpet. This allows the tiedown straps to be attached to the exposed loop, providing a secure place for the T-top panels during travel.

Carpeting around the Footman Loop

1 *Deep inside of the cargo area of the C3 coupe are the small chrome-plated footman loops. They are positioned at a slight angle on the top of the inner fender and attached with Phillips-head machine screws. The carpet and padding have been carefully removed, leaving just the footman loop undisturbed.*

2 *Before the new carpet padding is glued onto the inner fender of the cargo area, a small opening has been cut away, allowing the footman loop to be unobstructed from the pad. This allows for easier access of the tiedown strap hook to attach to the loop.*

3 *After the rear wheel cover carpet has been attached, a slit was cut through the carpeting with a sharp utility knife. It is easy to feel for the footman loop under the carpet and make the opening along the back side of the loop. The opening is cut the full length of the loop to allow the carpet to lay down around the loop.*

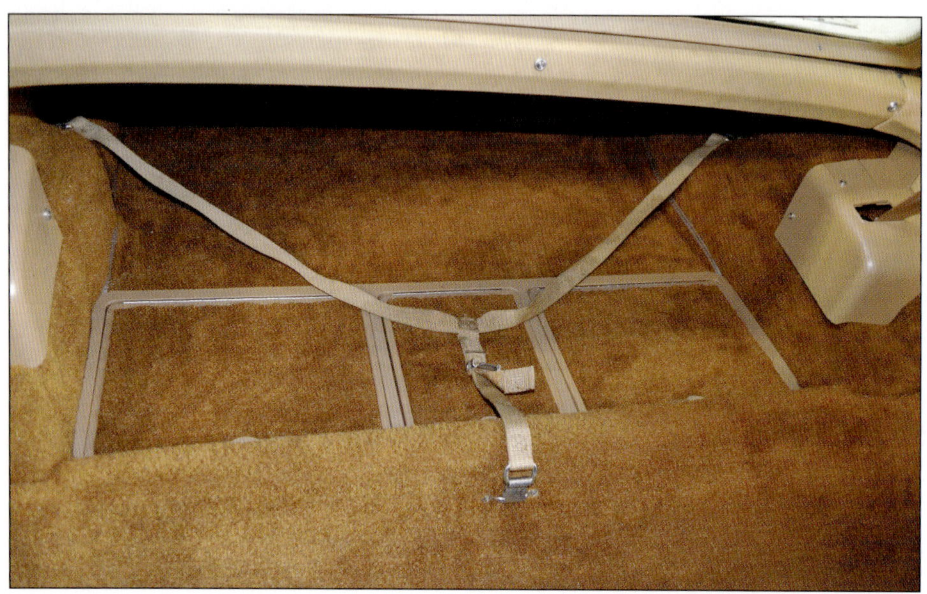

4 *Each end of the tiedown strap has a small hook that slides over the footman loop, locking it in place. After the T-tops are placed in their protective covers, they can be secured by the tiedown straps. Adjustments can be made to the straps to prevent the T-tops from shifting during transport.*

TRIM PANELS

There are many panels used to beautify and conceal the structural components of the interior. Most of these pieces can be serviced just by removing a few screws. Caution must be taken when working on the interior components. Often, they are used to conceal wires or mechanical components that are connected to wires. To be safe, always disconnect the battery before removing any of these pieces.

Hand Brake Cover

Nestled between the seats is the emergency brake console. Over time, the elements and passengers can take their toll on the interior panel, leaving it an eyesore. Because of its location, the surface of the cover is often used as an armrest, and the pressure placed upon the thin plastic causes it to crack.

To replace the emergency brake cover, the seats need to be removed from the car to access all of the trim screws that secure it to the floor mounts. This is one of those "while you are at it" projects, so if you are planning to replace the carpet in the car, this is the prime opportunity to add this item to the list of parts to order. There are a lot of pieces involved when bringing the cover back to life, but it is a simple task that can be completed in an afternoon.

Rear Console Removal

Begin by unbolting the seats from the car. Under the seat is a wire attached to the seat belt warning sensor. Disconnect the wire and lift the seat from the car. Now, unbolt the inner seat belt buckles from the floor of the car. Use a six-point, 1/2-inch drive, 13/16-inch socket to safely extract the retainer bolts.

On each side of the cover are two oval-head trim screws. Use a #2 Phillips screwdriver to remove the two screws. On the back side of the divider panel is a hidden bolt that needs to be removed. This can be difficult to get at if the rear compartment is still in the cargo area of the car. Remove the liner from the jack compartment to access the bolt. Use a 7/16-inch wrench to

This is what more than 40 years of hard use and abuse looks like. Because the interior panels needed to be removed for the new carpet installation, it just made sense to the owner of this 1974 Stingray to have the rear brake console replaced along with other worn interior components.

loosen and then remove the bolt and washer.

With the fasteners removed, lift the brake handle about a quarter of the way to relieve tension on the cover. Then, lift up on the back end of the cover to pull it away from the shifter console. The center bezel should stay with the shifter console.

While lifting the cover out, you will notice that there is a split in the brake handle slider. This is normal, as it allows the slider to be fit around the brake handle. To remove the slider from the handle, give the slider a slight twist to open the slot and allow the brake handle to come out of the slider.

If the car has the power-window option, there are wires connected to the window switches. Carefully lift the console to expose its underside, where the wire connectors are attached to the switches. Lift the connector straight up and off the terminal posts of the switch. Now, the cover should be free from the car, and it can be brought over to the workbench for further disassembly.

The last piece to remove is the center bezel. The piece simply slides off the rear of the shift console.

Removing the Rear Console

1 *Due to the compact cab space of the C3, it is difficult to directly service most of the interior components. Removal of the seats is vital to gain access to the emergency brake console fasteners. A Phillips screwdriver makes removal of the screws quick and easy.*

2 *Gaining access to remove this anchor bolt is not easy, but it is necessary. The bolt has an awkward location deep inside the rear compartment, just behind the center divider panel of the car. After the bolt is removed, the emergency brake console can be serviced.*

3 There are many little moves to make before the emergency brake console can be removed from the car. Lift from the rear while moving the hand brake lever and then slide the cover assembly backward. It is quite a dance, but that is how it's done.

4 Running up the center of the brake console is the brake handle slider. This flexible strip of plastic was designed to keep debris from getting into the ratchetting mechanism of the hand-brake lever. A small split in the slider makes it easy to fit around the brake handle.

5 Underneath the brake console is a reinforcement bracket that holds the power window switches in place. Power is supplied to each switch through a wire harness attached to the back of the switch with a modular connector. These connecters just pull off so the console can be removed.

6 This small panel is not just decorative, it also helps fill the gap at the end of the slider opening on the console. Small spring clips built into the center bezel are designed to hold it in place at the rear section of the shifter console.

Cover Disassembly

On the underside of the console, several stud fasteners retain the front and rear reinforcement pieces for the emergency brake lever. Cars that were equipped with a power-window option also had the window activation switches mounted to the front panel. Use a 3/8-inch socket to remove the retainer nuts holding the reinforcement pieces to the cover.

If you are going to use the original hardware in the new cover, it should be thoroughly cleaned and then painted before being reinstalled. Mask off any chrome areas that you do not want to get overspray on and then apply at least two coats of enamel to protect the metal.

Cover Assembly

New reproduction emergency brake covers are now made of ABS plastic. This material is more durable than the original rigid plastic. If the cover needs to be dyed to match the interior, follow the manufacturer's directions to obtain the best results. Also, give the piece several coats of satin clear finish to protect the color coat from scratches and normal wear.

If the window switches are in good working condition, they can be reused. As a general rule of thumb, I always replace them with new switches. This is a good practice since the parts are not very expensive, and it will save you a lot of grief later on when they do fail. Fit new window switches into the new cover panel. The switch should fit nicely into the holes of the new cover. A file may be needed to enlarge the opening if the switch does not seat properly.

Install the front reinforcement cover to lock in the window switches and secure the part with six of the proper retainer nuts. Do not overtighten

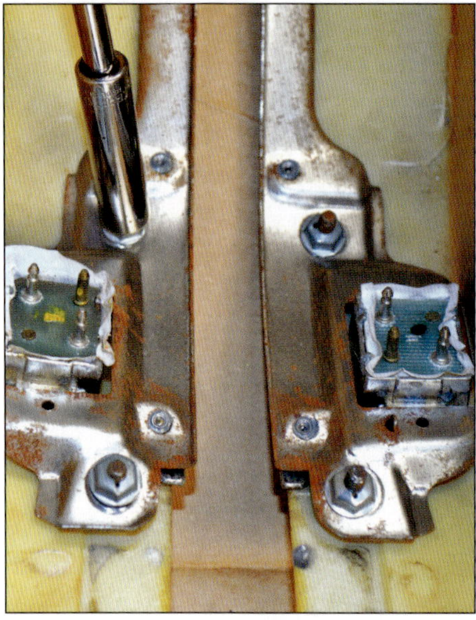

A socket wrench is used to remove the keeper nuts that are holding the reinforcement panels to the inside of the rear console cover. After the retainer panel has been removed, it can then be cleaned and painted, preserving the metal so that it can be reused.

All new hardware was used for the restoration of this rear console along with a reproduction reinforcement panel. Reproduction parts look and perform just as well as the original parts, and they make the restoration process faster.

New parts may need some caressing to make them work and fit properly. Small tweaks were made to make the new power window switches fit into the reproduction rear brake cover. After assembly, final adjustments were made to get the slider opening to look nice.

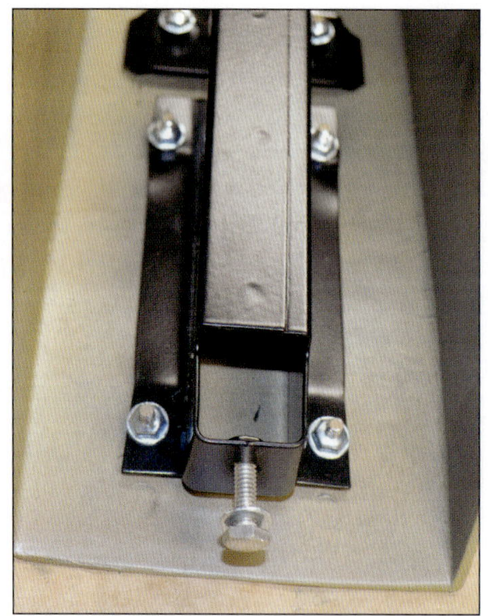

On the inside rear of the brake console, the rear reinforcement bracket provides a solid foundation for the casing. A 1/4-inch bolt is used to anchor the rear brake console to the car. These bolts are often left out of the car because of the difficulty to install them.

the nuts, as this could cause the cover material to distort or break.

Check the alignment of the chrome retainer along the center slot in the cover. Make any adjustments necessary to ensure that the slider moves freely and there are no gaps along the edges. Next, install the rear reinforcement using four retainer nuts. Make a note that the retainer bolt anchor should be facing the rear of the cover, and the bolt should be removed prior to installation in the car.

Installing the Console

Prefit the brake handle slider to the emergency brake handle by giving it a quarter of a twist to open the slot. The slider only fits one way over the handle with the curved end of the slot toward the back.

Next, attach the power window connectors to the switches. Temporarily reconnect the battery at this point and test the switches to make sure they function properly. You do not want to find out later that the switches are facing the wrong direction or there is a bad connection in the wire connector. If the switches function correctly, disconnect the battery and continue with the installation.

Now, insert the trailing end of the brake handle slider into the slot on the front reinforcement panel. Work the console panel at a down-ward angle to get the slider started. Be careful not to kink the brake handle slider as it enters the channels of the reinforcement panel. It also helps if the brake handle is lifted as the slider feeds into the cover. Insert the leading end of the slider under the trailing end of the shifter console.

Before the rear console can be positioned and secured, the small center bezel trim piece must be installed. Fit the center bezel in place on the shifter console. Each end of the bezel has small spring clips that are located on the underside of the bezel. These spring clips will hold the bezel in place. It only takes a little push and the bezel will stay in place.

Installing the Center Console

1 *It only makes sense that a new brake handle slider is installed with a new console cover. Fresh materials look better than old, scuffed pieces and will perform for many years to come. The fitment of the reproduction part is just as good as the original slider.*

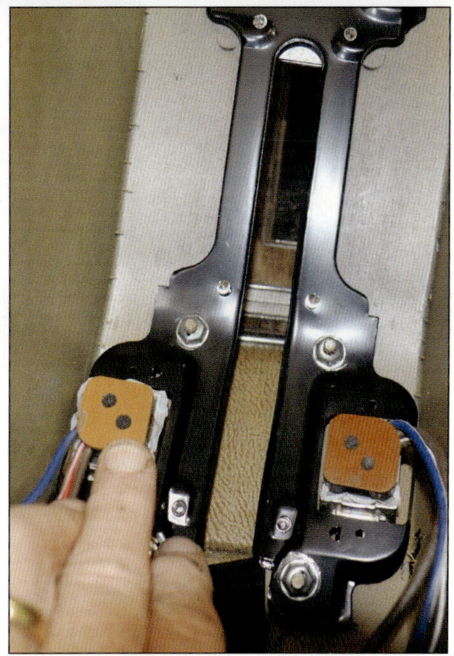

2 *Multiple wires lead into the modular connectors of the power window switch. They are keyed to fit only one way, ensuring that the connection works and will not cause a short circuit. Each connector is pushed onto the back of a switch for a neat and safe installation.*

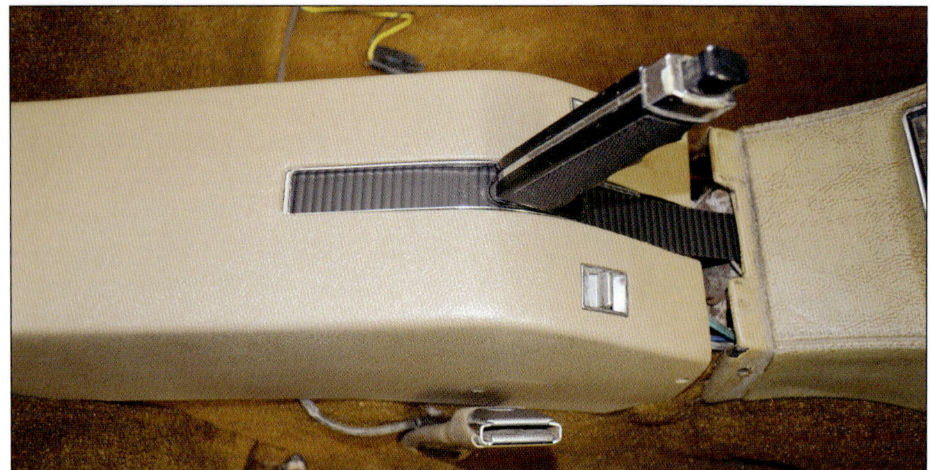

3 It takes a lot of patience to work the brake handle slider into the console while trying to fit the console cover back into the car. The new console looks so much nicer, and it is a much-needed improvement to the interior over the damaged original.

4 A small trim panel is used to fill the open space at the front of the slider slot. Built-in spring clips hold the filler bezel securely in place at the tail section of the shifter console. The best thing about this part is that you do not need any tools to install it.

5 This small bolt and washer are very important fasteners for the brake console. Installation may be a little difficult, but they give much-needed support that the rear of the console requires. Not only do they keep it in place but they also prevent the console from being crushed and broken if it is leaned on.

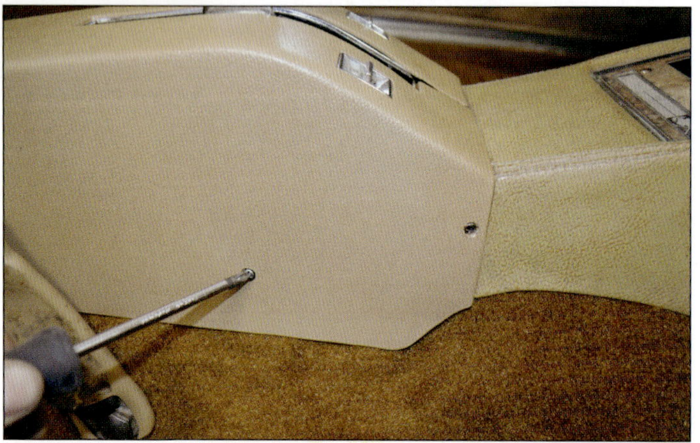

6 Small trim screws are used to fasten the rear brake console cover to the floor and shifter console. The screws provide a lot of strength to the console cover by helping the cover become more rigid. Without the trim screws, the sides of the console cover would widen, and the cover would become damaged.

Securing the Console

Slide the rear console cover up until the leading edge aligns with the shifter console. Make sure that the center bezel fills the gap in the rear console. Before the console is attached, check the operation of the brake handle. It should move freely without binding. If there are any issues with fit or function, now is the time to make any necessary adjustments to correct the problem.

Locate the anchor point in the rear compartment area and insert the 1/4-inch bolt through the hole in the compartment wall and into the rear reinforcement. Start the bolt with your fingers, and then snug it up using a 7/16-inch wrench. Do not overtighten the bolt, as this can damage the new cover.

The last step is to add the trim screws to the sides of the rear cover. Four oval-head trim screws are used to secure the rear cover to the car. Locate the anchor holes with the aid of an upholsterer's regulator or small awl. Insert the oval-head trim screws and use a #2 Phillips screwdriver to tighten them. Finally reconnect the battery.

Rear Compartment

Corvettes that were built after 1962 were no longer designed with a rear trunk. The spare tire was stored under the rear of the car, while the jack had a special place behind the seats, secured in a small compartment.

These interior compartments varied in size and design. As the compartments evolved, they became more complex. Locks, latches, and lights were added to the compartments, making them more useful.

Over time, exposure to the elements and normal wear and tear take

Storage space is very limited in the C3 Corvette. To help, a compartmented area behind the seats has been developed to house the battery, jack, and other items. Years of neglect and use has left the rear storage compartment in poor condition. It will take some effort to bring this unit back to life.

Independent compartment doors allow access to the specific components and keep the car organized. The current condition of this frame and doors will require new replacement parts to bring the unit back to a fully functioning unit.

Access to the car jack can be obtained simply by lifting the large storage bin from the compartment. After the jack has been exposed, a tiedown spring can be unhooked from the bottom loop of the compartment to release the lug wrench and jack. These items should be checked and lubricated annually to ensure performance.

a toll on the fiber board compartment covers. The pressed fiberboard would swell from moisture and sunlight, causing the plastic frames to crack. The latches and hinges also filled with grit and would begin to fail.

The easiest solution to correct these issues is to simply replace the compartment assembly with a new one. One big problem is that a completely assembled unit is going to set you back quite a few dollars. The good news is if only a few components are needed to restore the original unit, they are available. With patience and a little effort, the compartment unit can be renewed to its original condition.

Removal

Before the compartment unit can be removed, the covers need to be opened and the bin contents removed. Disconnect the battery and remove it to clean that compartment. There may be a few wires running to an internal light switch, but they just unplug, so it is not necessary to disconnect the battery to service the compartment unit.

Begin by removing the large storage bin. This compartment container simply lifts out of the storage area. Underneath the bin is the jack. It is secured to the bottom of the compartment with a spring fastener, keeping it from bouncing into the compartment. There is no need to remove the jack unless you wish to clean or oil it. The liner for the center compartment is clipped to the underside of the unit, and it will come out with the compartment frame.

To access the small screws used to secure the compartment frame to the car, remove the rubber gasket that runs around the perimeter of the battery compartment. Any small knife or scraper can be used to lift the glued-in gasket. Run the blade between the plastic compartment frame and the bottom of the rubber gasket, working your way around until the gasket is free. These gaskets sealed the battery compartment and prevented battery gases from getting into the car. A new rubber seal should be ordered to replace the old one.

Small flathead sheet-metal screws are used to secure the compartment frame to the car. These screws are located along the inside lip of the compartment frame and can be removed with a #2 Phillips screwdriver.

There are additional screws located along the hinge of the compartment lids that also need to be removed. Lift the compartment lid to expose the washer-head screws and remove them with a #2 Phillips screwdriver. Do not remove the compartment latch screws at this time.

If the compartment has a light switch, disconnect the wires to allow the compartment frame to be removed. Hold on to the connector casing (not the wire) and gently pull. The connector should easily come apart.

At this point, the compartment unit should be unattached and ready to remove from the car. Lift the entire unit from the rear-facing edge and pull up and outward to free it from the car. The unit cannot go forward because the vertical divider is in the way.

Be careful while removing the frame from the car so that you do not scrape any other interior components, as this will cause you more work. Once the frame is free of the car, place it on the workbench for further disassembly.

Storage Compartment Removal

1 *A rubber seal is used to prevent fumes from the battery compartment from entering the car. A small vent hose allows air to be exchanged in the compartment from the underside of the car. A small hobby knife is used to remove the seal to allow access to the compartment frame screws.*

2 A Phillips screwdriver makes quick work of extracting the small screws that secure the compartment frame to the car. Several of these screws are used on the inside lip of the compartment frame. Rust and debris can fill the head and make them hard to remove.

3 More screws are located under the compartment door hinges. These screws have washers attached, and they are larger in size than the perimeter screws used to secure the compartment frame to the car. After the screws are removed, the compartment frame can be removed from the car.

4 Two wires are connected to the center compartment switch of our C3 Corvette. One wire provides power to the bulb and the other returns the circuit to ground. Most of the wiring on a Corvette is done this way because the body is fiberglass and cannot be used as a ground for simple circuits.

5 Due to the size of the rear compartment frame and the limited amount of space available in the cargo area, the unit should be raised up from the back edge and moved backward out of its resting place over the wheel tubs. Now, the unit can easily be removed from the car for repairs.

6 When the rear compartment frame was removed from the car, the center compartment liner stayed behind. This was not supposed to happen, but it did. Small spring clip fasteners used on the top of the outside edges of the liner failed and did not keep the liner in place. New clips will be used to ensure a proper reassembly.

Compartment Frame Disassembly

Now that the compartment frame is safely on the workbench, inspect it for any salvageable components. Some parts can be cleaned and reconditioned for continued service, while others are damaged beyond repair. Reconditioning a part saves money and gives you the satisfaction of doing it yourself.

Look at the perimeter frame and determine if it is worth reconditioning. Most of these frames are cracked and cannot be saved. Lift up the doors and remove the small screws that hold them to the hinge. The compartment doors need replacement and most likely the thin plastic frames that surround them are too far gone. The door frames are held in place by small Phillips screws.

Remove the door latches by taking out the retainer screw on the back side of the door. Depress the latch button and push the latch through the door. Inspect the button and casing. With a little cleaning, they most likely can be reused. If the internal spring is broken or the keyed lock is jammed, they should be replaced.

Under the latch button are metal escutcheons. These act like a washer and keep the button from sinking too far into the surface of the door. Some escutcheons have a built-in finger pull, otherwise the door has a sewn loop to lift the door open. Check the metal for damage. If they are in solid condition, they can be cleaned, repainted, or polished to look like new again.

A machine screw and nut hold the sewn door loops in place. Use a screwdriver and wrench to remove the nut from the bottom of the door. The loop is then lifted up and off the top of the door.

Compartments that latch closed have a metal striker plate located on the forward-facing edge of the opening. These metal plates are held in place with two small screws and an anchor plate. A #2 Phillips screwdriver is needed to remove the screws, freeing the striker plate that is sandwiched between the underside of the compartment frame and anchor plate.

Each compartment has a small rubber bumper that prevents the compartment door from slamming into the fragile frame. The bumpers also give some upward resistance to the compartment door, which helps the latch keep the door closed securely. To help ease the bumpers from the frame, try using a little Windex on the rubber prior to removing them. As the rubber ages, it dries out and shrinks, becoming less effective and very prone to breaking.

If the compartment has a light, give the bulb a slight twist and then remove the bulb from the bottom of the switch. The switch can then be pushed upward through the frame. Check to see if the internal contacts are corroded and the wire leads are still securely attached. An internal spring is used to keep the plunger up to activate the switch when the compartment door is opened. If the plunger feels gritty or does not operate smoothly, the switch needs to be replaced.

A small machine screw must be removed from the latch retainer to allow the spring-loaded latch to be removed from the compartment cover. With just a few turns of a screwdriver, the screw comes out and the latch can be serviced or replaced. The retainer can be cleaned and reused.

Along the rear of the compartment opening, note that the hinge is secured to the frame with rivets. These must be drilled out if reusing the old hinges. Use a center punch prior to drilling. This helps the drill bit from wandering and creating an elongated hole in the hinge.

Replacement Components

After inspecting the compartment frame, compile a list of worn and damaged components. When placing an order with your preferred vendor, see if you can save money by buying a parts kit that contains many of the small parts you need, such has rubber bumpers and screws. The individual pieces can also be ordered to replace damaged and worn-out components.

Preparation

Plastic components, such as replacement frames, are available unfinished in black and prefinished in factory-correct colors. Refinishing the ABS frame can be done by properly applying the appropriate matching interior color.

Before the plastic pieces can be color coated, they must be cleaned and degreased. To remove contaminants from the surface of the frame, I prefer using a clean cotton rag soaked in lacquer thinner. Other solvents can be used; just be sure that the surface is free from any oils or fingerprints before spraying the parts.

Adding new color to interior trim panels can be done with special interior dye. These coatings are color matched to your specific interior trim code and can make a new or refurbished panel look factory fresh. It is always advised to follow the directions on the can when using these products to obtain the best results.

After careful preparation, the new trim pieces are ready for several light color coats of spray dye. A comfort grip spray can tool makes the task of spraying trim panels much easier. After the color has been applied, the new panels will match the interior and look amazing.

It is recommended to use an appropriate spray dye to color coat plastic interior components. Regular spray paint is not flexible enough for plastic or vinyl. These special dye colors can be obtained from a Corvette parts supplier in bulk or in aerosol cans. Always follow the manufacturer's instructions when applying color coats and use the proper safety equipment and precautions.

To help the spray dye stick, an adhesion promoter should be used. I have used SEM Sand Free for many years and have obtained excellent results. The key to getting the color coat to properly bond to the plastic is twofold. First, the surface has to be absolutely clean. Second, once the Sand Free is applied, a light dust coat of color is applied while the Sand Free is still wet.

When this base coat dries, it creates a strong bond that holds the next several lighter topcoats. After the parts have dried, a clear topcoat should be applied to ensure the color is protected from surface wear and dirt.

Cover Assembly

Before you begin to glue the carpet to the compartment doors, please note that each piece is designed for a specific location. Lay all of the components out and verify that they are lined up correctly. Pay particular attention to the center door frame, as it can easily become out of sync with the outer doors.

Each door has a section has that has been relieved to allow the hinge to mount flush. This edge faces the rear of the door. Also verify that the nap of the carpet for the center panel is the same as the outer pieces. If the carpet is rotated 180 degrees, it will appear different and spoil the look of the installation.

Start by dry fitting the plastic frames to the new cover board and make any adjustment to the door blank by sanding the edges down for a proper fit. Turn the pieces upside down and spray an even coat of contact cement on both surfaces. Then, allow the glue to tack (just dry to the touch).

Position the door over the carpet and square up the lower edge with the tuft line in the carpet. This keeps the carpet square to the door blank. Turn the door upright and work the carpet into the glue from the center of the panel outward in all directions. This makes the carpet lay flat and even on the door blank.

After the glue has set, trim the carpet to the edge of the door blank. If the carpet hangs over the edge of the panel, you will have great difficulty when installing the trim ring. It will also help to bevel the edge of the carpet on the face of the door with scissors. Relieving the bulk from the edge allows the trim ring to seat nicely against the carpet without distorting the plastic trim.

Make sure that the trim ring is oriented properly and then fit the trim ring over the carpet. Locate the screw hole in the plastic trim ring and predrill a hole in the panel with a 3/32-inch drill bit for the anchor screw. If the hole is not predrilled, the panel will split with the screw, and that causes the trim to be loose.

Push down firmly on the trim piece as you insert a trim screw and tighten it with a Phillips screwdriver. I use a manual screwdriver for this operation because the screw must be driven flush with the frame and not overtightened. If the screw hole becomes stripped, the trim will be loose. If the screw splits the plastic frame, you can buy new trim and start over. This is a very tedious job, but if you do it right, the result will be a panel cover that will last for a very long time.

Reassembling the Cover

1 New parts have been ordered to replace the old, damaged, and filthy compartment pieces. After a thorough inspection, adjustments have been made, and the reproduction door blanks, trim frames, and carpet sections have been carefully laid out and made ready for assembly.

2 Before the compartment doors are assembled, cardboard is used to protect the surface of the workbench. Contact cement is sprayed onto the front surface of the compartment door and the back side of the carpet section. An even coating of glue ensures a positive bond that prevents the carpet from lifting over time.

3 It takes a good eye to carefully position the new door blank onto the carpet section while keeping everything straight. The carpet pieces are made larger than needed to ensure that they can be applied properly. Some trimming of the carpet will be needed after the glue has set.

4 After the contact cement has dried, scissors are used to trim the excess carpet flush to the edge of the new compartment door. If the carpet backing extends past the door blank, the plastic trim ring will not fit around the door properly.

5 *To ensure a great fitment of the new plastic trim ring, the edge of the carpet is cut with scissors at an angle. The beveled edge has less bulk, which will allow the thin trim piece to fit better. Any bulges in the trim will cause the compartment door to bind in its opening.*

6 *A pilot hole is drilled into the edge of the compartment door before a screw is added. The small hole gives the screw enough room to seat properly without splitting the door. If the door material is damaged, the screw will not hold and will compromise the installation.*

7 *Orientation of the plastic trim ring is vital to the proper assembly of the compartment door. A slight recess is built into the trim ring, allowing enough room for the hinge to mount flush with the underside of the compartment door. Color has also been added to the screw heads to make them blend in with the trim.*

Latches

Clear the latch opening by cutting away the carpet covering the hole with a sharp hobby knife. Trim the carpet right up to the edge of the panel board. Any overlap of material will make the insertion of the latch through the door difficult.

Use the tip of the hobby knife to open up the bolt hole for the finger loop. Insert the bolt through the eyelet in the loop and then insert the bolt through the carpeted side of the door. Secure the loop in place by holding the bolt with a screwdriver and then tightening a nut on the back side of the door panel.

There are standard and keyed types of spring-loaded latches

To prepare the compartment doors for the latches and pull rings, a small section of carpeting is cut away from the latch hole in the door with a very sharp trim knife. After the opening has been made, the latch will be installed and secured in place.

available for the compartment covers. The center compartment typically is fitted with a locking latch to provide that extra security for important papers or valuables. They install by slipping the latch through an escutcheon before inserting it into the top of the compartment panel.

Place a latch retainer over the back side of the latch and secure it to the latch with a small Phillips machine screw. This draws the latch and escutcheon into the carpet, keeping the latch button from coming out of the panel.

Hardware

If the car has a lighted compartment, a through hole will need to be added to allow the placement of the light switch. Reproduction compartment frames are produced without this provision for the light switch. The switch requires a 5/8-inch opening. Mark the center point for the opening on the tab in the compartment opening and use a step bit to create the through hole. If you use a hole saw or single-size bit, you can run the risk of damaging the plastic frame. When completed, insert the switch and then install the light bulb.

Install the small rubber bumpers into the frame. First, wet the bumper with Windex to lubricate it. This prevents damage to the bumper and helps it pop into place. Feed the tail end of the bumper through the proper opening in the frame and use a little downward circular motion. The bumper will come through and seat correctly. If you just pull the dry rubber bumper through the plastic frame, it can break. There is also a thick rubber gasket that will be installed along the inside

A small nut and machine screw are used to hold a finger loop to the top of the compartment door. The finger loop is made of a color-matched upholstery material, and it will help when lifting the door to gain access to the storage compartment below.

Compartment latch assemblies are simple devices that consist of a metal escutcheon, a spring-loaded latch, a retainer, and a screw to keep the compartment doors from popping open. Some escutcheons may have a finger loop built into them, and there is also a keyed option available for the spring-loaded latch.

It took just a few strokes with a small wire brush to clean up the original latch retainers to restore them to like-new condition. Our keyed latch was working perfectly, so we reinstalled it into the center compartment door and secured it in place with the retainer and small screw.

perimeter of the battery compartment, so do not install rubber bumpers in the battery compartment.

Add the metal strikers to each compartment. They are held in with two small Phillips sheet-metal screws. Place the striker plate under the forward edge of the compartment and sandwich it in place with the retainer plate. Insert the screws and tighten them just enough to hold the striker firmly in place without damaging the plastic frame. The holes in the striker plate are elongated and give some adjustment to help the latch work better.

At this stage, the striker should be pushed all the way inward to allow the most room for the compartment door to close without binding. Final adjustment can be made after the compartment assembly is installed in the car.

Each compartment door is mounted to a piano-type hinge along the rear edge of the compartment opening. Rivets are used to attach the compartment hinges to the frame. Begin by closing the hinge and dry fitting it in place. We do this to ensure that the hinge is oriented correctly prior to it being permanently attached to the frame. The right-angle portion of the hinge should face forward into the compartment opening. When the hinge is opened, the flat part of the hinge will be riveted to the plastic frame with 3/16-inch rivets.

There are several holes in the hinge and compartment frame. Some are for the hinge rivets and others are used to anchor the frame to the car with screws. If you are not sure which holes are used for the rivets, refer to the old frame as a reference guide.

Load a pop rivet tool with a 3/16-inch rivet with a grip range of 1/8 inch and then properly align the hinge to the compartment frame. Insert the rivet in an appropriate anchor hole. Set the rivet and check that the hinge operates smoothly, as it can deflect and distort from the pressure of the rivet. Correct any problems before continuing with the rest of the rivets.

Secure the compartment doors to the hinge with the appropriate fasteners. Use a manual screwdriver or a nut driver to tighten the fasteners. Be careful not to overtighten or strip out the fastener. Check the fit and make any adjustments to prevent the door frame from rubbing on the compartment opening.

Installing the Compartment Hardware

1 *A hole is needed in the center compartment of the frame to hold the light switch securely in place. A step drill bit is the perfect tool for this task. After the hole has been created, the switch can be inserted into the frame and a new light bulb installed.*

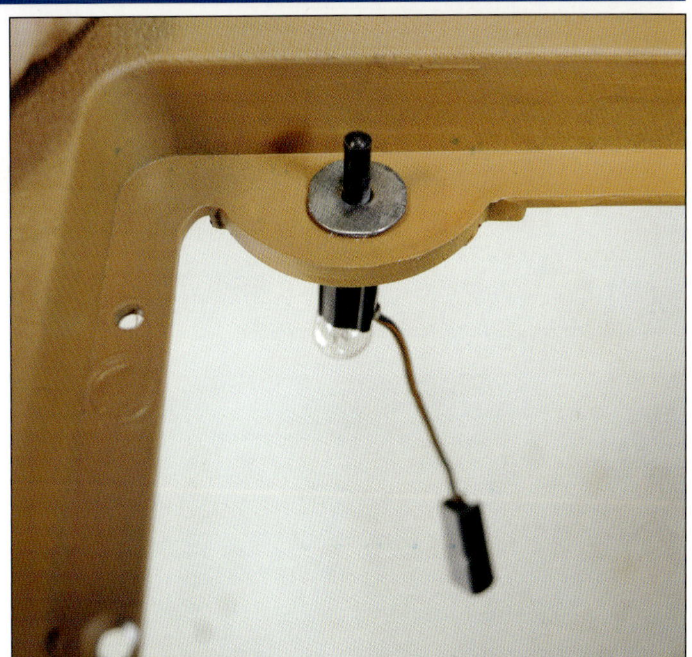

2 *After pressing the small spring-loaded light switch into the mounting hole of the center compartment, it fits nicely. A small bayonet-based light bulb is installed after the switch is seated. When power is connected and the compartment door is opened, the light comes on.*

3 These little rubber bumpers are easy to install, and they serve more than one purpose. Primarily they cushion the compartment door when it is closed, and they also put positive pressure on the underside of the door, which helps keep the spring-loaded latch from rattling while the car is in motion.

4 New striker plates are installed on the compartment frame to replace the rusty and bent originals. The fresh hardware also dresses up the compartment, giving the latches a solid surface to grab onto. Two small screws are used to hold the plate to the frame, and the installation only takes a minute.

5 A pop rivet tool is used to anchor the new compartment door hinge to the back edge of the frame. The stainless-steel hinges can be painted to match the frame or left alone. The shiny new hinges add a little touch of bling to the rear compartment assembly.

6 Our new compartment doors were made with T-nuts installed. They require a small machine screw to attach the door to the hinge, giving the door a solid connection. The original door used a sheet-metal screw that often would come loose over time, which would cause the door to operate poorly.

Rear Compartment Installation

Place the assembled compartment facedown on the workbench and set the center compartment liner in place. There should be a small spring clip on the top edge of each side of the liner. These clips hold the liner to the underside of the compartment frame. Push down on the bottom of the liner just over the clip position to seat the liner in the frame. Turn the assembly over and carefully put it into the rear compartment of the car.

Guide the front edge of the compartment assembly forward into the opening in the rear deck of the cargo area. Push down on the rear of the compartment frame to seat the assembly into position. The lip around the frame should now be sitting on top of the carpet edges, which will finish off the carpet.

You may need to push down on the compartment frame to help seat it securely into place before the small screws can be tightened.

Open the compartment doors and insert the small Phillips-head screws along the inner lip of the compartment frame. Carefully tighten them with a manual screwdriver to prevent damaging the compartment frame. Add the larger washer screws to the back side of the hinges to finish securing the compartment frame. Test the operation of the compartment doors and make any further adjustments to the striker plates or doors until they open and close properly.

Install the rubber gasket to the battery compartment. Depending on the replacement part, the seal may have a self-adhesive tape already applied to the bottom of the gasket. If this is true, peel the protective paper from the gasket and press the seal into position and trim it to fit. Gaskets without this tape must be glued into position. Apply a bead of 3M weatherstrip adhesive to both surfaces and press the seal into place. The adhesive dries fairly quickly, but follow the directions on the package to achieve the best results.

Insert the compartment liner into the storage compartment with the lock. The liner just sits in place without any need for tools or fasteners. To get that authentic factory look, install new jack instructions and fuel requirement labels to the inside of the compartment lids. Make sure that the surface of the panel is clean and dry before peeling the backing paper off. Position the sticker and press it onto the door.

Reinstalling the Compartment

1 *To give the shallow center compartment liner more storage area, it was designed to extend past the front edge of the compartment frame. A drop-in installation is not possible, so the frame must be tilted in with the rear edge raised to allow the compartment to enter the opening first, and then it can slide forward and down.*

2 Because access to the rear lip of the compartment frame is blocked by the door hinge, larger screws are used under the compartment door hinges to secure the frame to the car. These screws also provide more stability for the compartment doors to open and close without damaging the plastic compartment frame.

3 The battery of the Corvette resides inside the car and is concealed in one of the compartments. A rubber seal is used to prevent fumes from the battery escaping into the cab. For the safety of the passengers, a new rubber seal should be installed around the inner perimeter of the battery compartment.

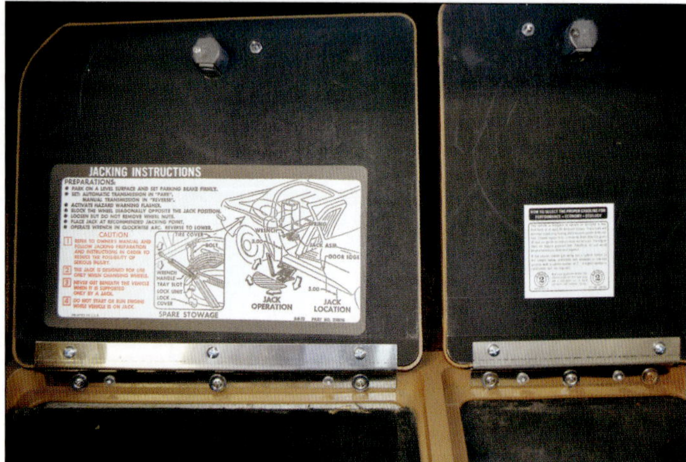

4 To prevent the car's jack from becoming buried and difficult to extract, a new drop-in liner is positioned in the compartment. The liner can hold many items and be quickly lifted out of the compartment to gain access to the jack in case of a flat tire.

5 Restoration of the rear compartment would not be complete without the addition of new information decals. These reproduction pieces are true to the originals and make the new compartment look just like it rolled out of the factory. The best part is that there are no tools required for installation.

A-Pillar

A tattered corner on interior trim panels is all too common. The soft, padded upholstery is often exposed to passengers entering the car, weather, and everyday use. They can only take so much abuse before they begin to show signs of wear and damage.

Reconditioning these dried-out panels is only a temporary fix, as they quickly crack and fail again. The proper solution to these wear issues is to replace the damaged component with a fresh new part.

One of these panels is located on the inside of the metal windshield post. This soft trim panel has a vulnerable outer corner that is exposed to everything after the convertible top is lowered or the T-panels are off. Replacement of the panel is simple and quick.

Panel Removal

Start by removing the sun-visor screws. Use a Phillips screwdriver to extract the screw located in the loop of the bracket on each end of the visor. Under the sun visor is a padded header panel that is also held in place with several trim screws. You only need to remove the two screws on the outer end of the panel, which allows the upper inside of the A-pillar to release.

Before the pillar panel can be detached, there is another trim screw that needs to be removed. It is located just under the top inside contour of the pillar panel. One word of caution here, some cars are equipped with a built-in map light on the rearview mirror. These cars have a wire that runs up on the inside of the driver-side A-pillar molding. Be careful not to cut or

One of the first things we notice about entering this car is how badly the upper corner of the pillar panel looks. This area of the interior is prone to damage, and it often goes years without being addressed. With the removal of a few screws and the addition of a new panel, this damage disappears.

Many layers of interior panels and components must be removed to allow access to the damaged pillar panel. Screws holding the sun visor to the windshield header are extracted from their brackets with a Phillips screwdriver. Some of these pieces will be reused, so extreme care is used during their removal.

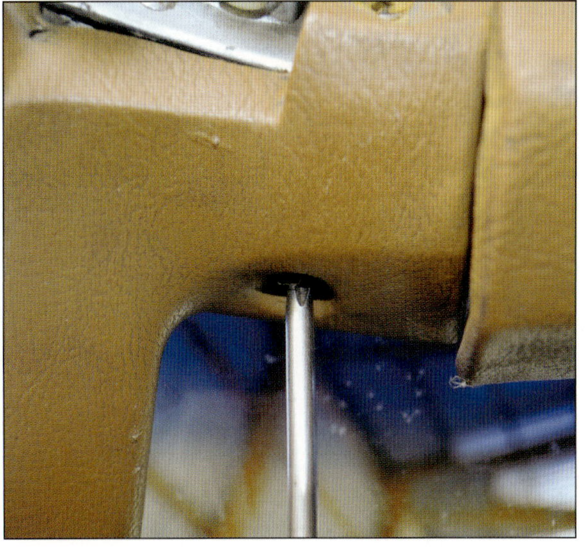

There are many small trim screws used to secure the interior panels to the car. Use the correct-size screwdriver to fit the screw and always look under and around the panels before pulling on the pieces, as this can damage the trim panel.

pull on the wire, as this may cause the map light to fail.

After the screws have been taken out of the panel, there are two sets of dual-lock nylon fasteners under the panel that are holding it to the inside surface of the pillar. Use a panel-lifting tool and insert it about 1 inch down from the top of the panel between the metal post and the panel.

Pry the panel outward to release it from the top dual-lock nylon fastener that is holding it in place. Slide the panel-lifting tool downward another 3 inches and repeat to separate the panel from the lower fastener. After the panel is free of the metal post, it can be removed from the car by lifting it up and outward from the post.

Panel Installation

Prior to installing the new panel, verify that the nylon fasteners are going to mate up by holding the new panel next to the pillar post when the panel is correctly positioned inside of the car. Insert the lower end of the panel between the metal post and the end of the dash pad.

The top of the new pad should be no taller than the top of the windshield trim. If the pad is too tall, it will interfere with the fitment of the latched roof. There is also a cutout area on the driver-side panel that must allow the car's VIN to show. Make any adjustments prior to setting the panel in place.

Check the placement of the map light wire to keep it clear of the nylon fasteners. If the wire is pinched between the fasteners, the panel will not seat properly and will come loose. It may help to tape the map light wire to the metal post to prevent installation problems.

Under the trim panel are some nylon fasteners that do a great job of holding the panel in place. The angled end of a panel-lifting tool provides a lot of leverage and makes the separation of the pillar panel from the windshield post seem almost effortless.

These nylon fasteners are designed to mate with each other to draw the interior trim panels tightly to the car. Checking their alignment prior to installation is a great idea because they need to be oriented properly for them to work. A brisk slap forces them to interconnect, making a tight bond.

When installing trim panels, attention to the small details is very important. Provisions have been designed into the pillar panel that allows the vehicle's VIN to be seen through the windshield of the car. For this feature to work, the panel must be positioned correctly as it is secured in place.

When the panel is properly positioned, tap the panel directly over the fastener area sharply with a soft mallet to drive the fasteners together. The surfaces of the nylon fasteners are not like Velcro. They have small ball-like ends that knit together to hold the panel in place and need to be snapped together for them to work properly.

Use an upholstery regulator or small awl to pierce the cover material to locate the underlying anchor hole for the bottom trim screw. Replace the screw and hand tighten it with a Phillips screwdriver. Replace the trim screws at the outer ends of the header panel and hand tighten them as well.

Reposition the sun visor and secure it in place to the header with the appropriate trim screws. Tighten the screws by hand until the visor bracket is firmly in place. Do not crush the soft padded panel under the ends of the visor brackets.

Dash Pads

Removing and installing a damaged dash pad on any Corvette is not an easy task. There are many components that need to be removed just to get to the worn-out dash. The battery must first be disconnected, the steering column dropped, and on some models, the windshield and frame should be removed. Extreme care must be taken when working with the instrument cluster so that the wiring is not damaged during the process of removal and reassembly.

Although this task can be accomplished by a do-it-yourselfer, I highly recommend that you have a qualified professional do the work for you, especially on a C1 Corvette.

It didn't take too much effort to replace the damaged pillar panel, but what an improvement a new panel makes to the appearance of the car. After all the pieces have been installed, the car can be put back into service for many more miles of driving pleasure.

This dash pad was replaced many years ago by someone who wasn't as careful as they could have been. The crack in the instrument bezel was caused by the part being mishandled. Overtightening of the passenger grab-bar end cap has damaged the edge of the dash pad, and now it has distorted and cracked.

CONVERTIBLE TOPS

The inception of the Chevrolet Corvette came from the brilliant mind of Harley Earl. Earl was the chief designer for General Motors from 1927 until he retired in 1959. In 1951 at Watkins Glen, Harley Earl first saw and fell in love with the Jaguar XK120. The two-seat European-designed open roadster impressed Earl enough for him to develop an absolutely unique American sports car that the world had never seen or imagined before.

In June 1953, the first Corvettes rolled off the assembly line. Once the Corvette was introduced to the public, it soon evolved as the first true and ultimate American sports car. Unique to the Corvette was the wraparound windshield and its fiberglass body. The one-piece Euro-design drop top gave the new American sports car a fresh look that had not been used on any other model car up until this time.

What Makes a One-Piece Top?

One of the unique features of the Corvette is its Euro-influenced one-piece articulating top. The one-piece top refers to the built-in rear curtain. This one-piece design meant that the top was made to fit the frame with little error. Although the frames on the first model years were very crude in design, the top provided some protection from the elements as well as a stylish dome cover for the occupants of the car.

Another feature of the original Corvette was that it had no side windows. This bodystyle was considered an open roadster. The bodies were fitted with removable side curtains that attached to the doors of the car to help repel the weather. An all-metal articulated frame consists of a header

This 1954 Corvette is truly an American sports car. One feature of the C1 Corvette was the Euro-designed top. This simple frame was not very durable and quite awkward to operate. It was best to have some help when you wanted to raise or lower the top.

The influence that this 1951 Jaguar model XK120 had on the design of the early Corvette is clear. The carriage top with the small roof bows had a unique appearance that made it stand out against all other cars that came before it.

bow, inward-folding side rails, two top bows, and the rear deck bow.

Variations

I will explain the top removal and installation process of the C1 (1953–1962), C2 (1963–1967), and C3 (1968–1975) Corvettes. There are many similarities to these different models and a lot of variations that I will point out. Each and every Corvette that I have worked on is a unique experience and rewarding to complete.

Remove the Old Top

Most often owners of a Corvette keep the top lowered because they enjoyed the openness of the car. I tend to believe they kept the top stored because the car was small and there really was no headroom for the passengers. For whatever reason the top was not kept in the up position, you can bet that the top material had shrunk and eventually would not be able to be latched to the windshield. It is this reason that many top frames became damaged due to tugging and pulling while trying to get them latched to the windshield of the car.

Replacing the top begins by first draping the car to protect it from any accidental damage that may occur while working on the top. Be careful when using masking tape on the painted surface of a Corvette. The C1 Corvettes are most likely painted with lacquer, and the finish is very delicate.

Use a good grade of painter's tape if taping draping to the body of the car. Also, remember that the decklid will be opening from time to time during the installation of the convertible top on all models. Do not seal the drape over the edges of the decklid so that it will not open.

Without roll-up windows, the first Corvettes relied on side curtains to seal the car. Although they are crude, the side curtains did provide some protection from the wind and rain. Thumb screws and guide pins were used to hold the side curtains in place.

Because of the many frame issues associated with this 1959 Corvette, the top was kept in the lowered position. The material had shrunk and was damaged because it had not been able to fold properly. The frame will soon be stripped and then repaired.

Unlatch the top from the windshield and then the decklid. Remove all the rubber weatherstripping from the outer edges of the frame. This allows access to the side flaps that are glued to the side rails of the top frame to be lifted off.

Unscrew the chrome tips from the wire-on welting with a #1 Phillips screwdriver. Use a staple puller to remove the tacks and the staples holding the wire-on to the rear bow of the top frame. Continue to pull the additional staples that are under the wire-on holding the top material across the rear bow.

To remove the top material from the header, it needs to be unlatched and the top retracted about halfway down to expose the underside of the header bow. There is a variation on how the materials are attached on the C1 models. Several screws hold a metal retainer strip across the rubber weatherstrip seal that must be removed to reveal the tack strip that the top decking material is attached to.

C2 and C3 models have a front sewn 1/2-inch rubber core weather seal stapled across the leading edge of the header bow. This is removed by lifting the staples that hold it to the header bow. Under the weather seal are staples that secure the top material to the header bow. There is also a second rubber weather seal that is attached to the header bow with small trim screws and plastic tee fasteners that also need to be removed.

With the staples removed from the header bow tack strip, the top material can now be peeled back from the header bow.

Before the rest of the top material can be removed, the tops of the rear straps must be loosened from the rear bow by pulling the staples that secure them to the rear bow.

See what happens when you put fresh paint and a new top on an old 1964 C2 Corvette? The car takes on a whole new appearance. This car came in with a bare convertible top frame that needed a lot of adjustment and parts to make it operate correctly.

Years of neglect and abusive practices have taken a toll on this beautiful 1972 C3 Corvette Stingray. The broken rear window is a result of too many automated car washes that left a lot of soap residue on the top, resulting in a prematurely failed window.

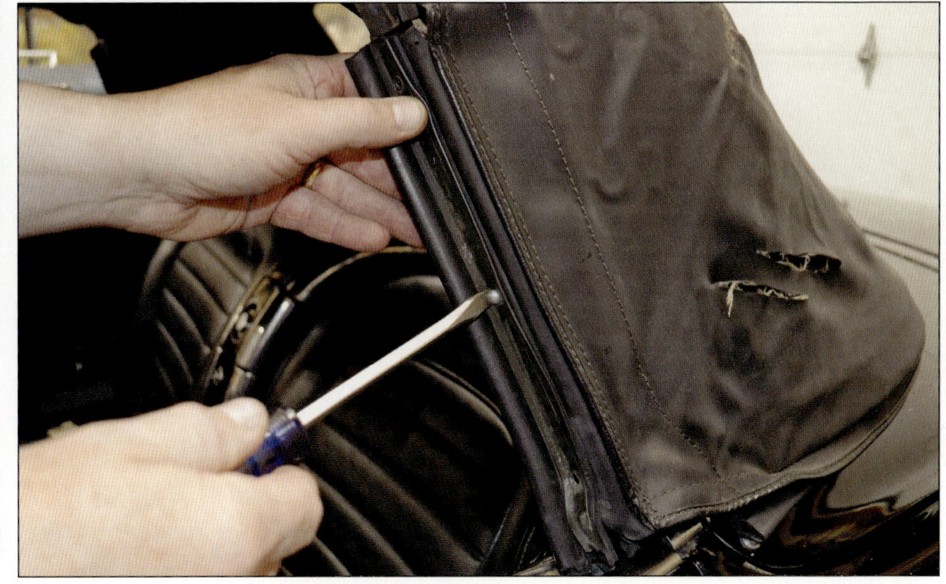

One of the first items to be removed from the old top is the worn-out rubber weatherstripping that is attached to the side frame rails of the car. A screwdriver is used to remove the small screws and T-nuts that hold the weather seal in place.

Having the top lowered a little helps with the accessibility to the trim screws during the removal of the rubber weatherstrip. This old rubber will be replaced with a new set after the new convertible top has been installed on the car.

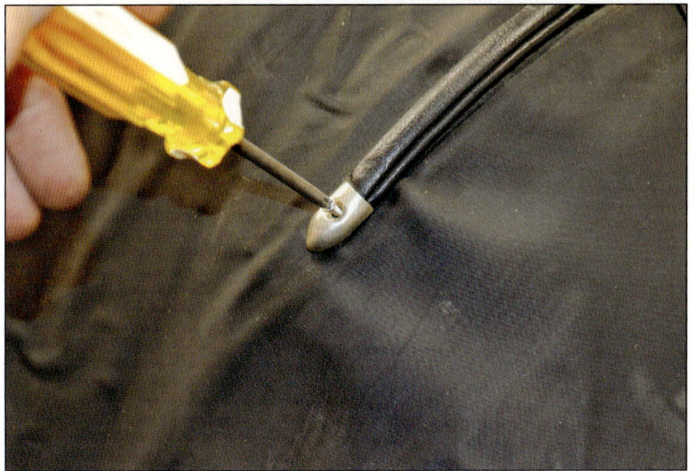

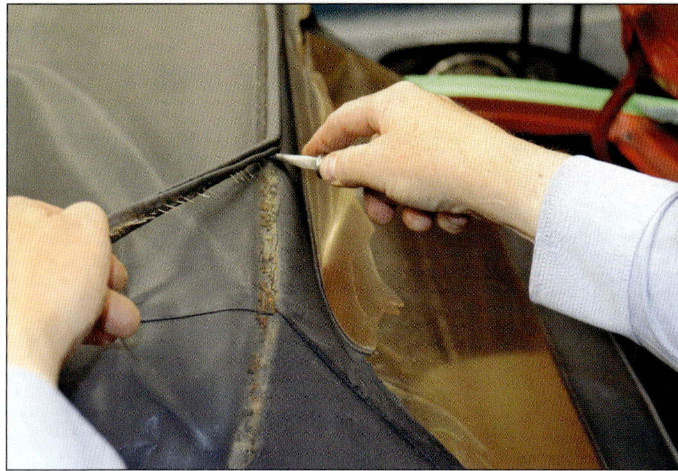

A screwdriver is used to free the small trim screw that is holding the stainless-steel wire-on welt tip to the rear bow of the convertible top. The shiny metal trim pieces cover up the cut end of the decorative wire-on welt cord.

Wire-on welt is used along the top of the rear bow to conceal the staples used to hold the top material to the bow. The special decorative cord also keeps the weather off the staples, which would be prone to rusting if they were left exposed.

There are a lot of staples that need to be removed from the rear tack bow. This is the place that all the convertible top components come together and are attached. The next row of staples to be removed holds the convertible top decking material in place.

Many errors were made by the last installer of the C1 convertible top. Staples were used to hold the rubber header bow weather seal in place instead of the metal retainer and screws. After the header bow is reconditioned, the correct hardware will be used.

Small sheet-metal screws were used to attach new tack strip material to the underside of the header bow. All this incorrect material will be discarded, and the correct original-type tack strip and weatherstrip hardware will be installed into the beveled tack strip channel.

With the top partially retracted to expose the underside of the header bow, a staple puller is used to remove the old worn-out front foam core weather seal. A new weather seal is included in the convertible top kit we received from Al Knoch Interiors.

After the staples were pulled, the top material is pulled back to reveal the condition of the header bow tack strip. There are no surprises here, just the typical rust and rot that we always see. The header bow will be restored and put back into service.

Staples are removed from the anchor point at the top of the rear strap. A lot of tension is put on these straps, as they help to contour the top and give support to the rear window. The old straps will be discarded and replaced with new materials.

Before the rear deck bow can be removed from the C1, this small rubber deck seal is removed. Two small screws hold it in place on the rear deck bow. The condition of this seal makes it no longer serviceable, and a new rubber filler seal will be installed with the new top.

On the C1, the small rubber deck weather seal will need to be unscrewed from the leading end of the rear deck bow tack rail.

Bow Measurement

Before the rear deck bow is removed from the car and the balance of the top material removed, a critical measurement must be taken. Without this measurement the new top will not fit the car properly, and you will have a very difficult time trying to make it fit.

Measure the distance between the vertical side rail and the front edge on the rear deck bow and write down the measurement on the instruction sheet that came with the convertible top kit. This measurement will need to be referenced when you are ready to fit the new top to the rear deck bow. The measurement can vary from side to side on each model of Corvette, so do not assume that it will be the same every time.

Side Tension Cables

An added feature on the C3 was the side tension cables to help keep the convertible top from buffeting while it was driven at higher speeds. The cable is connected to the forward section of the side rail near the header bow. The cable is held in place with a rivet or a small sheet-metal screw. Relieve the tension on the cable by lifting the header bow about a foot off the windshield and then remove the fastener.

The rear of the cable is fastened to the top of the vertical section on the side rail with a pop rivet. The rivet is removed by drilling it out with a 3/16-inch high-speed drill bit. Use care when drilling. Do not enlarge the hole in the side rail. Once the cable has been disconnected from

A measurement is taken from the edge of the vertical side rail to the leading end of the rear bow before the rear bow of the C3 is removed. To get the proper fit on the new top, this distance must be observed, otherwise the top material will not fit correctly.

Each Corvette top installation can vary a little, and getting the deck bow measurement correct is vital to the top material fitting the top frame. Transferring the correct measurement to the new C2 top material will make all the difference in the final appearance of the installed top.

The rear deck bow measurement on a C1 is taken from the face of the vertical side rail to the center point of the deck bow pivot bolt. This distance must be observed when installing the new top to ensure that the top will fit the top frame without any extra wrinkles.

Side tension cables were a welcome addition to the C3 Corvettes to help with the buffeting issue when they were driven at higher speeds. The front of the tension cable is secured to the side rail of the frame with a small sheet-metal screw.

the frame, the rear deck bow can then be removed.

Rear Deck Bow

After the bow distance has been measured and recorded, the rear deck bow can be removed from the car. On the C1, use a wrench and a screwdriver to remove the pivot bolt that goes through the bow and pivot point on the convertible top frame.

Once the bolt is removed, reinsert the bolt through the bow and replace the washer and acorn nut to keep the bushing in place and prevent the accidental loss of the attaching hardware.

On the C2 and C3, there are two Phillips-head machine screws that hold the rear deck bow to a pivoting bracket on the inside of the leading end of the bow. Use a #3 Phillips screwdriver to remove the machine screws to release the bow from the pivot bracket.

Place the old top and rear deck bow on the workbench. The C1 top is attached to the rear deck bow by staples. Remove the staples with a staple puller to free the material from the rear bow. On a 1961 and 1962 C1, the top material and rear rubber weather seal was held in by a nylon cord that is pressed into a channel in the bow. Pull the hold-in cord out to release the top material.

The hold-in cord was also used on the C2 and C3 models. Use a small screwdriver to pry the nylon hold-in cord from the retaining channel to release the rubber weather seal and top material from the rear deck bow. Set the old top aside for later reference if needed.

Top Pad

Underneath the convertible top is a set of protective pads that hold the

Removal of the side tension cable requires that the rivet anchoring the rear of the cable to the frame should be drilled out. The use of a 3/16-inch drill bit makes quick work of eliminating the rivet to release the cable from the top frame.

With the convertible top material pulled back, the rear deck bow attaching pivot bolt can be easily accessed for removal. Simple hand tools, such as a wrench and a screwdriver, are used to remove the locking acorn nut that secures the pivot bolt to the top frame.

Removal of this rear deck bow requires the use of a large Phillips screwdriver to remove the machine screws that secure the pivot bracket to the rear deck bow. The screws are accessed from the inside near the front of the rear deck bow.

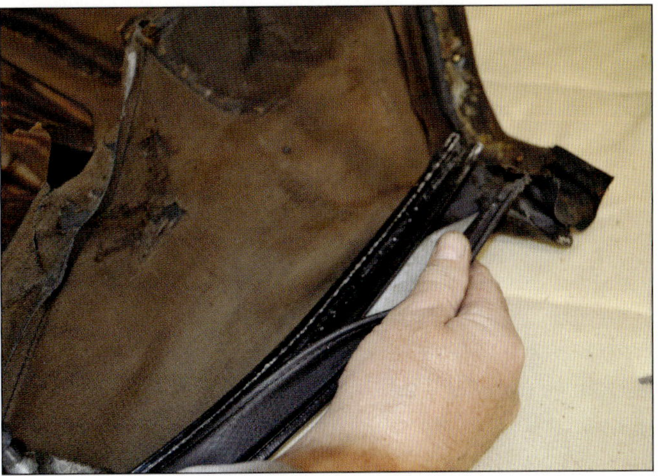

While working on the bench, the hold-in cord and rear rubber weather seal have already been removed from the rear deck bow. The top material is release by prying out the small, beaded flap from inside the channel in the rear deck bow.

correct position of the cross bows and keep the top material from becoming damaged from the hard steel top frame. Removal of the top pads requires pulling the cover tape that is over the staples along the front of the pad and the staples at the rear of the pad material. This allows the material inside the pad to be removed.

After the staples have been lifted, the pads can be opened to reveal the padding. Remove and discard the old padding material.

You should now be able to see the small screws and washers that hold the pad in place on the cross bows of the frame. The screws can be removed with a Philips screwdriver. Be careful not to break them off while removing the screws from the bow. If they do break or have been replaced by some other method, do not panic. Please refer to the restoration section of this book about how to repair the bow screws.

Removing the Top Pad

1 *Now that the convertible top material has been removed from the top frame, we can see that years of wear have taken their toll on the protective top pads. The old pads will be removed and replaced with a new pair to protect the new convertible top.*

2 *At the front of the top pads, the body tape is removed to access the staples that secure the pads to the header bow. The protective tape was placed over the staples to help prevent them from damaging the inside of the top material.*

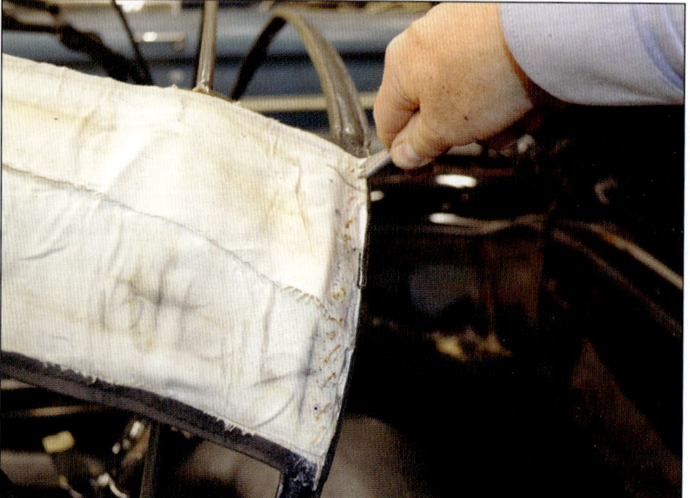

3 *More staples are removed from the rear bow. The back end of the protective top pad is removed so that the top frame can be inspected and serviced. A new set of convertible top pads will soon be installed on the newly reconditioned top frame.*

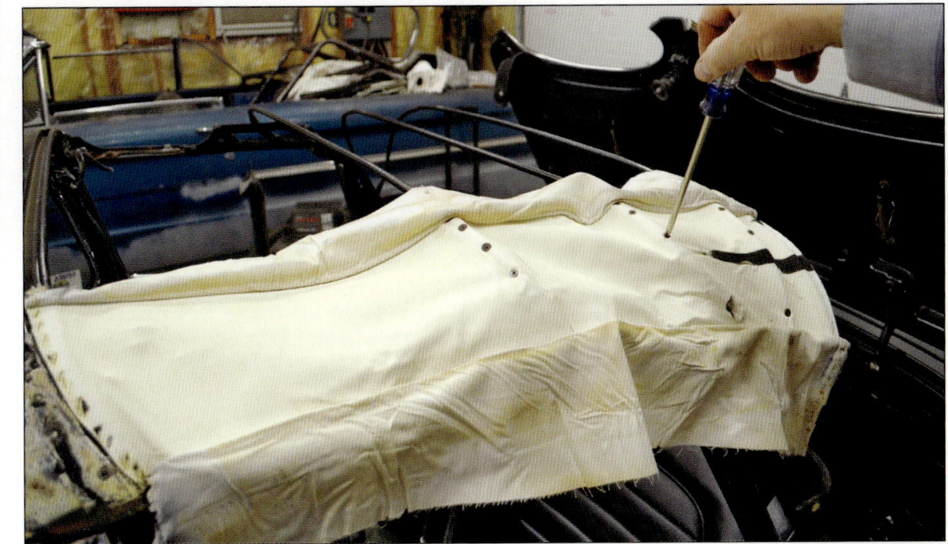

4 Inside the convertible top pads are many small machine screws that hold the protective pad to the cross bows of the convertible top frame. The screws are also necessary to maintain the position of the cross bows that give shape and support to the convertible top material.

Inspecting the Frame

With the pads removed, we can now evaluate the condition of the top frame. The first thing to look for is any obvious problems with the frame, such as missing bolts or broken rivets. These need to be replaced before the frame can be serviced. Other issues that are often found are stress cracks or failed welds in the top frame. When one component fails, it most likely will have an adverse effect on the top frame, causing other parts to compensate and develop problems that must be corrected.

The most common issue associated with a Corvette frame is a rusty header bow. Typically, the retaining tabs for the underlying tack strip are broken or too weak to retain the new tack strip. This condition must be repaired before continuing. Also, check for broken screws in the cross bows and repair them.

Once the frame is serviceable, begin to fold the top frame up and down and listen for any grinding noises or binding of the frame. This indicates a bent component that needs to be corrected before proceeding. Sometimes all the frame needs

This vital pivot bolt is missing, and it is the major cause of the convertible top frame not operating correctly. The remedy here is to replace the missing bolt with the correct shoulder bolt and then proceed with fixing the other damage caused by folding the top without the bolt.

Broken welds were found on the left side rail due to the missing pivot bolt. This condition must be properly repaired before a new convertible top and pads can be fitted to the top frame. If this damage is not fixed, the new top will surely become damaged.

is a good cleaning and some light lubrication to get it to fold correctly again. After the top has been proven to fold properly, proceed with the reinstallation of the top.

Header Bow Tack Strip

Inspect the header bow for rust and damage and make the necessary repairs before proceeding with the new top installation. On the underside of the header bow is a long tack strip that holds the top material and front weather seal to the header bow. This tacking material should be replaced to ensure that the new top will be secured tightly to the bow.

On the top side of the header bow are two smaller tack strips. These are used to secure the front end of the pads. Please refer to the header bow restoration section of this book on how to replace and repair the tack strip and header bow.

A lot of grinding has been done to remove the old welds that had failed on the top frame. It was necessary to go to the trouble of getting the metal back to a condition that the top frame can be reassembled to the way it came from the factory.

A lot of care went into draping the car with a welding blanket to protect the car and prevent any unforeseen problems during the welding process. The new welds have made the convertible top frame strong and have restored its function to like-new condition.

More top frame problems were found and needed to be corrected. The header bow was welded to the side rail of the frame and was no longer able to be adjusted. Removing the welds and incorrect mounting hardware and then installing the correct hardware made the joint adjustable again.

Before the header bow can be removed and serviced, the retainer screws are removed from the header trim panel on the C3. This allows us to properly recondition the panel and then weld in new retainer tabs for the header bow tack strip.

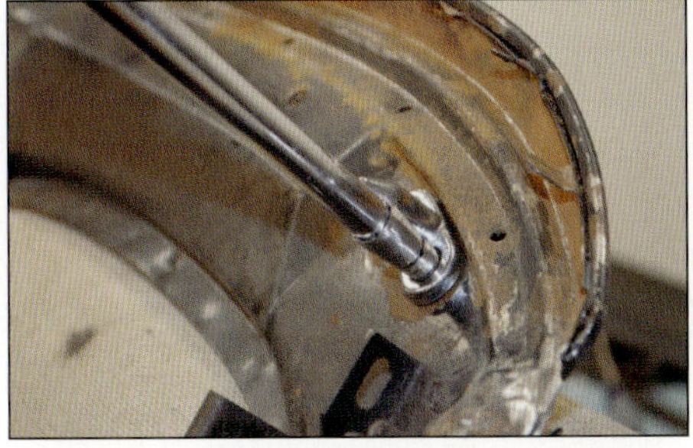

Removal of the alignment pins from the header bow requires a 12-point 1/4-inch socket to loosen the guide pin bolts. The socket used to remove the bolt has been ground down and modified to be thinner to fit the close proximity of the bolt head to the alignment pin.

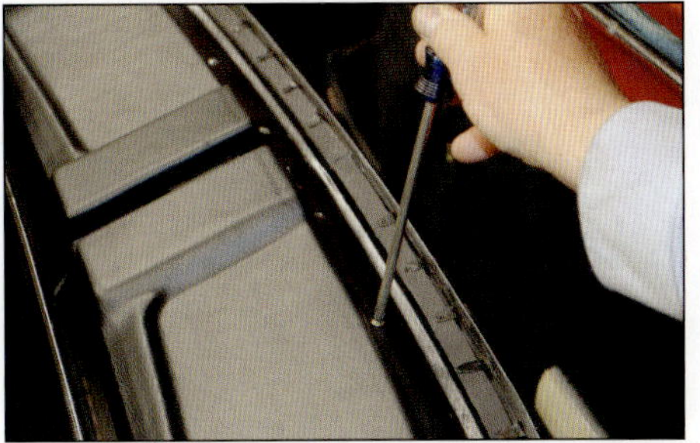

The reconditioned header trim panel is refastened to the header bow with the correct hardware after it was cleaned and given a fresh coat of color. A new fiber tack strip was also installed after the missing retaining tabs were welded in to replace the ones that were rusted away.

It is obvious that the top frame is not properly adjusted by the large gap in the side rail of the frame. With a little finesse, the top frame will be repositioned to eliminate the gap in the side rail and also have the proper spacing around the door glass.

Adjustments are made to the C1 top frame by loosening the outer locking nuts and moving the frame either up or down to correct the window gap. After adjusting the tension on the inner balance link, the gap in the side rail will be straight.

Top Frame Adjustment

With the reconditioned header bow back on the car, the convertible top frame can be adjusted so that the window gaps and frame operation are correct. These adjustments must be done before the new top and pads are fitted.

Rubber Side Rail

Begin by attaching the rubber side rail weatherstrip sections to the convertible top frame. This serves as a reference point for the correct positioning of the top frame as the door glass meets the rubber weather seal. Roll the door glass up all the way to get the proper adjustment for the top frame.

Door Glass

It may also be necessary to adjust the door glass to make the top frame fit better. This requires the removal of the door panels to gain access to the inner door window regulator. If you are not familiar with the procedure on how to adjust the door glass, it may be helpful to consult the Corvette service manual to help make these adjustments. While the door panel is removed, it is also a good time to inspect the internal regulator and replace or repair any worn or damaged components before reinstalling the door panels.

I find it the easiest to work on one side of the top frame at a time. Loosen the retaining nuts at the rear attachment point of the frame and the header bow fasteners so that the top frame can be moved into proper alignment.

Rear Vertical Rail

Vertical adjustments are made by moving the frame up or down into

To get the proper frame gap around the door glass, the rubber weather-strip is installed on the convertible top frame. When the door is closed with the window up, the glass should have an even margin across the top and rear edge of the door glass.

We can see that the top frame has been properly aligned to meet the perimeter of the door glass. The rear edge of the top frame was brought into adjustment by loosening the header attachment hardware and moving the frame into the correct position before tightening all the hardware to lock the adjustments in place.

A ratchet is used to tighten the mounting points of the top frame on the C2 Corvette after the frame has been brought into adjustment. The same procedure is performed on only one side at a time to align the frame with the door glass.

Adjustments to the rear vertical rail are made on the C3 by loosening these two header screws on the underside of the side rail. The spacing of the vertical rail can be moved by extending or retracting the top frame rail with the header bow adjustment.

Here, the rear vertical and horizontal frame rails are in perfect adjustment with the door glass. The convertible top frame can now be tightened down to retain the position of the properly adjusted frame. With the top adjusted, the new top can now be installed.

Each and every section of the convertible top frame is wiped down to remove the years of dirt and grime that has accumulated. After covering the car with a poly drape, a fresh coat of satin black enamel will make the top frame look like new again.

After the new paint has cured, it is time to recondition and reinstall all the chrome hardware that was removed. Adjustments to the guide pins and latching hardware may be necessary so that the header bow aligns properly with the windshield.

the correct position over the top of the door glass. The rear vertical frame adjustment is made by loosening the header fasteners on the side rail and moving the frame forward or backward to fit the rear edge of the door glass.

Once you are satisfied with the way the frame is positioned, tighten all the fasteners to lock the frame in place. Raise and lower the frame several times and make any other adjustments that are necessary for a proper fit.

After the top frame is adjusted to fit the glass as well as it can, remove the rubber weatherstrip moldings from the frame rails before cleaning and painting the convertible top frame.

Clean and Paint

After the top frame has been inspected and all adjustments and corrections have been made, the convertible top frame can be thoroughly cleaned and painted with a fresh coat of satin black enamel. This is the only time that this can be done, and it gives the car a like-new appearance.

Clean the convertible frame with a small chip brush and 409 cleaner to remove any dirt and light grease that has built up. Stubborn areas may need special solvents and cleaners to remove old glue and grime. Be careful not to get any of the solvents on the interior or paint of the car.

When the frame is clean, rinse it with clean water to remove any residue. Then, wipe down the frame to dry it.

It is very important to drape the car with at least a 1-mil poly sheet, and mask off everything that you do not want to get overspray on. After the new paint on the top frame has dried, refit the top latches and other trim pieces before installing the top pads.

Top Latches

You may need to adjust the header bow latches and guide pins after adjusting the top frame. Having the proper tension on the latches makes locking the top frame in place easier and causes less strain on the latch.

The old, worn nylon guide-pin bushings should be replaced with new ones. They are a low-cost item, and they will help the top and decklid close without damaging the painted surfaces or chrome on the guide pins.

Fitting a New Top

When it comes down to what top kit to buy, I always choose Al Knoch Interiors convertible tops and seat covers for my Corvette projects. These are the best products that can be obtained for your Corvette, and you can rest assured that the quality and authenticity is always correct. The Al Knoch top kits are shipped complete with the top, pads, and trim accessories that are needed to complete the installation of the new top.

Additional parts that are needed can be acquired by contacting Corvette Pacifica in California. They have all the correct weatherstripping and hardware that may be needed to bring your Corvette back to perfect operating condition.

It is advised that you replace the worn or missing guide-pin bushings with new bushings to prevent the windshield corner moldings from getting torn up. The small nylon bushings are easy to replace and cost a lot less than new corner moldings.

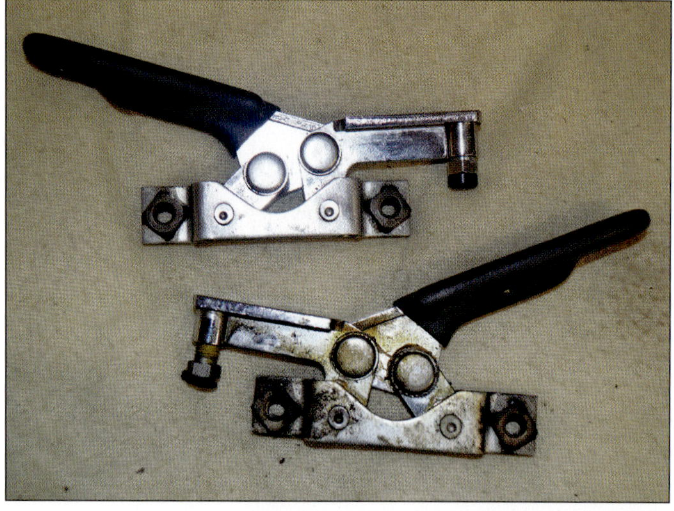

Sometimes all you need to do is give your chrome pieces a little attention to get them in top condition. These top latches needed to be cleaned and new rubber tips added to make them function like new. After they are cleaned, they can be reinstalled.

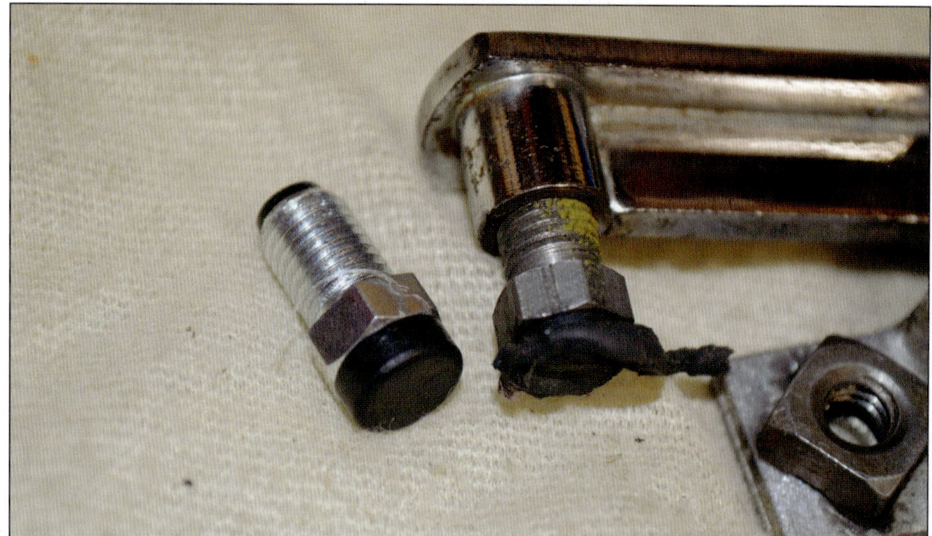

There is a lot of force that is exerted onto the tip of the top latch, and the rubber will mushroom out and fail. A worn tip on an adjuster bolt can scratch the surface of the windshield trim, and they are not safe to use. New adjustment tips are readily available from Corvette Pacifica.

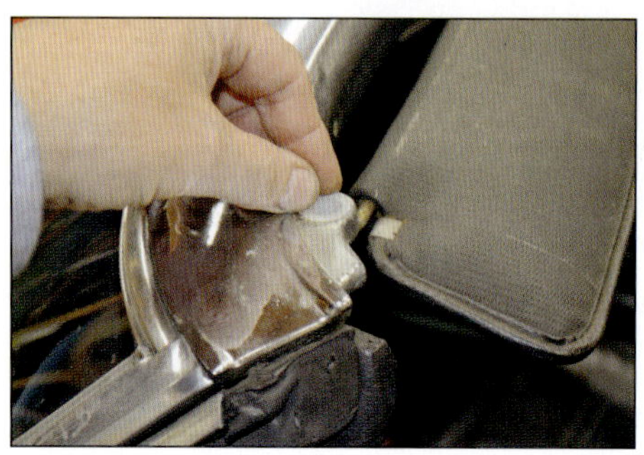

A small mallet is used to help set the rear deck bushings into place. These nylon bushings are often missing or broken and aid with proper rear deck alignment. They will also help keep the decklid from rattling while you are driving.

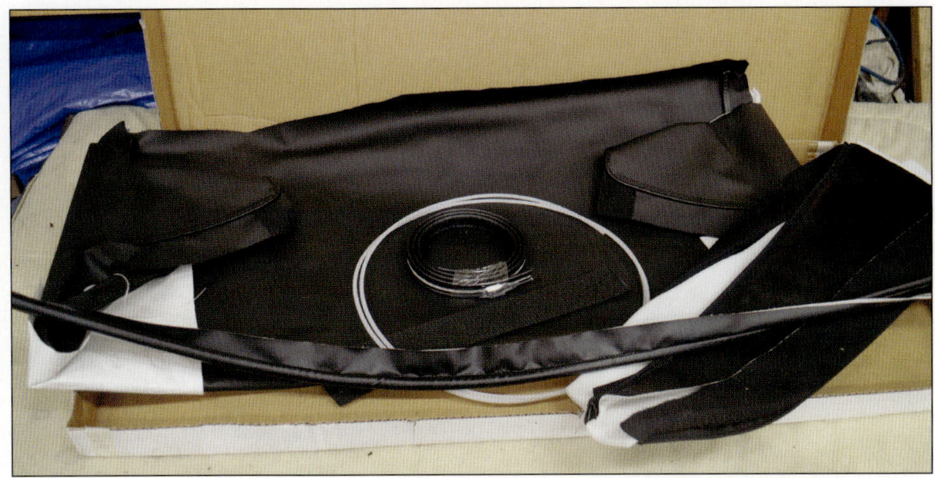

You will find everything you need to replace the top on a Corvette inside the box of an Al Knoch Interiors convertible top kit. Each top has been made from the finest materials available, and it has been designed to exact specifications to fit your car.

New protective pads are a must-have for every new convertible top installation. It all starts with the forward end of the pad getting stapled to the header bow tack strip. This pad has been premarked for its placement on the top frame.

A staple is placed on the inside of the pad to hold it in place as it is positioned along the rear bow of the convertible top frame. After the pad has been stretched into position, additional staples will be added to keep the pad from shifting.

Top Pads

Installing the new top pads on the frame could not be simpler. There is no guesswork installing the Al Knoch convertible top pads because they are marked on the inside of the pad decking where the cross bows are supposed to line up. The kit does come with a chart showing the exact measurements of the bow placement so that you can double-check the fitment, but if you just line up the marks to the cross bows you will have great results every time.

Stapling the Pad

Begin the pad installation by laying the pad over the top frame and opening the flaps to expose the inside of the decking material. Here, you will see some pre-drawn lines that indicate the bow alignment. The pads are precut to size and are ready to install.

Staple the front outside corner of the pad to the top header bow tack strip. Then, pull the pad taut and staple the inner rear corner of the pad to the rear tacking bow just before the indent in the bow. The indent compensates for the thickness of the pad material.

Pull the pad down across the rear bow and staple the lower corner. Move up to the front inner corner and secure it to the tack strip. By attaching the corners of the pad in a cross pattern, you get a tighter fit, making the pad conform to the curvature of the top frame. Once the corners are set, additional staples can be added to the inside ends of the pad.

With the flaps on the pad open, staple the deck material of the pad to the bows with tack strips. On the bows that require screws, align

Al Knoch Interiors has precisely marked the bow positions on the inside of the pad material to make the pad placement much simpler. You will still need to pull on the pad to help it contour to the cross bows as it is stapled in place for a wrinkle-free fit.

An upholsterer's regulator is used to prepunch a screw hole in the base material of the pad. The hole makes it possible to insert the small machine screw through the pad material. A tapered washer is also used to hold the pad to the bow.

Some pads use both staples and machine screws to hold the material in the correct position on the cross bow of the convertible top frame. All of the fasteners must lay flat after they are applied to minimize any bumps in the surface of the pad.

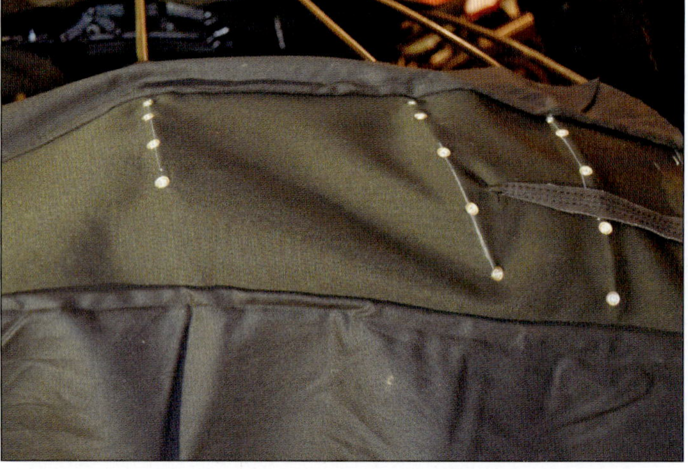

The C1 Corvette uses a total of 28 small machine screws and washers to secure the protective pad material to the cross bows. Each cross bow has a specific place and spacing to offer the correct amount of support for the convertible top.

Modern convertible top pads use a foam filler to soften the convertible top frame. The pad has flaps that are folded over the top of the foam padding to keep it in place. Each end of the pad is stapled closed, locking the foam padding inside.

Contact cement is brushed along both of the facing edges of the flaps to seal in the foam padding. Gluing the pads closed also helps to keep the pad from ballooning up if air gets under the top while the car is being driven at highway speeds.

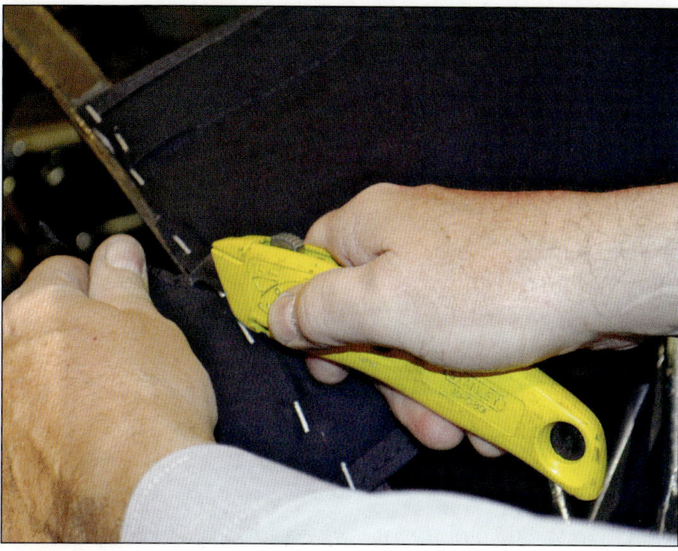

A sharp utility knife is used to trim the excess material from the ends of the convertible top pad. There would be too much bulk on the inside of the car if the pad was not trimmed. Trimming leaves the pad with a cleaner appearance.

Staples along the front end of the convertible top pad are covered to prevent any chafing against the underside of the convertible top. Gorilla tape makes a strong bond and adds a little extra padding to smooth out the pad-to-header transition.

the inside edge of the pad with the indent on the bow and center the alignment mark inside the pad with the cross bow.

Before the small screw and washer can be set in place, use an awl or an upholsterer's regulator to pierce a hole through the pad decking and then insert the screw. Snug the screw down until it locks the pad material to the bow. Pull on the rear bow to make sure that the pad will lay smooth and then continue adding screws until they are all in place.

Insert the new burlap webbing and foam padding by fitting it into the open pad and then stapling the materials in place along the front and rear of the pad. The top flaps can then be folded over the padding to seal it in place and stapled across the ends to finish off the pad. The flaps are also glued down to keep them from billowing when the car is driven.

The ends of the pad can now be trimmed flush with a utility knife to remove the excess material and pad-ding. Apply a layer of Gorilla tape at the front of the pad to cover the staples. The tape protects the top material from rubbing on the surface of the staples. Before the new top material can be applied to the rear deck bow, move to the workbench with the top material and rear deck bow so that some preparations can be made.

Rear Straps

To give the top a fuller appearance, the Corvette uses a pair of additional straps in the rear of the top frame. These straps are either stapled in place or held on the rear deck bow by a small metal retainer plate and machine screws.

The straps on the C1 Corvette are stapled to the inside of the rear deck bow and wrap under the bow and then up over the outside of the bow before they are attached to the rear bow with staples. The placement of the rear straps is determined by a small notch in the rear deck bow.

In the case of a reproduction rear

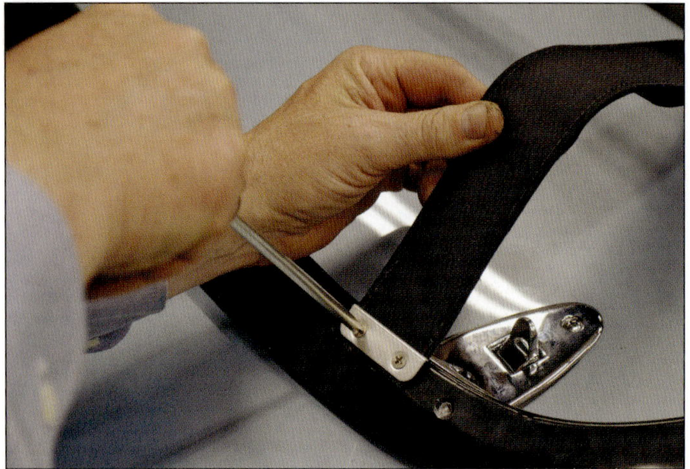

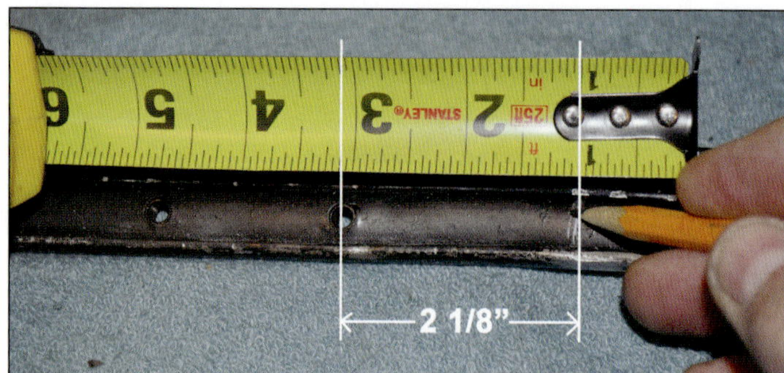

A reproduction C1 rear deck bow is marked for the correct positioning of the rear strap. An original deck bow would have a small indentation in it that indicated the position for the rear strap. Careful measuring and marking are needed, otherwise the strap will show in the rear window of the top.

The rear strap is fastened at the bottom edge of the rear deck bow with a small metal plate and two machine screws. This strap extends upward and attaches to the rear bow, concealing the seam in the top material and giving support to the rear window.

deck bow, the straps are fitted $2^1/_8$ inches from the center of the outer latch screw hole on each side of the rear deck bow. Measure from the inside of the bow and mark the tack strip material where the inside edge of the strap will be attached.

Attaching the straps on a C2 and C3 rear deck bow is a little different. The strap is attached to the outside of the rear deck bow with two small machine screws that hold a metal retainer plate across the lower end of the strap.

Prep the strap to accept the retaining hardware by holding the retainer plate in place on the end of the strap and then with a China marker, mark the placement of the screw holes. Remove the retainer plate and use a rotary punch to make the through holes in the straps for the anchor screws.

Attach the strap to the outside of the rear deck bow by placing the strap in position on the rear bow and then setting the retainer plate on top of the strap with the cleat end up

Aligning the rear strap to the outside of the measured mark ensures the proper placement of the rear strap. Staples are used to secure the strap to the rear deck bow. A lot of pressure will be placed on the strap once the new top is fitted.

and facing toward the strap. Insert the screws into the bow through the retainer and strap and tighten them down with a Phillips screwdriver.

Prepare the Top

Now that the straps are in place on the rear deck bow, the top material can be marked for proper alignment. The one-piece top has no adjustment, and this measurement is a key step for the proper fitment of the top. If this process is not followed correctly, the top will not fit the rear deck bow at all.

You must refer to the measurement taken when the rear deck bow was removed from the car. This measurement needs to be marked on the inside of the top material for proper installation of the top. The object here is to have the vertical seam of the new top line up with the vertical side rail of the convertible top frame. If the seam is too long or too short, the top will not fit correctly, so it must be exact.

To mark the top, lay the side panel of the top on the workbench and measure from the side flap seam inward the distance of our measurement, and make a mark on the top material with a pencil. This is where you will line up the rear deck bow and begin attaching the material.

Attach the Top

Along the lower inside rear edge of the convertible top is a short flap that is on top of a thin rubber liner that emerges from the sewn-on edge binding. The rear deck bow is placed between the flap and the rubber liner with the rubber liner on the inside next to the top material.

Preparing the rear strap on a C3 requires prepunching the screw holes in the base of the rear strap. A China marker was used to indicate the position of the screw holes on the strap material so that a rotary punch can be used to make them.

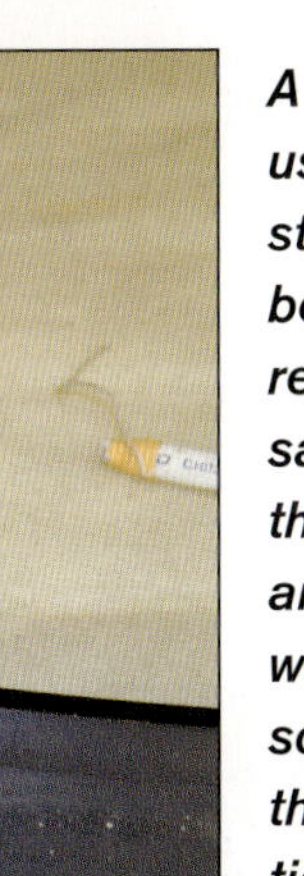

A small metal cleat is used to lock the rear strap to the rear deck bow of the C3. The rear strap material is sandwiched between the rear deck bow and the locking plate while small machine screws are fed through the plate and tightened.

Laying the Top Material

At the front of the flap on the C1 top, you need to cut through the flap material up to the binding behind the vertical seam without cutting the thread. This allows the top material to lay correctly on the rear deck bow.

Align the pencil mark you made on the inside of the top with the center of the deck bow bolt and then position the top material over the bottom edge of the rear bow so that the flap seam is just on top of the bottom edge of the bow. The material must be positioned this way otherwise it will not lay right when there is tension on the top.

Before the top can be installed on the rear deck bow of the C2, the bow position must be measured from the seam of the vertical flap to the inside of the lower top attachment strip. There are no other adjustments to the top, so this must be exact.

The one-piece top for the C1 Corvette is laid out flat on the workbench to transfer the measurement for the rear deck bow position. A mark is made on the inside lower flap of the top material, referencing off the binding seam of the convertible top.

A precise mark is made on the inside of the C3 convertible top to serve as a reference point on where the end of the rear deck bow will be placed. Installation of the top begins at this point to ensure that the vertical seam will line up properly with the vertical side rail.

Staple the flap onto the rear deck bow to keep it in place. Now, check that everything is lined up correctly and add a few more staples along the deck bow to secure about 5 inches of the flap material. Repeat this process on the other end of the deck bow.

Laying Top Material Over the Deck Bow

After the ends of the top have been properly secured in position, the rest of the top flap material can be worked over the deck bow and stapled in place. Continue to observe that alignment of the material on the bow so that it will lay smoothly and evenly across the length of the deck bow with the rubber liner on the outside against the top material.

Do not worry about centering the top material, as it is already self-centered from attaching the ends first. If you started by attaching the top material in the center and working your way outward, the outer seams would not line up correctly with the vertical part of the frame.

A cut has been made in the attachment flap on the C1 top so that the top material lays correctly against the bottom edge of the rear deck bow. Care is taken not to cut any of the existing stitches in the convertible top material.

After a lot of manipulation, the convertible top is temporarily stapled to the rear deck bow to verify that the top material is in the absolute correct location before proceeding any further. After the positioning is verified, the top can be permanently attached.

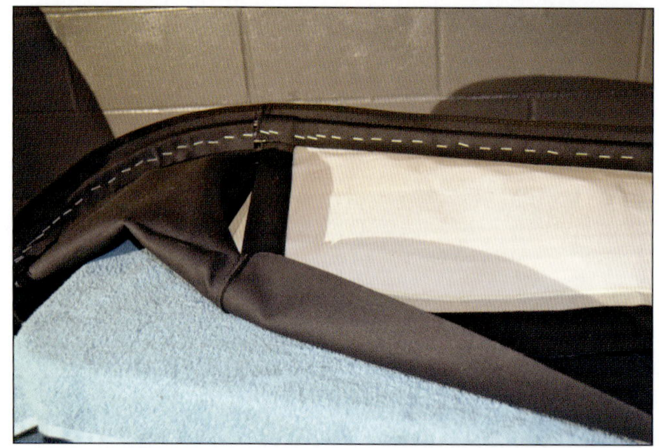

The process of keeping the top material positioned on the rear deck bow while it was stapled in place turned out well. This is one operation that could not be rushed. After the top was stretched, imperfections would show up along the outside of the top as a wavy mess.

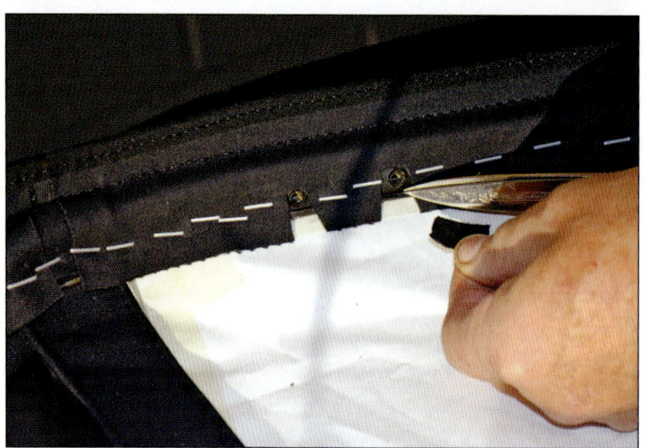

Access to the rear latch mounting holes is revealed by cutting away the attachment flap material. The top edge of the flap material will also be trimmed even with the top edge of the rear deck bow to allow the installation of the rear rubber weather seal.

HOW TO INSTALL CORVETTE INTERIOR KITS

Trim the flap material flush with the upper edge of the rear deck bow and notch out the material to reveal latch-mounting T-nuts in the bow. Fit the rear weather seal to the deck bow and then install the latch brackets in position on the top side of the rubber seal. There will be a lot of force put on the rear latches, so be sure that the screws are secured firmly to the bow to prevent the bolts from bending when they are latched.

1961 to 1975 Deck Bow

Attaching the top to the rear deck bow on the 1961–1975 models is a little different. There are no staples used at all. The flap on the inside of the top has a welt or bead sewn to the flap that is tucked into a small channel inside the rear deck bow. Begin by aligning the mark you made on the inside of the top to the forward edge of the deck bow.

I like to give just a touch more material on these models, so make sure the mark is fully visible on the outer edge of the bow. Use a large flat-blade screwdriver to push the bead into the channel on the underside of the deck bow by working the screwdriver against the bead as it is pushed it into the channel.

To lock the bead in place, set the rear rubber weather seal in position over the channel and push the nylon lock-in cord into the channel in the rubber weather seal. Then, push the weather seal and lock-in cord into the channel on the rear deck bow. Work about 6 inches of the lock-in cord into the channel and then repeat the process on the other end of the deck bow.

With both ends secured, the top material flap can be worked over the edge of the deck bow. The top will self-center itself so the small bead can be worked into the small channel on the deck bow. Work from one end of the deck bow and continue locking in the top with the weather seal and lock-in cord.

When you get about 3 inches from the other locked-in section,

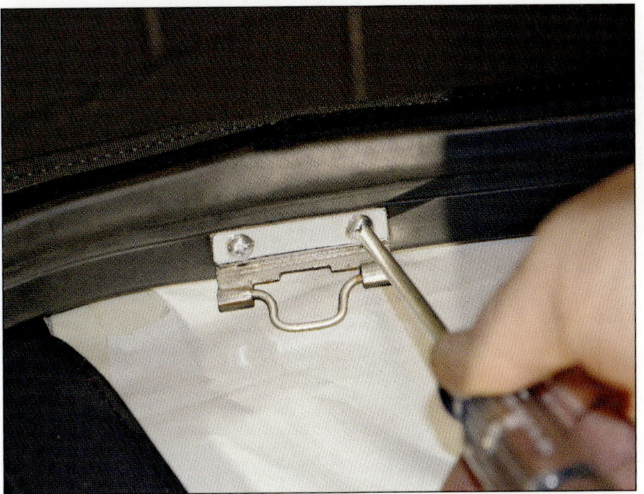

After the rear rubber weather seal is fitted onto the rear deck bow, the rear deck latches can be attached. New machine screws are used to mount the laches to the rear deck bow. The latches will be under a lot of pressure, and the screws must be secured tightly.

After the reference point on the top material has been lined up with the end of the rear deck bow, a flat-blade screwdriver is used to work the bead on the hold-in flap of the convertible top into a little channel that is machined into the rear deck bow of the later-model Corvettes.

A nylon lock-in cord is pushed into place with a large flat-blade screwdriver to hold the rear rubber weather seal in the channel of the rear deck bow. As the cord is worked into the open channel, the weather seal locks the top material in place.

there will be extra weatherstrip material that has bunched up. Pull the lock-in cord from the weather seal and remove the first 6 inches from the channel. Now, continue installing the lock-in cord until you reach the end of the deck bow. The excess rubber weather seal can now be carefully trimmed flush with the end of the rear deck bow.

Attach the Deck Bow

After the top material is attached to the rear deck bow, the assembly can then be reattached to the top frame. Remove the acorn nut, washer, and bolt from the C1 deck bow and reposition the top assembly into the well of the car. Align the end of the rear deck bow with the mounting point on the top frame and insert the pivot bolt. Install the washer and the acorn nut on the pivot bolt and tighten the hardware with a wrench and a screwdriver.

The C2 and C3 rear deck bow mounts to the pivot bracket with two oval-head machine screws. A #3 Phillips screwdriver is used to tighten the screws to the inside of the deck bow.

Rear Strap Fitment

The rear straps on the Corvette run up the inside of the top along the outer edges of the rear window. The top of the strap is positioned on the rear bow so that the seam in the top is centered on the strap, concealing the seam from view on the inside of the car.

With the top frame unlatched from the windshield, some tension is put on the straps. They are secured to the rear bows with staples. After the straps on both sides are secured, the deck can be lowered and the top latched to the deck. Pull the top frame forward and check the strap tension and fit of the top at the vertical side rails.

Each end of the rear deck bow is reattached to the top frame pivot point with a shoulder pivot bolt and an acorn nut. A washer and the acorn lock nut are placed on the inside of the frame and tightened with a wrench and a flat-blade screwdriver.

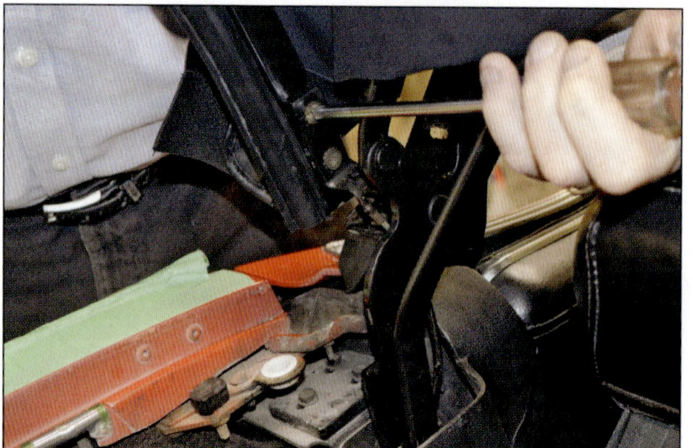

Two machine screws are used to attach the rear pivot bracket of the C2 and C3 to the rear deck bow. The screws are tightened with a #3 Phillips screwdriver from the inside of the car. After the rear bow is attached, the rear bow deck lock can be adjusted.

When the end of the rear strap is flush and centered to conceal the seam along the rear of the top, it can be anchored to the rear bow with staples. The C1 rear strap also helps give shape to the top and adds support to the rear window.

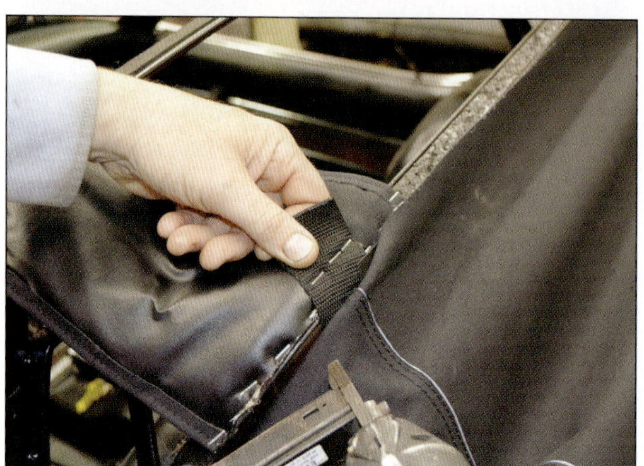

While the top frame is unlatched, the rear strap on the C3 can be pulled tighter and positioned to be in the center of the top seam before it is secured to the rear bow. Adjustments can easily be made to the rear strap before it is permanently anchored and then trimmed.

Make any adjustment necessary to ensure that the top is aligned correctly and will be wrinkle free. Unlatch the top from the windshield and rear deck and trim any excess strap material from the front edge of the rear bow.

Rear Bow Detail

While the top frame is still unlatched, the top of the rear window can be attached to the rear bow. Gently pull upward on the top material at the top center of the rear window and tack it into place at the center of the rear bow. Pull the top material slightly upward and outward at the seam on the rear window and tack it in place at the inside corner seam along the rear bow.

Now, latch the top to the deck and then to the windshield to check the tension on the rear window. The top material should be snug and lay smoothly across the rear bow. Unlatch the top and make adjustments until there are no wrinkles in the rear window.

It can help to use a little heat to soften the rear window and relax away any wrinkles that may have formed. After you are satisfied with the appearance of the window, finish stapling across the top of the bow to hold the window in position.

Trim off the excess material that hangs over the front edge of the rear bow. Be careful not to cut into the pad material while trimming. Latch the top to the decklid and then to the windshield to give the top and rear window a good stretch. Work the sail panel material upward and forward to remove any wrinkles in the top material and staple the top material to the rear bow from the seam outward about 4 inches.

Top Decking

Square up the top decking by pulling on the decking from front to rear to verify that there will be enough material to fold over the header bow. Place a staple at the center of the rear bow to hold the top material in place.

At this stage, there is extra material and some bunching at the rear outer corners of the top as the

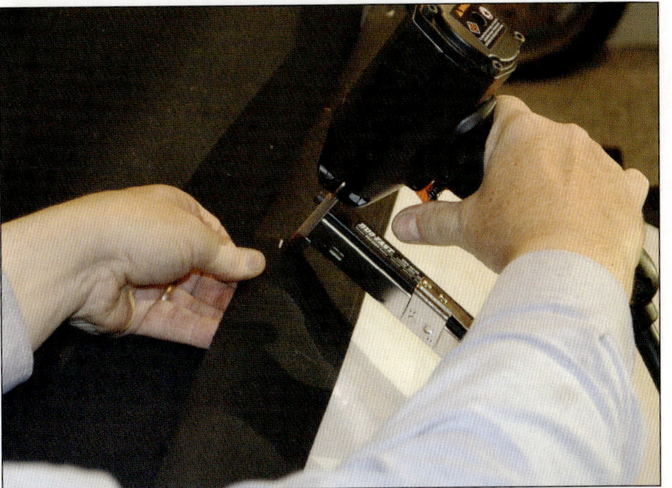

A single staple at the top center of the rear window provides a good reference point on the adjustment of the rear window. The top frame can be unlatched to give the top a lot more movement, and the rear window can be drawn tighter to remove unwanted wrinkles.

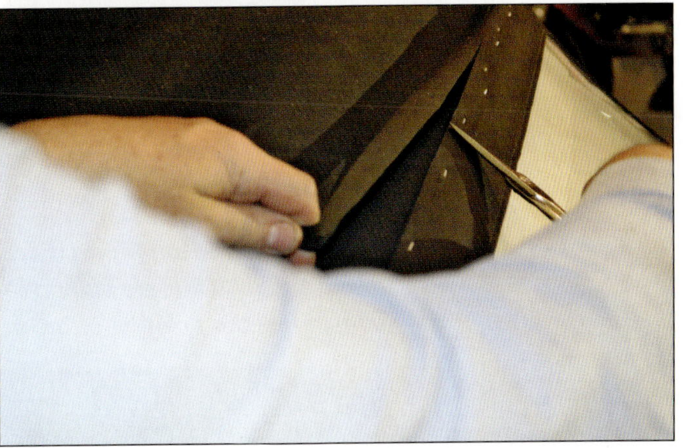

Trimming the excess rear window material from the inside edge of the rear bow not only makes the inside of the car look nicer along the rear bow but also relieves a lot of extra bulk from along the rear bow top decking.

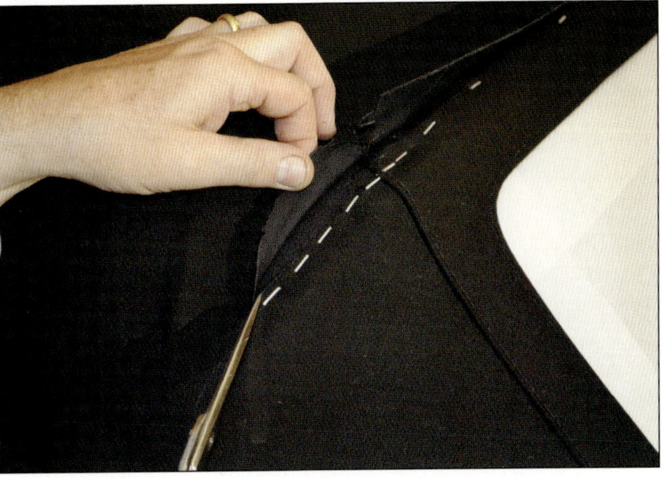

Cutting the top material closely along the forward edge of the rear bow will help relax the pucker in the top decking material. The cut in the material should only go as far as the last staple without causing a gap in the top material.

material curves over the rear bow. This is a normal occurrence. To relieve the top material, cut the top decking material along the front edge of the rear bow down to the last staple so that the top material can lay smoothly over the top of the rear bow.

Do not overcut the material or you will end up with a hole in the corner of the top. The top decking must overlap itself at the curve in the rear bow to create a seal at the bow.

Use your fingers to pull the decking over the rear bow and staple the material to the bow so that it will lay smooth and wrinkle free up to the seam in the top. Pull the top material forward and recheck that the top decking is going to be wrinkle free. Continue adding staples across the rear bow until the rear portion of the top decking is completely attached to the rear bow.

Wire-on Welt

To cover up the staples and protect them from the weather, a decorative piece of wire-on welt will be applied to hide the seam along the rear bow. A good gauge for the wire-on placement is at the end of the underling pad. This makes the wire-on finish about 6 inches past the seam on the C1 Corvette and about 4¾ inches on the C2 and C3.

Measure down from the seam in the top to the desired distance and make a small reference mark to indicate the end point of the wire-on welt. Position the end of the wire-on welt with the small bead facing the rear of the car just above the mark and staple it to the center of the rear bow.

Move to the other side of the car, pull on the wire-on to straighten it,

Pulling the top material forward at the seam causes it to lay smooth. Now, the top material can be stapled to the rear bow without any folds or wrinkles. This can be done to both ends before securing the center of the decking.

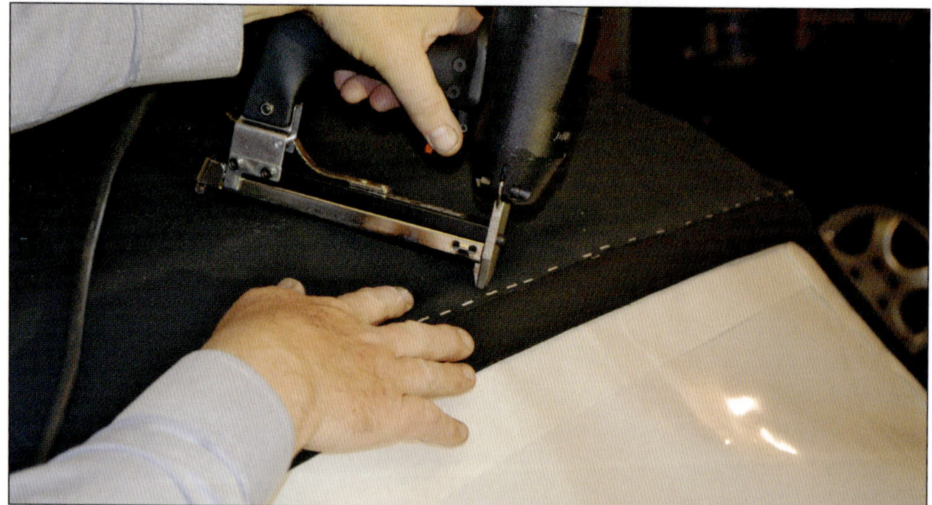

To make sure that the staples end up in a straight line along the center of the rear bow, place your fingers along the inner and outer edge of the bow. This way you can feel the position of the bow and staple in the center.

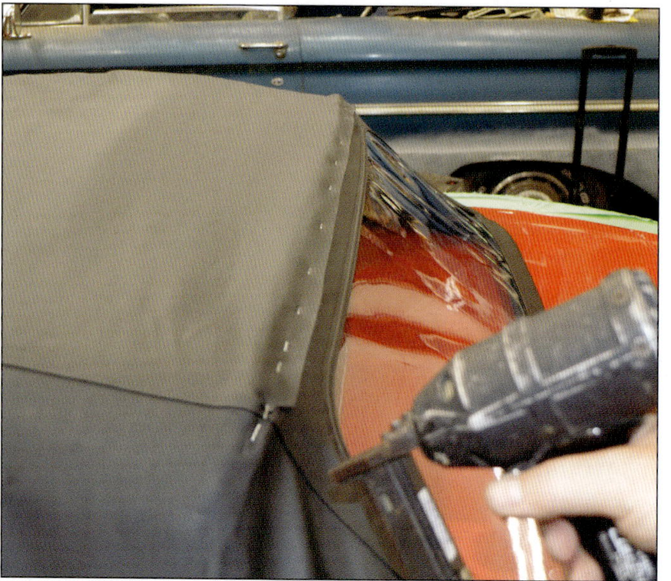

Staples are used to secure the rear decking to the rear bow of the car. Staples are placed every few inches from the center point on the rear bow to ensure that the top material lays flat and smooth along the top of the rear bow.

and add a staple to hold it in place. Trim the wire-on so that it finishes just like the other side. The wire-on should be applied so that it conceals the staple line along the rear bow and hides the overlap seam. Continue to staple the wire-on to the rear bow, fold the top of the wire-on over the staples, and tap the wire-on down with a mallet to seal the staples inside.

Fit the decorative tip over the raw cut end of the wire-on so that the screw hole is just over the wire-on material. Use a small awl or an upholsterer's regulator to make a pilot hole for the small screw. Use a #1 Phillips screwdriver to tighten the screw down. The tip must be held snugly in place, or it may come loose and damage the top when it is folded.

Installing the Wire-on Welt

1 The deck seam in the convertible top is used as a reference point to measure from to set the end point for the wire-on welt. By measuring down equal distances from both seams, symmetry can be reached for the end point on the rear bow.

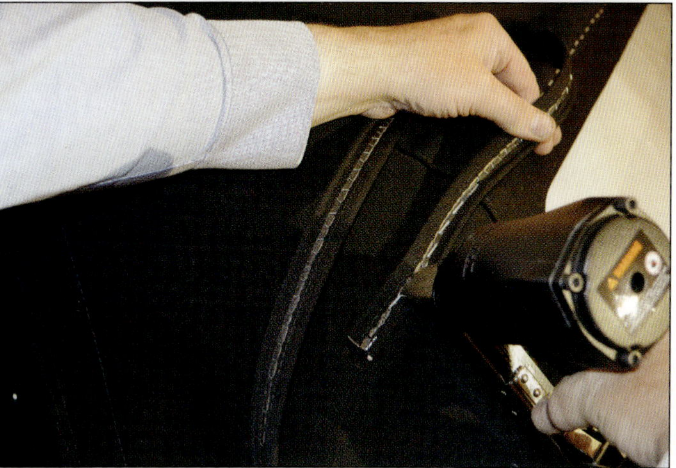

2 The wire-on welt is fastened just above the finishing point that was marked on the top material. After a few inches have been secured, the wire-on welt is then stretched to straighten it out and then anchored in place on the other end.

3 A plastic mallet is used to flatten the wire-on welt after it has been stapled in place. By its design, the wire-on welt stays flattened because of the internal zigzag wire that runs throughout the material. Once it is flattened, it seals the attaching staples.

4 A screwdriver is used to tighten the small screw that holds the wire-on tip in place on the rear bow. The wire-on tip conceals the raw end of the wire-on welt and gives the new top a little splash of bling.

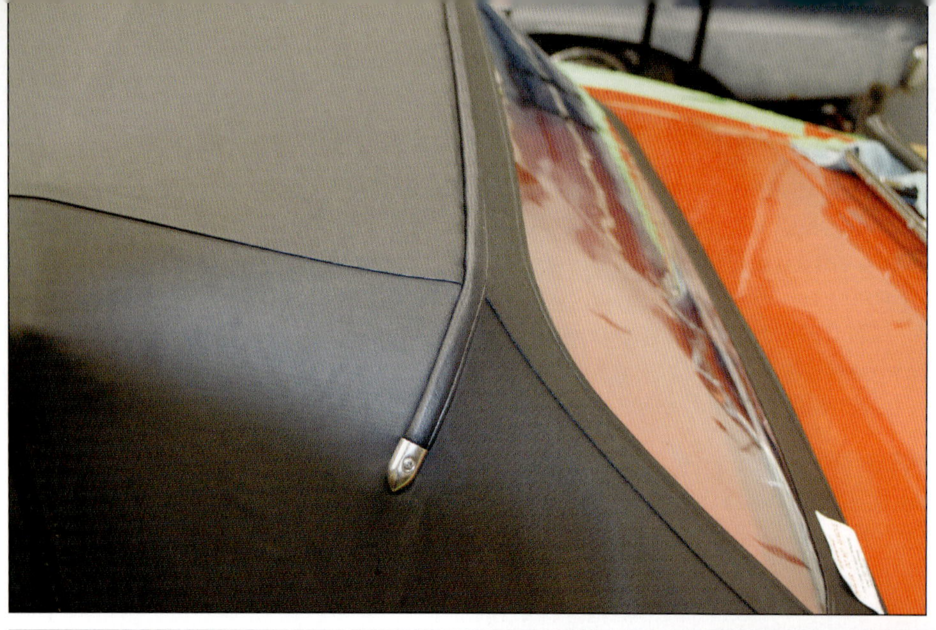

The finished wire-on welt conceals all the staples along the rear bow and keeps them from direct contact with the elements. As a finishing touch, the chrome dresses up the convertible top with a simple touch of elegance.

Side Tension Cables

Side tension cables were added to the 1968–1975 convertible tops to help hold the tops tighter to the side of the top frame. The idea was to help with the buffeting issue caused by driving the car at highway speeds. The tension cable runs along the inside of a special sleeve that is sewn into the outer edge of the top over the door glass. A string is supplied to draw the cable through the sleeve. To install the tension cable, fold the top material back to expose the cable sleeve. Now, tie the string to the front end of the cable and pull it through the sleeve until it emerges.

The tension cable is attached to the rear side rail with a 3/16-inch pop rivet. Unlatch the top and retract it about halfway down to give enough slack so that the front of the tension cable can be secured. The spring end of the cable is attached to the front side rail near the header bow with a small sheet-metal screw or a 3/16-inch pop rivet. Raise the top and latch it to check the fit and function of the side cable.

Top-to-Header Bow

To get a good fit on the top decking, the top frame should be latched so the top material can be pulled as

A string has been tied to the end of the tension cable to help draw it through the cable sleeve that has been sewn into the inside edge of the convertible top. The tension cable will keep the top material from buffeting as the car is driven at highway speeds.

Rivets and screws are often used to secure the side tension cables to the convertible top frame. Anchoring the side tension cable to the convertible frame allows the cable to keep the top from ballooning up as the car is driven at highway speeds.

far forward as it can go. With the top material pulled over the leading edge of the header bow, use a piece of chalk or a pencil to make a reference line on the material the full length of the header bow. Now, unlatch the top and lower the frame so that the top material can be wrapped over the header bow about a 1/4 inch past the reference line you made.

Line up the corner of the top and front flap with the edge of the header bow. Pull the flap under and the top material over so that the reference line is about 1/4 inch past the leading edge of the header and put a staple into the header bow tack strip to hold the corner of the top in place. Now, do the same to the other corner. You need to pull the top material across the header to make the side flap seam line up with the outer edge of the header.

Latch the top frame and check the tension on the top material. You want the top material to be tight but not overtight. Unlatch the top and make any adjustments necessary to get a proper tension on the top material. If you are satisfied with the way the top decking is stretched, unlatch the top and staple the material to the underside of the header bow tack strip. Latch the top and recheck that the fit and tension are correct. Make any adjustments necessary before moving on.

Front Weather Seal

Unlatch the top and lower it enough to expose the underside of the header bow tack strip. On the C1, remove the material covering the T-nuts in the tack strip. To expose the T-nuts, carefully lift the top material to locate the nut and then make a U-shaped cut around it. The U shape will not cause the top material to tear out when there is tension put on it.

Fit the rubber weather seal to the underside of the header bow and begin installing the weatherstrip retainer screws through the metal retainer strip into the T-nut in the header bow tack strip. Work from the center outward, and be careful about cross threading the retainer screws.

A chalk line is made across the leading edge of the header bow onto the top material as a visual reference for the tensioning and positioning of the top decking. Being able to see how much to move the fabric makes adjusting it much simpler.

A temporary staple was used on the underside of the header bow to retain the top material in place after it was positioned on the corner of the header bow. After the top material is checked for fit and tensioning, additional staples will be added to secure the material.

After the top decking was checked for the correct tension, a nice row of staples was added to retain the top material in place along the underside of the header bow. The top material was also trimmed to allow room for the weather seal to be added.

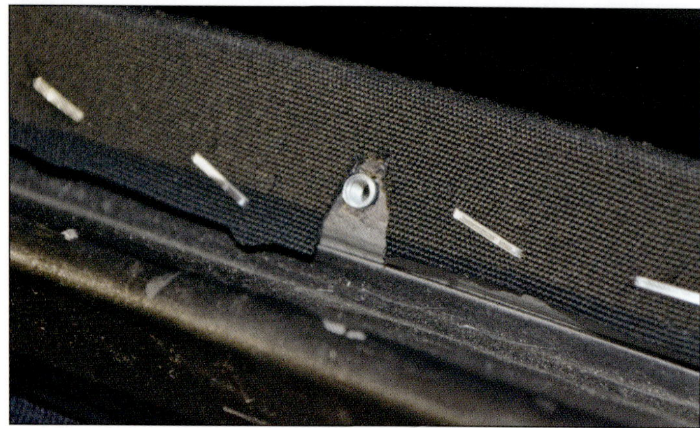

Excess material is cut away from the weather seal mounting hardware to allow the retainer screws access to the T-nuts mounted in the header bow tack strip. Being neat also helps with the installation of the rubber seal, making it much easier.

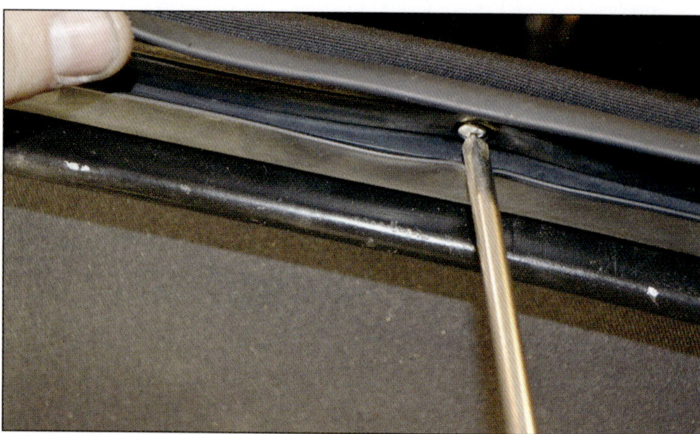

A metal weatherstrip retainer is used to even out the pressure of the retainer screws as they keep the thick rubber seal in place along the underside of the header bow on the 1959 Corvette. Without the retainer strip, the rubber weather seal would become distorted and leak.

Hidden on the underside of the header bow is a secondary rubber weather seal that is designed to keep out most of the wind and rain as the car is driven down the road. The seal also acts as a cushion when the convertible top frame is clamped to the windshield.

Fastened along the front of the header bow is a soft rubber core seal that will act as the first line of defense to repel wind and rain from the occupants of the car. The weather seal also eliminates the small gap that is created as a result of the top frame and windshield meeting.

If you jam one up, the top material needs to be removed along with the tack strip to repair the T-nut, so be careful.

Do not tighten the retainer screws all the way until you have them all in place. The T-nuts can move from side to side, and a little movement will help get the thick rubber seal set in place much easier. After the retainer screws are in place, they can all be tightened.

Installing the weather seals on the C2 and C3 is a little different. The inner rubber weather seal is attached to the outer ends of the header by small trim screws. The main body of the seal is attached to the underside of the header bow with small plastic tee fasteners. The tee fasteners are just pushed into the retainer holes in the header bow.

There is also a sewn weather seal that runs along the leading edge of the header bow. This 1/2-inch foam-core seal is blind stapled to the underside of the header bow.

Rear Weatherstrip

One of the last things to be completed on the top installation is the rear flap and rubber weather seal. There is a small rubber filler seal that is attached to the rear bow on the C1 Corvette and connects to the lower end of the rear vertical rail on the top frame. Two small screws secure the seal to the rear deck bow before the rear flap is glued to the vertical side rail.

After the flap has been positioned on the side rail, a small sheet-metal screw is added to the flange on the front of the small deck bow seal. The other hole in the flange is secured by the bottom rubber weather seal screw. Attach the rubber weather seal to the side rail along with the metal seal retainer, insert the machine screws into their appropriate places, and secure the screw through the side rail frame with a T-nut.

There is also a small rubber seal that attaches to the rear deck bow on the C3. This seal is held in place by a small machine screw on the end of the deck bow. After the seal is secured, the vertical flap can be glued in place and the last piece of rubber weatherstripping can be installed.

The filler seal on the C2 attaches to the bottom of the vertical rail and fills the gap at the rear corner of the door. It may be easier to install this seal with the top partially retracted and the door open. The seal attaches with a machine screw and is retained by a washer and nut on the inside bottom of the vertical side rail.

The Finished Top

Latch the top frame and inspect the top for any imperfections. A little steam can remove almost any box wrinkle and help relax the top material to make it fit and look better. The convertible top will need to be in the latched and up position for at least two weeks so that the top material can conform to its new shape.

This small rubber filler piece will help keep noise and dust out of the convertible when the top is in the raised position. Small machine screws are used to hold the filler piece in place on the rear deck bow while the flange on the front will be attached to the top frame.

Contact cement is applied to the inside of the rear vertical side flap on the convertible top and to the surface of the vertical side rail of the top frame. The sail panel of the convertible top completely smooths out once the flap is pulled tight and set in place.

Attaching the new rubber weatherstrip seals to the side rail of the convertible frame is the last thing that is required to finish off the installation of the new convertible top. Small screws hold the metal retainer in place, keeping the seal in the correct position.

With the top frame fully restored back to like-new condition, the 1959 Corvette will once again turn heads as it cruises through town. The stylish new Stayfast convertible top from Al Knoch Interiors gives this baby a lot of class and some real attitude.

Nothing beats the classic styling of the 1964 Corvette. The distinctive rib down the center of the back panel really sets this beauty off along with the new vinyl convertible top. Look out Route 66, this 'Vette is ready for the road!

Now that all the repairs have been done and the new top has been fitted, the owner can enjoy her 1972 Corvette Stingray for many years to come without the worry of getting wet when it rains. With the top up or down, this is one sweet ride.

Header Bow Repair

The most common repair on a header bow is missing or weak tack strip retainer tabs. Restoring the retaining tabs on the header bow is a simple process. New tabs can be cut from sheet metal and then welded into place on the header bow

Begin by marking the header bow with a permanent marker to indicate the location of where the new tabs will be attached. This also provides an accurate count as to how many tabs you need to make. After the positions to the tabs have been marked, the stubs from the old tabs can be removed by grinding or filing them away to prevent any surface distortion after the new top material is installed.

New retainer tabs can be cut from 22-gauge sheet metal. Each tab starts by cutting a 1/2 inch by 1 inch piece of sheet metal and then tapering the tab to a rounded point to mimic the original retainer tab. To help with the attachment of the new tab, a welding base needs to be bent at a right angle along the bottom edge to create a 1/8-inch flange. These tabs can now be aligned with the marks on the header bow and welded into place along the tack rail of the header bow.

After the new retainer tabs have been welded in place, the welds can be dressed down a little with a small die grinder to even out the metal. Use a small file to remove any sharp edges that may be on the edges of the sheet-metal tabs. The welded replacement tabs now are able to hold the new tack strip material securely to the header bow without failing.

Broken Screws

The most common repair is a blocked hole from a broken screw. Extracting the old screw may be very difficult due to the physical size of

Replacement tack strip retainer tabs are not available from a supplier, but they can be made from light-gauge sheet metal and simple tin snips. Cut the retainer tabs to width and then shape them to match the original tabs that are on the header bow.

Reconditioning the header bow with new metal retainer tabs provides ample holding power to secure the new tack strip material in place. This prevents the new convertible top material from coming loose as the car is driven down the road.

the screw. The original screw used to secure the pad to the bow is a #6 machine screw with 32 threads per inch and 3/8 inch long. These small screws often have the heads snap off while being removed.

The simplest way to extract the remaining screw piece is to use a small punch and drive it through the bow. This may sound barbaric, but by trying to drill out the remainder of the old screw, the drill bit may wonder and crate an elongated hole. By supporting the bow, you can drive the screw fragment through the bow, saving a lot of time and frustration.

If the screw hole becomes oversized and a #6 machine screw will no longer hold securely into the metal, the hole can then be drilled out with a #29 drill bit and then re-tapped to fit a #8 machine screw with 32 threads per inch. Although the screws are a little bit larger, they work the same without any further issues.

Too often, the bow has had the pad secured in place with 1/8-inch aluminum rivets. This type of repair is considered to be a major fail and the screw holes have become too large to re-tap.

To repair this damage, remove the rivet first by drilling through the aluminum rivet with a 1/8-inch drill bit.

Carefully weld the hole closed. Then, drill a new pilot hole with a #36 drill bit and chase the hole with a #6/32 tap to create new threads for the pad screw. The repaired bow can now be sanded, cleaned and prepped for a fresh coat of satin black paint. After the paint has cured, the bow can be reinstalled on the frame.

These cross bows are from a C1 Corvette. There are several broken pad screws that need to be repaired before the new convertible top pads can be installed. The small metal bows are fragile, and care must be taken to make them strong again.

After a broken screw has been removed from the cross bow and the hole has been repaired, run a threading tap through the hole to create clean threads for the machine screw that holds the convertible top pad in place.

Al Knoch Interiors
9010 N. Desert Blvd.
Canutillo, TX 79835
800-880-8080
alknochinteriors.com

Auto Custom Carpets, Inc.
800-325-8216
accmats.com

Berry's Staple Remover
Lubbock, TX 79423
806-799-5252
berrysstapleremover.com

Corvette Central
13550 Three Oaks Rd.
Sawyer, MI 49125
800-345-4122
corvettecentral.com

Corvette Pacifica
8981 La Lina Ave.
Atascadero, CA 93422
800-488-7671
corvettepacifica.com

Eckler's
7980 Grissom Pkwy.
Titusville, FL 32780
800-815-5799
ecklers.com

Fabric Supply Inc.
3434 2nd St. N.
Minneapolis, MN 55412
800-645-9998
fabricsupply.com

Hydro-E-Lectric
5530 Independence Ct.
Punta Gorda, FL 33982
800-343-4261
hydroe.com

Jiffy Steamer Co. LLC
4462 Ken-Tenn Hwy.
Union City, TN 38261
jiffysteamer.com

Master Appliance Corp.
2420 18th St.
Racine, WI 53403
800-558-9413
masterappliance.com

Metro Molded Parts Inc.
11610 Jay St. N.W.
Coon Rapids, MN 55448
800-878-2237
metrommp.com

Milwaukee Tool
13135 West Lisbon Rd.
Brookfield, WI 53005
800-729-3878
milwaukeetool.com

Osborn Tools
125 Jersey St.
Harrison, N.J. 07029
973-483-3232
csosborneupholsterytools.com

Rochford Supply
7624 Boone Ave. N. #200
Brooklyn Park, MN 55428
866-681-7401
rochfordsupply.com

Top Flight Automotive
100 Classic Car Dr.
Reedsville, PA 17084
833-486-7354
topflightautomotive.com

Trim Parts
2175 Deerfield Rd.
Lebanon, OH 45036
513-934-0815
trimparts.com

Wolfsteins Pro-Series
3040 Amwiler Rd., Suite A
Atlanta, GA 30360
800-377-4700
raggtopp.com